D1068785

BORDER CROSSINGS

BORDER CROSSINGS

Mexican
and
Mexican-American
Workers

Edited by
John Mason Hart

A Scholarly Resources Inc. Imprint
Wilmington, Delaware

Scholarly Resources Inc.
104 Greenhill Avenue
Wilmington, DE 19805-1897

Library of Congress Cataloging-in-Publication Data

Border crossings : Mexican and Mexican-American workers /
  edited by John Mason Hart.
    p.   cm. — (Latin American silhouettes)
  Includes index.
    ISBN 0-8420-2716-5 (hardcover : alk. paper). —
ISBN 0-8420-2717-3 (pbk. : alk. paper)
    1. Mexican Americans—Employment—United States—
History. 2. Mexican Americans—Employment—Southwest,
New—History. 3. Alien labor, Mexican—United States—
History. 4. Alien labor, Mexican—Southwest, New—History.
I. Hart, John M. (John Mason), 1935–   . II. Series.
HD8081.M6B673   1998
331.6'272073—dc21   98-22834
                                                                CIP

⊖ The paper used in this publication meets the minimum requirements of the American National Standard for permanence of paper
for printed library materials, Z39.48, 1984.

To the memory of Cesar Chavez,

a Mexican American who devoted his life

to the betterment of his people

About the Editor

JOHN MASON HART joined the University of Houston faculty in 1973. He served as a visiting instructor at the Centro de Documentación Intercultural in Cuernavaca, Mexico, in 1969 and as a Distinguished Visiting Scholar at the Dirección de Estudios Históricos of the Instituto Nacional de Antropología e Historia in Mexico City in 1992. He researched in Mexico City as a Social Science Research Council-American Council of Learned Societies Post-Doctoral Scholar in 1975; at the U.S.-Mexico Center of the University of California as a Visiting Scholar in 1988; as a Shelby Cullom Davis Visiting Scholar at the Department of History, Princeton University, in 1991; and held a Senior University Research Fellowship from the National Endowment for the Humanities in 1992.

Professor Hart has served on the editorial boards of *The Americas* and *Mexican Studies/Estudios Mexicanos*. His special interests include modern Mexican history and U.S.-Mexican relations. His publications include *Los anarquistas mexicanos* (1974), *Anarchism and the Mexican Working Class, 1860–1931* (1987), *Revolutionary Mexico: The Coming and Process of the Revolution* (1988, 1998), with "Empire and Revolution: The Americans in Mexico since the Civil War" forthcoming. Hart presently teaches Mexican history at the University of Houston.

Contents

Introduction

The following essays treat the experience of the Mexican and Mexican-American working classes from their cultural beginnings and the rise of industrialism in Mexico to the late twentieth century in the United States. A distinguished group of authors identify the problems that they confronted and explain the survival strategies and adaptations made by communities in Mexico to internal migration and industrial change as they coalesced into new groups and established working and living arrangements that met the challenges presented by seemingly insurmountable obstacles. Mexican-American workers have applied many of these strategies, such as mutual aid and the emphasis on local problem solving, to the resolution of the challenges that they faced in the United States.

The Mexican and Mexican-American working classes draw upon a rich experience of collective action and personal and community-wide mutual aid practices that began with the holocaust of the sixteenth and seventeenth centuries. During that period, over 95 percent of the population of Meso-America died from disease, starvation, or forced labor, but those who managed to survive were innovative. Often using the Church as a vehicle for guidance and support, the adults adopted the offspring of deceased neighbors and began to guarantee protection in advance for each other through vows of compadrazgo. They further developed mutual aid, practiced in pre-Conquest Tenochtitlán of the Aztecs, to establish formal societies that guaranteed support to the membership in case of personal calamities.

Mexican artisans, masters, journeymen, and apprentices learned the metal, textile, and leatherworking skills of their Spanish counterparts during the era of the Conquest and carried forward those skills, educational processes, and mutual assistance practices into the period following independence. During the last third of the nineteenth century, union members united the mutual aid practices of the earlier guild workshops and patios with liberal, anarchist, and socialist political consciousness into the factories of the industrial age.

The prevailing illiteracy did not exclude political discourse; it helped shape the demand for schools controlled by workers. The Mexican Labor Congress of the 1870s established self-instruction programs that anticipated the Escuelas Racionalistas of the Casa del Obrero Mundial (Casa) during the 1910 revolution. They learned political consciousness in shops, factories, bars, and at home. The artisans, especially tailors in the nineteenth century and typesetters in the twentieth, served as the intellectuals of the class. Most artisans could read a little, while typesetters were the personification of literacy.

From the inception of Mexican factory organizing during the 1860s the radicals and anarchists demonstrated resentment for extreme differences in wealth. Their demands paralleled the rise of a political press that addressed labor. Stories disseminated by the working-class newspapers *El Socialista* and *El Hijo del Trabajo* equated great individual wealth with perversion. Workers, including women employed in the textile mills, sought assistance from the national labor movement in order to defend their collective interests.

By the first decade of the twentieth century, *El Hijo del Ahuizote*, read by artisans, intellectuals, students, and leftists, mocked the president while demanding wider freedoms and justice for workers. Writers using nationalist terminology protested the mistreatment of working women and the rural poor. Author Heriberto Frías in *Tomochic* epitomized the concern for "Indians" and a peasantry dispossessed by the Liberal land reforms. During the revolution the anarcho-syndicalist Casa leaders organized thousands of women factory workers in central Mexico. They sought workers' control of factory and field production through local self-management after breaking the power of the government and capitalists.

After the Casa's defeat in 1916 the government took a more active hand in the labor movement, but the anarchist and radical impulse toward self-management remained strong during the 1920s. *Resurgimiento*, the anarcho-syndicalist newspaper in the state of Puebla, thrived for years, filling the plaza of the capital city with tens of thousands of demonstrators in support of anarchist Enrique Flores Magón in 1923. By the late 1930s a flood of patriotic and antiforeign sentiment pervaded the popular press and the working class as the Mexican government nationalized all but one of the multinational oil companies. The oil workers chose to support the government when forced to make the choice between it or their employers. The crisis blurred the distinction between the government and the patriotic notion of "Mexico."

In cases such as Poza Rica, in the twentieth century, the workers had created their own towns and forms of self-government where settled life previously had not existed. The early Mexican migrants to the American Southwest brought the same know-how with them. The miners of Arizona, the farm laborers of California and Texas, and the urban workers of Chicago and San Antonio used their experience with self-help and the wider application of mutual aid to optimize their conditions of segregated housing and services and counter discrimination in employment.

In Mexico the rural working class shared a cultural commitment to the land that implied, sooner or later, some share in its ownership or control over production. A priest defending the autonomous rights of local citizens against the intrusions of the government or private estate landowners was only fulfilling his obligations. In Mexico, as in the United States, the overwhelming power of capital and the emergence of the modern state prevented the success of independently controlled workers' unions that challenged the distribution of wealth or the general contours of society.

When the largely rural citizens of Mexico arrived in the United States, they found improved material conditions but faced tenuous legal status, prejudice, and a different property and political regime. Accordingly, these migrants shifted their concerns from the issues of municipal autonomy and the control of land and water to face those of human rights, fair treatment, the right to organize, and a living wage. In the new struggle they employed the survival strategies learned in the past—that is, the collaborative employment of clergymen, community leaders, mutual assistance societies, cooperatives, and a wide range of labor-organizing strategies including accommodationist and radical tendencies.

Meanwhile, their American counterparts reflected the cultural diversity of the many European nations from which they had come. They also experimented in consumption, manufacturing, and trade cooperatives, thereby resulting in a wide range of organizations. The Knights of Labor, the Industrial Workers of the World, the American Federation of Labor, and the Congress of Industrial Organizations reflected all imaginable ideological and tactical approaches. From the midnineteenth century the two cultures, American and Mexican, existed side by side, distinct and yet melting inexorably together. Working people on both sides intermingled and married, even under the segregated conditions of the Rio Grande Valley, the Arizona mining camps, and the fields of California's San Joaquin Valley. Their upper- and middle-class as well as urban counterparts also participated in the process.

It is no accident that in the 1960s, during the first days of the United Farm Workers' organizing effort in the San Joaquin Valley, Mexican-American clergymen supported migrants of Mexican and Philippine descent in their demands for union recognition, labor contracts, living wages, occupational safety, and decent housing on the enormous farms where they worked. Clergymen and Anglo sympathizers joined in to help set up soup kitchens, housing, and other services for those adults who needed assistance, and in the effort to provide educational services for the children. Farm workers and their leader, Cesar Chavez, demonstrated a deep religious and community commitment as they applied the strategies of social action learned from their forebears, many of whom are described in this book.

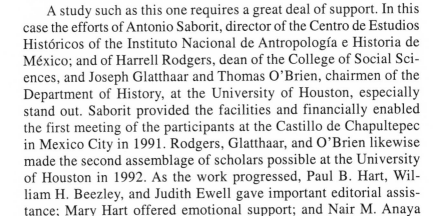

A study such as this one requires a great deal of support. In this case the efforts of Antonio Saborit, director of the Centro de Estudios Históricos of the Instituto Nacional de Antropología e Historia de México; and of Harrell Rodgers, dean of the College of Social Sciences, and Joseph Glatthaar and Thomas O'Brien, chairmen of the Department of History, at the University of Houston, especially stand out. Saborit provided the facilities and financially enabled the first meeting of the participants at the Castillo de Chapultepec in Mexico City in 1991. Rodgers, Glatthaar, and O'Brien likewise made the second assemblage of scholars possible at the University of Houston in 1992. As the work progressed, Paul B. Hart, William H. Beezley, and Judith Ewell gave important editorial assistance; Mary Hart offered emotional support; and Nair M. Anaya Ferreira translated large parts of the manuscript.

J. M. H.

CHAPTER ONE

The Evolution of the Mexican and Mexican-American Working Classes

JOHN MASON HART

U ntil now the social, cultural, and political continuities in the history between the Mexican and Mexican-American working classes have remained largely unexplained by scholars. The history of the greater Mexican working class has been segregated by the political boundary that separates the United States of America from the United States of Mexico. However, many scholars, especially the participants in this volume, are now demonstrating the important linkages between the heritage derived from the country to the south and the history of their people in the nation to the north.

Unfortunately, this effort has been asymmetrical. Until now, scholars from both countries who treat Mexican history have largely ignored the impact of American values and organizations on the working class of that country. The importance of migratory labor as an influence on Mexican-American customs and practices has been studied far more than the effect of those workers returning to Mexico with new ideas and aspirations after residency in the United States. Even the more obvious structural and individual linkages between unions and organizers in the United States and Mexico have been examined only rarely.[1]

This book is an endeavor to understand better the historical process behind the formation of the Mexican and Mexican-American working classes. In developing historical continuities, its authors explore the depths of Mexican labor history. They treat both the more remote yet formative past and the more immediate present; and they explain the similar social experiences and strategies of Mexican workers in both countries, the formation of communities and community organizations, mutual aid efforts, the movements of people across the border, the roles of women, and the formation of political groups. The authors also study the interactions between Mexicans and Mexican Americans. Finally, they address the special conditions of Mexicans in the United States, including the creation of a Mexican-American middle class, the impact of racism on Mexican communities, and the nature and evolution of border towns and the borderlands.[2]

The Premodern Background

Two of the most important practices of the Mexican working class, those of mutual aid and strategies for the formation and maintenance of communities, can be linked to the ancient past through the industrial artisans of Teotihuacán in pre-Columbian Mexico. That well-researched city was archetypical of the technologies and artisanal methods applied by the workers of other cities in the prehistoric era. It dominated central Mexico as the trading and cultural center for more than five hundred years. From before the first century B.C. until the seventh century A.D. the people of Teotihuacán organized and developed a city that now serves us as a model of the pre-Columbian way of life.

The artisans lived and worked together, perhaps even on a familial or extended lineage basis, but almost certainly with a high degree of intimacy and cohesion. The architectural layout of their buildings reveals a workshop or patio, sometimes in the center but often on one side of a rectangular or squared design of residential construction. The other sides of these usually one-story buildings featured sleeping quarters and dining areas capable of accommodating as many as fifty persons. The industrial workers used the patios, whether for work or leisure, on a communal basis. This type of design also served on a larger scale outside of the family.

At Teotihuacán and later in the Aztec capital of Tenochtitlán and the other cities of Mexico, the working class formed its familial workshops together with their living spaces as parts of larger designs that centered on community plazas and squares where the general citizenry came together. The planning of cities and their architecture paralleled the organization of human beings. Larger communities reflected the underlying system of personal, familial, and communal interactions found in the workshops. The people carried out larger construction projects for transportation, the movement of water, or civic buildings by utilizing a mass-based system of corvée labor based in part on the proportional representation of workers from each identifiable communal unit within the urban area. Under the Aztecs each of the four great communities of Tenochtitlán carried an assigned allotment of obligations to the whole.[3]

Beginning during the Conquest age, which extended from 1519 to 1570, the Spanish version of private property blended with the pre-Columbian one to create a mixture of private and communal values. Most pre-Columbian and colonial-era communities shared a common property that belonged to the incorporated entity itself (*calpulli*), but individual families held claims to specific parcels marked off by walls made of stone or maguey. Clan-like origins and birthrights bound the communities of small property holders together. The Mexicans had a system of mutually interactive and supportive labor long before the Europeans arrived and made their contribution to its further development. The Spanish viceregal state encouraged the mixture by sponsoring the creation of Church or Christian-based community landholdings and mutualist assistance societies known as *cajas de comunidad.*

Endorsed by the Spanish Crown and the indigenous population, the *cajas* and community landholdings grew and endured for the next three centuries. The *cajas* derived their income from *vecinos* who held individual parcels of land by virtue of their citizenship in the community. The *vecinos*, as a part of their civic responsibility, made donations to a common coffer in order to offer personal loans and health, death, and education benefits, including care for the aged and crippled, to their fellow *vecinos*. The ejido lots, or privately held properties whose ownership resided within the community, provided the basic source of funding for the *cajas*. Taxes and *caja* income served as the principal sources for the construction of civic buildings, streets, roads, drainage ditches, sewers, and agricultural development projects.

Ideally, the people practiced local government through town meetings; usually, however, a smaller group of more powerful people governed in the name of the community. Whatever its flaws, the merged pre-Columbian and Spanish systems of private and public property, and mutual support responsibilities represented by the *caja de comunidad*, prospered in Mexico well into the modern era and still exist alongside the omnipresent government in unions, cooperative societies, and communities throughout the nation. That manner of supporting one's fellow citizens is evident among the Mexican-American people studied in the chapters in this volume written by Antonio Ríos Bustamante, Gerardo Necoechea Gracia, Devra Weber, and Emilio Zamora.

In the towns and cities of New Spain the pattern of working-class history differed from that of the smaller rural communities. The citizenry rebuilt and reorganized the cities and towns in accordance with Spanish practices following the violent initial disruptions of the Conquest. However, the experience derived from the industrial workshops concentrated in pre-Columbian trade and manufacturing centers such as Teotihuacán and Tenochtitlán helped to maintain a sense of community cohesion and mutual responsibility among the indigenous population. Spanish-style artisans' guilds, or workers' organizations based on skilled workers in an applied art or trade, emerged and gradually changed in composition. They evolved from a merger of practices associated with pre-Columbian and European manufacturing and new conditions. In Spain, guilds identified with specialized trades such as those of shoemakers, carpenters, metal workers, and silversmiths were already well developed when the practitioners of those arts came to Mexico.

As the European skills spread across New Spain, large numbers of guilds appeared in the areas removed from Mexico City where most of the people lived. As mestizos entered the artisan trades, so did the surviving communalist social practices of pre-Columbian Mexico that had persisted in the countryside. Most guilds were officially recognized in their hometowns, although informal organizations also existed. They became centers for the generation of a new workers' culture. The guilds established schools for industrial arts training, laid out guidelines for the quality of merchandise, and established mutual aid funds to help needy members and their dependents during times of emergency. Away from Mexico City a new system of practices evolved from the combination of American and European experiences.

Even the colonial viceregal state took an active social role in the cities. In response to overwhelming need and public demand during the famines of the sixteenth century, the government introduced several institutions including *alhóndigas* (granaries), which ensured the supply of sustenance to the local citizenry during times of shortage. The *alhóndigas* marked the most significant instance of state intervention or assistance in community self-help activities. In the towns, *cajas* actively supported civic betterment projects and provided social services. Hence, well before the advent of modern industrial capitalism, the Mexican working class had a long and pervasive experience with local self-help organizations, guilds, the practice of mutual aid, and the expectation of state assistance for those projects deemed too expensive to be satisfied with local resources alone.

During the colonial era, which endured until Mexican independence in 1821, the undercapitalized nature of the economy meant impoverishment for many people. That unredeeming situation encouraged artisans to organize for the preservation of their mutual interests. Artisans, as skilled industrial workers who specialized in one particular craft, were the key element of industrial society before the emergence of factories. Anticipating modern state strategies, the viceregal government recognized their importance and, through its *ordenanzas de gremios*, offered a legal framework for the guilds and regulated their activities. The results were mixed. Given the colonial nature of the society, the Spaniards were able to use some guilds to preserve their power and exclude other people; in that way they offered a hierarchy of inherited status for their members.

At first the state reinforced the colonial caste order by restricting membership and therefore legitimate practice to Spaniards and their descendants, the criollos. Despite the seeming lack of mobility, however, the guilds offered a source of social cohesion to industrial workers, especially in the towns and provinces away from the concentrations of wealth found in the capital. Throughout New Spain the guilds moved toward broader membership, but the process was slower in more conservative locales. With the pressure for more democratized artisan guilds growing during the late eighteenth century, the state issued new *ordenanzas* during the 1790s. Those edicts decreed that anyone, regardless of his caste, could practice a trade and belong to a guild. The stage was set for the formal creation of Mexican mutual aid and cooperative societies and the onset of modern unions.

The Working-Class Response to Industrial Capitalism

In the first half of the nineteenth century the guilds continued to serve as important social, economic, and political forces. They played a direct and powerful role in local economies, charities, and town governance, and, along with the Church, were the basic providers of education and social welfare. Following independence, in the 1820s and 1830s, mestizo guild leaders participated in government by sitting on town and city councils, lobbying for local and state tariffs, and establishing quality standards for goods. But, despite the fact that the overwhelming majority of the Mexican population (82 to 87 percent) as well as the vast majority of artisans lived in rural areas, continuing poverty and decreasing real income plagued the rural communities.

The working class responded to growing material hardship by sharing residences and farm properties, extending aid to the aged, and continuing the practice of voluntary group labor in the villages under the leadership of local *comisarios*. Instead of the visible institutions of the cities, the working-class members of rural guilds continued informal systems of mutual support for loved ones and neighbors through the assumed responsibilities of *compadrismo* and the parish church. The rural economic malaise clearly limited the possibilities of formal mutualist endeavors, characterized by large savings deposits and even buildings, to the cities. The average rural artisan had lost the economic well-being to provide social benefits through formally endowed institutions. That poverty, and the fragmented, more introverted nature of rural society, left the formation of the more highly evolved forms of working-class organizations to the factory towns and cities.

While the ever more demanding members of the rural and provincial working class continued to practice intimate and less formalized mutual support services, the people of the urban centers struggled to maintain communal traditions while living in an increasingly more modern capitalist economy, diverse polity, and less personalized existence. If they did not know their new neighbors as well as their rural counterparts did, they might overcome that condition of alienation by forming larger mutual assistance units and unions. But they realized, as Mario Camarena Ocampo and Susana Fernández Apango point out in their study of the workers of San Angel, that they needed to struggle against unfair treatment and to have their interests represented in the face of arbitrary actions carried out by the increasingly powerful and more assertive factory owners and capitalists. The new factory workers in the small industrial towns on the periphery of the larger cities created many of Mexico's first *sindicatos*, a combination of mutual aid society and union. While the workers formed these *sindicatos* in order to compete more effectively with modern capitalists, they also used them to provide mutual aid and self-help such as basic education, health care, and industrial training. In cities such as Guadalajara, Mexico City, and Puebla, the absence of government social programs plus employer opposition to all forms of employee insurance caused the workers to create even more mutualist societies. They increased in numbers and size for the rest of the nineteenth century.

In the 1840s a group of artisans in Mexico City created the Junta de Artesanos de México, by far the largest mutual aid organization that the country had yet seen. They adopted a relatively open membership policy in order to bring as many artisans as possible to their group. To members they offered loans, health care, and educational services, and they established a life, disability, and survivors insurance program that supported orphaned children. To the south, the workers and artisans of Orizaba, an industrial town of 20,000 inhabitants, formed the first *caja de ahorro*, or independent mutualist bank. Instead of maintaining an account at a commercial bank, they created their own financial institution. Like the Junta in Mexico City, the workers of Orizaba distributed loans to members at 6 percent interest, which was the same discounted rate offered by the Church to hacendados (great estate owners), miners, and merchants, who placed their properties in escrow as security.

In December 1843 the director of the Mexico City Junta reported a membership of 1,683, drawn from across south and central Mexico: Acapulco, Oaxaca, Puebla, Mexico City, and the state of México. In 1844 the members established a Lancasterian adult night school in Mexico City in order "to advance the skills" and "elevate the moral values of the membership and the artisans in general, through instruction that included religion." The inclusion of religion constituted a bold move in a society where the Church claimed the sole right of religious indoctrination. They then created a fund for the alleviation of "misery," another inroad by those advocating workers' self-help into the previous clerical monopoly on social welfare. In addition, they founded the newspaper, *El Seminario Artístico*, which they published during 1844 and 1845. In Orizaba the *caja* leaders reported a reserve of 1,251 pesos in its coffers in 1840. A year later they had made outstanding loans of 9,374 pesos. The total reached 17,882 pesos in 1842 with a reserve of 2,347 pesos. While not rich, they demonstrated the pride and unity of Mexican workers, however fraught with hardships their lives might have been.[4]

When members joined the Mexico City Junta, they accepted explicit "mutualist" obligations. Created in the 1840s, these obligations became the basic framework under which formally recognized mutual aid organizations, whether independent or provided by unions, have operated ever since: the payment of regular dues, one month of tenure before eligibility for benefits, government oversight of finances, a *caja de ahorro* for the development of artisanal skills and shops, and a *fondo de beneficio* to assist members in cases of illness, death, marriage, and the baptism of children.[5]

Beyond mutual assistance and insurance needs the workers also addressed political issues. They aligned themselves with and against regional and national political leaders. Those ties caused some government officials to encourage and others to oppose mutualist associations regularly from the 1850s onward until the revolution of 1910. The politicians recognized the power of organized labor and offered charters and official sanctions "in order to create a more powerful and prosperous nation." Politics and morality joined self-help as constant themes for Mexican mutualists. During the 1840s and 1850s the Mexico City Junta de Fomento de Artesanos directed its loans toward day laborers and female domestic workers as well as to the artisans in order to uplift the moral character of all producers. Its members expressed concern for the welfare of women, citing reduced gambling by women and less alcohol consumption by men as major victories for its programs.[6]

In 1853, 33 artisans in Mexico City formed the Sociedad Partícular de Socorros Mútuos. Within a month it claimed 130 artisan members. It combined the usual program of loans, life and disability insurance, and educational services for self-improvement with a new level of political activism. The members declared that their Sociedad was the basis of their effort to resist the "modern slavery" of industrial capitalism "that strips away the gains of our labor." The Sociedad was the first group that took on the label "resistance society." This group, a combination of union and mutualist society, became the first prototype unit of what would become the Mexican labor movement. It anticipated the *sindicato*, which goes beyond the usual functions of an American union and offers other benefits, including housing, child care, and food programs, in addition to the older functions of Mexican mutualist societies.[7]

At the same time, the rapid decline of certain trades radicalized those artisans affected, such as the tailors and weavers who were being overwhelmed by the factory production of textiles. That problem became identifiable in the 1860s. The anguish of the tailors and weavers would be experienced a generation later by the typesetters, stonemasons, and stone and quarry workers in the face of the rising Linotype and portland cement industries. The displaced workers and artisans combined with radical intellectuals to supply militant political leadership to the emergent mutualist, cooperative, and labor movements spanning the next 150 years.

In addition to material well-being, the leaders articulated the goal of defending traditional forms of community, working-class, and artisanal culture. Their "associations" combined the defense of tradition with a spirit of unity, "fraternity" in order to "defend society" from advancing capitalism and its corollaries, extreme individualism, alienation, anomie, the growing abandonment of long-accepted social responsibilities, and the commodification of culture. Beginning in the 1860s and continuing through the era of the revolution of 1910, the workers and artisans composed titles for their mutualist groups that frequently included the words "Unión" or "Sociedad de Resistencia."

During the 1860s and 1870s, Mexican workers began to organize on a larger scale and to incorporate the broader strategies of the Sociedad. They organized factories and modified several of the mutualist groups into "resistance societies." Many of them, in some cases a majority of the workers' organizations in central Mexico, adopted anarchist-socialist agendas. They supported anarchism because it meant workers' power and the rejection of government and elite interference in their affairs. Capitalism was still young, and the working people of the small industrial cities and even the urban areas remembered the workshops and autonomous realities of the old order. They practiced self-help and advocated self-management by the workers, often achieving the latter goal in the artisans' workshops. Some of them favored limiting the role of the state in their domestic affairs, while others supported socialist programs.

As Camarena Ocampo and Fernández Apango demonstrate in this volume, technology made the emergence of modern Mexico City possible and deeply affected the workers on the urban periphery. As urbanism developed, the workers of San Angel and similar towns attempted to integrate field, factory, workshop, and family. They strove to combine the rise of capitalism with the achievement of adequate support for their families and the maintenance of comfort, if not luxury. While creating unions, they sought to defend traditional values, including the practices of interfamilial and workshop mutual aid and the forms of local self-determination associated with decentralized and precapitalist production. That meant the survival of a prosperous workshop, a team-based concept of production, and the frequently attendant small store. In the cities, artisans and workers often supported the political liberalization associated with the rise of capitalist democracy. Artisan leaders duly took their places on town councils. All of these factors combined to give artisans and less-skilled workers a degree of security and social standing in their neighborhoods. By the 1870s a more urban culture was emerging among San Angel's factory workers, who began to emphasize demands for higher wages and better working conditions along with the continuing quest for mutual aid.

The towns in the central valley around Mexico City supplied the artisans, laborers, and radical intellectuals who formed the first confederation of Mexican workers. By 1871 the tailors of Mexico City, the vendors, carpenters, streetlighters, beauty shop workers, candlestick makers, alcoholic beverage deliverymen, schoolteachers, carriage makers, typesetters, musicians, weavers, button makers, and tobacco and textile workers had organized. In 1871 they sent representatives to a labor congress that met in the capital with delegates from workers' groups from the cities of Durango, Guadalajara, Oaxaca, San Luis Potosí, and Veracruz, and many smaller towns. They created the nation's first workers' council, the Círculo de Obreros de México, whose purpose was to coordinate union business such as negotiations and strikes over broad areas.

In the meantime, the focus on mutual assistance that Devra Weber reveals among the farm workers of California during the 1960s, 1970s, and 1980s became a universal effort. In the 1870s the mutualists of Durango and Guadalajara formed banks in order "to alleviate misery among the artisans, improve their arts, and educate their children." In Toluca, the capital of the state of México, they published a newspaper in addition to offering support for those members in need. Only the felicities of writing style and space preclude a list of virtually all of the towns and cities of any size throughout the country where emergent working-class groups combined mutual aid with labor militancy.[8]

With a contingent of highly motivated anarchists espousing a mix of Proudhonist and Bakuninist ideas among the leadership, the Círculo de Obreros claimed its strongest following from the typesetters, tailors, musicians, hat makers, carpenters, and textile and tobacco workers. These craftsmen, in addition to radical students from the Colegio San Ildefonso, were particularly articulate as well as more literate and prosperous than their impoverished fellow workers, and they produced the principal leaders of the labor movement. Beginning in 1867 the textile workers of central Mexico used their embryonic unions and mutualist associations as the basis of strikes. Anarchist organizers, some from the new subclass of factory-based industrial workers and a handful of intellectuals, but largely composed of artisans and students, stimulated and led most of these efforts.

In rural Mexico the striking workers at the mines around Pachuca in the state of Hidalgo provide an outstanding example of the *sindicato*. In 1869 they went on strike protesting newly imposed wage reductions and longer working hours. The striking miners won not only by closing down the mines but also by providing support for their members through mutual aid. Their success provoked a cry of alarm from the Mexico City press in favor of suppressing the union and its anarchist leaders before they grew any stronger. During the 1870s a violent strike by textile factory workers in Querétaro and several others in the central valley of Mexico brought direct and fatal interventions by the police and army.

After the strikers enjoyed some initial successes, the successive governments of Emperor Maximilian (1864–1867) and Presidents Benito Juárez (1867–1872), Sebastian Lerdo de Tejada (1872–1876), and especially Generals Manuel González (1880–1884) and Porfirio Díaz (1877–1880, 1884–1911) increasingly repressed legitimate union activity. While González used heavy-handed tactics, Díaz mixed the club with the carrot, offering workers the opportunity to organize unions sponsored by the Church and strictly apolitical mutualist societies regulated by the government.

During the 1870s an estimated one-fifth of the population of Mexico City, or 50,236 persons, belonged to one or more unions, cooperatives, and mutualist societies. Nationwide, the working class had formed over one hundred co-ops and mutualist groups with 125,000 members and beneficiaries. That membership is impressive when it is remembered that only 700,000 Mexicans lived in cities and towns counting over 10,000 people. The industrial working class comprised only about 10 percent of the urban population. The rest of the membership was rural, drawn from the over 8 million people who lived in the countryside. Community and group-help efforts were a key part of their way of life. They adopted positive goals: "fraternity, friendship, pride, savings, study, and hard work." Union, cooperative, and mutualist leaders also expressed political concerns: they protested the extreme poverty endured by the unskilled and unemployed workers and contrasted it with the "greed and vulgarity of the rich."[9]

As the pace of industrial expansion intensified and capitalists continued to broaden their role in the economy, a deepening sense of crisis swept the working class. Union and cooperative leaders increased their complaints of abuse by factory supervisors and "capitalists." More workers than ever sought relief in mutualist societies, but these institutions were underfunded and unable to meet the challenge. Claims of death through neglect by hospitals, capitalists, and mutualist society administrators surfaced and led to more militancy. Members accused some directors of having "forgotten their origins and those of their organizations." Underlying these tensions was the sense that militant unions were needed if the workers were to rescue themselves from the worsening conditions. Labor activists advocating socialism and anarchism multiplied during the 1870s.

During the 1870s the leaders of the Mexico City Gran Círculo de Obreros, or workers' council, complained bitterly about their "prostration." They demanded an end to the "illusion" that mutualist social insurance could save the situation and called for "production and consumption cooperatives" capable of foreign exchanges in order to establish an alternative to what they saw as the unsatisfactory new system of capitalism. In 1874 the Gran Círculo created the Compañía Cooperativa de Obreros de México, capitalized with 10,000 pesos and enjoying a wide base of support headed by the mutualists from the carpenters' union. They opened a discount store stocked with food and dry goods staples, established free schools, set aside land for housing, and offered construction assistance and working-class neighborhood development plans. Their members included virtually every segment of the working class, even a society of Mexico City policemen. The labor leaders became increasingly radical in their opposition to the capitalists. By the late 1870s the Mexican Congress of Workers, comprised of 50,000 cooperative and mutualist society members and union workers from virtually all of the country, from Chihuahua in the north to Oaxaca in the south, claimed representation at anarchist-led labor congresses in Europe.

The workers in Durango, some six hundred miles northwest of Mexico City, defined the labor movement's basic goals: to create a "bank of assistance" to serve the artisans belonging to the association; to heal the suffering of those artisans; to procure the betterment and perfection of their skills and duties; and to educate the artisans' children, beginning with the establishment of a trade school where the children of poor artisans would be given preferential consideration for admission, but which would be open to all those who aspired to a brighter future.[10] A lack of monies undermined the Durango effort, but the modern application of long-standing working-class mutual aid practices had been accomplished.

As early as 1881 workers from the Contreras textile factory south of Mexico City formed a housing cooperative at Tlalpizalco in the state of México. They opened their own grocery and dry goods outlet in order to provision the community at minimal cost. They named their community Colonia Cerícola and organized the real estate in individual rather than communal parcels. Teams of workers at Colonia Cerícola took on semipermanent community duties such as street maintenance, pest control, irrigation, fence and other public construction, and police work. Colonia Cerícola opened the way for others. Beginning in the late nineteenth and continuing through the twentieth century, Mexican workers have strived to provide themselves with adequate public housing through volunteer construction projects known as *colonias obreras*. They have done so with the know-how or empowerment derived from centuries of self-help and mutual aid. The Mexican government has never provided the support needed for adequate public housing. Chronically undersupported and underpaid, Mexican workers partially overcome their poverty by continuing to organize as self-helping, self-managing, and dedicated *vecinos* living in self-built neighborhoods made up of private parcels.

Beginning in the 1870s the first Mexican unions "guaranteed" that women would be able to escape "the humiliating conditions in which they find themselves." The largely male leadership sought to "protect" women from the tedious and heavy labor of some factories and to see to it that they would work at less strenuous jobs "as bookkeepers, telegraph operators, and in similar [white-collar] occupations." To achieve this end they crafted strike demands that included protections for women from the heavy work and long hours in mines and factories generated during the Industrial Revolution and at a time when pregnancy was a regular occurrence. Working-class men, however, persisted in maintaining divisions of labor in factories and workshops that excluded women from advancement to positions of greater authority and higher salaries. The women formed their own mutualist societies and unions. One of them, the Sociedad de Costureras, comprised of seamstresses in Mexico City, even attracted presidential attention. The First Lady of Mexico, Carmen Romero Rubio de Díaz, accepted the title of honorary lifetime president of the group. In their appointment message the seamstresses described her as "adorable and tender, reflecting in a breath, kiss, phrase or tear, the cultured women of the Americas."[11] Carmen Ramos Escandón demonstrates that working-class Mexican women redefined themselves as a result of the factory experience and the struggle to better their working conditions and incomes. Ramos Escandón places them in the mainstream of Mexican working-class history and points out their exceptional experiences based on an understanding of gender as an everchanging process defining relations between the sexes.

Despite lacking the numbers developed during the Industrial Revolution in England, Mexican women produced their own leaders. Whatever the designs of Carmen Romero Rubio, who accepted the status of "role model" for working-class women, they responded to the new conditions that they encountered in the factories. As they mobilized, they transcended the roles imagined for them by the state and their employers. When their unions demanded special protection for the Native Americans of Mexico, they reflected the ever widening experience of the membership. By 1900 the meaning of the term "feminine" had irretrievably changed among the working class and was still evolving. The process explained by Ramos Escandón had defining moments during the revolution of 1910 when women factory workers from the greater Mexico City area formed a corps of fifteen hundred nurses for service with the revolutionary army and adopted the name *acratas*, or those opposed to all authority.

Bernardo García Díaz, in his discussion of the textile factory towns that took shape at Orizaba in the late nineteenth century, demonstrates the varied character of the immigrants who came to Orizaba and created a new community with a consciousness based on their backgrounds and their new experience. His presentation anticipates the dramatic findings by Alberto Olvera Rivera and the Mexican-American scholars in this volume. Olvera Rivera examines the formation of a community by oil workers during the late 1920s and early 1930s. His explanation of mutual aid, cultural development, and independent politics parallels the findings of Antonio Ríos Bustamante, Devra Weber, Emilio Zamora, and Gerardo Necoechea Gracia in their examinations of the Mexican-American experience in the twentieth century.

Olvera Rivera, in an interesting contrast with Camarena Ocampo and Fernández Apango, finds that the workers of Poza Rica manifested a class-based cultural nationalism and little antagonism toward foreigners in the oil industry before President Lázaro Cárdenas nationalized it in 1938. Camarena Ocampo and Fernández Apango offer another perspective on the complexity of the process of class formation in their analysis, where heroism on the part of several workers in the war against the French invaders of the 1860s helped them win elections in the mutualist societies and represent them in the workers' congresses of the 1870s. The formation of new communities is a major dimension of Mexican working-class history, and García Díaz uses the textile towns of Orizaba as graphic examples of the dynamics of polity and social regeneration. The coming together of Poblanos and Oaxaquenos meant the mixing of peoples with widely divergent experiences and expectations. The perceived need for mutual aid societies intimately merged with unionization. The deepening sophistication and modernity of mutualist societies and then unions corresponded with the adoption of the term *sociedades de resistencia*.

Meanwhile, throughout the late nineteenth and early twentieth centuries, the Church maintained an important, though often ignored, role in social issues. Priests have acted with the working class as organizers and supporters since the time of the Spanish missionary friars and parish priests who helped the Native American villagers obtain common lands from the Crown during the sixteenth century. In the early twentieth century the Church organized some Catholic mutualists and unions in response to government encouragement and the papal bull, *Novarum Rerum*. The government did not object to the organizing effort because it represented a preferable alternative to a rising tide of anarcho-syndicalism, which advocated the control of the factories by the organized working class. In a famous speech during a Catholic labor congress held in Guadalajara in 1906, a clerical speaker protested that a "lack of credit is the greatest enemy that the small property owner can have." He complained that without unity the small farmer or rancher had no other recourse than the "outrageous moneylenders" who, "like jackals, force the producers into contracts for less than one-half of the value of their production." Even the most conservative mutualists distrusted the exploitative behavior of the new banking class.[12]

There is a strong tradition of Church-assisted working-class projects including orphanages, schools, food banks, savings fund societies, and, in rural Mexico, the defense of the community against outside intruders. Workers have traditionally expected the Church's participation even in the most radical of causes such as the Zapatista insurrection during the 1910 Mexican Revolution and the farm workers' strikes and boycotts in California from the 1960s through the 1980s. For the most part, clerical participation in the Mexican and Mexican-American working-class movement has been informal, usually involving caring local priests who join industrial or farm workers and community defense projects on an individual basis.

In the years immediately preceding the great social revolution of 1910 many Mexican workers took part in strikes, and a few even rebelled, largely stimulated by the faltering of the textile industry in 1898. Over the next decade a recession in that industry led to labor cutbacks, reduced wages, lockouts, and strikes. The unrest began in 1898 with a strike that paralyzed the textile mills in the state of Puebla. In 1906 the unrest spread to Cananea, Sonora, the mining town near the border with Bisbee, Arizona, where rebellious unrest among the Mexican workers there led to repression but did not deter them. As Ríos Bustamante points out, the workers in that area of Mexico and Arizona were already forming self-help societies and resisting the racial discrimination practiced by corporations such as Phelps Dodge, Amalgamated Copper, and Anaconda. Radicalism in favor of democratic voting rights and equal wages for equal work swept the mining camps of northern Mexico and Arizona. In 1907 a workers' rebellion erupted at the Rio Blanco textile-manufacturing complex on the edge of the highlands between Puebla and the coastal state of Veracruz. After Rio Blanco the unrest spread throughout central Mexico. When the revolution of 1910 began, the working class was already joining new *sindicatos* with revolutionary aims in unprecedented numbers.

The Mexican workers, frustrated by their lack of access to aid from their government and unable to obtain redress for their political isolation through the ballot box, joined with alienated local and provincial elites in the revolution. The latter two groups had found that they were losing ground between 1900 and 1910 as a result of a precipitous fall in the value of Mexico's silver-based currency. Their calls upon the centrist national government for relief from their economic plight had fallen on deaf ears because it was using the devaluation of silver as the mechanism through which it could recruit investments from advanced economies such as that of the United States, which used the gold standard against which silver steadily lost strength. Foreigners were attracted because purchases and labor paid for in Mexican pesos saved them great amounts of money. The alienated elements among the workers and elites shared the same lack of access to political redress when they turned against the government. Ten years of revolutionary conflict ensued.[13]

The Workers and Revolutionary Mexico

In the opening years of the revolution the majority of miners in some parts of the north, such as the large mining camps of Batopilas, Chihuahua, and Cananea, supported radical efforts. A group of some seventy miners at Batopilas joined Pascual Orozco in armed support of the Maderista revolution, a movement named after Francisco Madero, who unseated President Díaz in less than a year. The revolt enjoyed the support of workers all over Mexico. When Orozco rebelled against Madero a year later, the most radical elements in Chihuahua and Sonora fought under radical leaders such as Prisciliano Silva in support of the new revolution and in favor of giving land to the landless. When that effort failed, many fled into Texas, Arizona, and California carrying their egalitarian political convictions with them.

In the meantime, the workers in Mexico City reached new levels of political activism on behalf of organized labor. They formed two rival organizations based on the well-established working-class demands for unions and mutual aid programs. One, the Centro Mútuo-Cooperativo, enjoyed the support of the short-lived Madero government in 1911 and 1912, but it died out in competition with the other, the Casa del Obrero. At the height of its power in 1915 the Casa, a workers' central that tried to maintain independence from the government, established medical clinics with the aim of creating hospitals based upon mutual aid, schools, and trade centers. It had some success and counted 150,000 members from the larger cities throughout the nation and in the smaller towns and factory settlements across central Mexico. The range of Casa membership included petroleum workers in Tampico and miners in Sonora and Chihuahua. The industrial working class in Mexico at the time of the revolution numbered no more than 1.5 million in a nation of 15 million souls. The fact that some 25 percent of the industrial workers enrolled in Casa affiliates, mutualist societies, and cooperatives during the revolution is testimony to the strength of their heritage and consciousness. As the articles written by Ríos Bustamante, Necoechea Gracia, Weber, and Zamora demonstrate, Mexican workers carried this hard-earned awareness forward through time and space into the twentieth century and to the United States. The Mexican and Mexican-American workers created a continuity of thought and action which justifies the argument that theirs is one history, albeit complicated by the many different situations as depicted in this volume.

One example of the carrying forward of working-class organizing efforts took place in 1915 at the height of the revolution. By that year Juan Francisco Moncaleano, a Casa leader exiled by the Madero government as a foreign subversive, had founded the Casa del Obrero Internacional on Yale Street in Los Angeles. Moncaleano, an anarchist of Colombian birth, and his equally political Mexican-born spouse Bianca had extensive ties with the Mexican-American community, which included a sizable number of refugees with experience in the labor movements of both Mexico and the United States. His meeting hall served as a gathering place for Mexican workers in East Los Angeles for more than a decade.

Hoping to increase the power of the "modern" industrial workers, the Casa sent "red battalions" to fight in the revolution. But the leaders of the Casa largely adhered to the ideology of anarcho-syndicalism, which basically meant workers' control of the means of production through unions. That objective led to inevitable conflict with the majority of their Constitutionalist allies, who had no interest in seeing labor unions in control of the country. In 1916, after the Constitutionalist alliance had defeated their rivals the Villistas and Zapatistas, the Casa challenged the new government by calling two general strikes. The strikers demanded wage increases and more self-management in industry. However, the revolutionary army, under the control of what Casa leaders called the "national bourgeoisie," defeated the anarcho-syndicalists and abolished the Casa. In 1917 the government encouraged the successful replacement of the Casa with the Confederación Regional de Obreros Mexicanos (CROM). With government financial support, the CROM used the desire among the workers for union power, mutualist societies, and cooperatives to secure a large following. The CROM continued the older efforts to develop workers' housing, social insurance, and full employment. It also deepened the ties of Mexican workers and their unions with the American Federation of Labor in the United States by establishing a formal relationship with the Americans. In the decade that followed, the new Mexican government, always searching for more popularity, enlarged upon its support of the CROM by underwriting a large number of cooperative and mutualist undertakings.[14]

President Venustiano Carranza recognized the depth of the ties of the working class to the survival of the community and to mutual aid. During his term in office from 1916 to 1920 he established the National Agrarian Commission to begin a program of giving back land to the peasantry, and he committed 150,000 pesos of the national budget to the National Consumers Society (NCS) despite the fiscal bankruptcy of the government. The NCS enjoyed wide support among the workers and revolutionary leaders. President Carranza made the NCS allocation in order to alleviate hunger during a time in which famine stalked Mexican cities. He intended for the program to help the working class escape rampant food speculation characterized by hoarding, excessive price increases, and opportunistic distribution. It was logical that the money was given to the NCS as a self-help group rather than to a government agency.

The merger of state programs with popular demands continued to develop after Carranza left office. At the end of his term the new Cooperative Party, which appealed to both the urban and rural working class, entered the political arena. In the 1920 national elections the Cooperative Party won sixty seats in the House of Deputies and five state governorships. In 1921 the party issued a manifesto that stated that "the Cooperative Party has arisen from entirely local sources," a claim that was partially true. The government had encouraged its creation, but its popularity rested on the nature of the program that it offered the voters. It had brilliant successes in Mexico City and other municipalities during its brief history. The 1921 Cooperative Party platform effectively merged the social aspirations of the workers as expressed throughout Mexican history with the political ambitions of the new state-building elites:

1) The action of political parties should not be simply in the arena of political power. They should participate in all aspects of collective life.

2) The state is not simply a political organization. Its purposes are essentially social.

3) Political, academic, and intellectual freedom should be guaranteed and limited by the general interests of society.

4) Educational services should be dispensed throughout the nation, at farms, factories, and in cities. They should provide autonomy to the universities and advance technological skills.

5) Each municipality should have an autonomous cooperative entity with a democratically elected administration dedicated to the efficient and equal distribution of services and benefits.

6) Large landholdings should be equitably subdivided with fair compensation to the owners while rural schools and cooperative agricultural credit banks assist the new landholders in employing modern means to farming. Practical means should be adopted to ensure the progressive socialization of agricultural land and production.

7) Land taxes should be abolished and the fiscal system simplified in order to free small transactions and family inheritances from taxation.

8) The state should undertake infrastructure development, serving the communities with irrigation projects, roads, canals, and ports.

9) Large industries and public services should be collectivized.

10) A far-reaching labor code should encourage the development of workers' associations, that is, the adoption of a system of cooperatives and unions.[15]

Elizabeth Norvell shows how a merging of class consciousness rooted in the traditional values of community and family with modern nationalism came together in the 1920s at the port of Veracruz to forge a major confrontation between the workers and elite business and property owners. A broad-based coalition of working-class and even middle-class citizenry united to defend local customs and work practices in the face of the insensitive application of modern technologies and the rationalization of labor by the capitalist owners of the port facilities. The Veracruz experience was exceptional for cultural as well as economic reasons. The Porteños had developed their own unique work schedule, music, cuisine, and even ethnicity during the previous century. Veracruz's locale on the Gulf Coast meant scorching daytime temperatures that called for rest periods during the heat of the day. Its geographic position also gave it immediate exposure to Caribbean and European political and cultural influences. The leadership of the strikes came from anarchists and other radicals, while participants included port workers, waiters, housewives, seamstresses, and even prostitutes. The government attempted to mediate between the contending parties, limit the unrest, and eventually control the citywide unions that emerged. Both sides issued nationalist imagery. Similar to their success in other parts of Mexico, the officials outmaneuvered the anarchists and suppressed them in order to assert authority. That suppression constituted a major setback for the development of democracy in Veracruz.

During the 1920s and 1930s the revolutionary programs carried forward by the government gave it much closer contact with the working classes than had existed during the Porfiriato. The state's encouragement of unions and successful strikes, followed by the creation of the nationwide Mexican Confederation of Workers in the 1930s, complemented a longer-running agrarian reform program in which perhaps one-third of the national territory was returned to the rural working class through the National Confederation of Campesinos and the Secretariat of Agrarian Reform. The government's promulgation of nationalism after 1915 corresponded with its sponsorship of unions and massive agrarian reform programs. It sought to demonstrate to the working class that if the members wanted to make gains, there was an official way to accomplish their goals. The Party of the Institutional Revolution (PRI) gained popular support from the masses and created a modern political machine as a result.

In the context of the new modernity, Olvera Rivera demonstrates the process of community formation at Poza Rica, an oil center that grew rapidly in the 1930s. He highlights both the heterogeneous origins of the workers who migrated to Poza Rica in search of opportunity and the increasing importance of the government. The workers' localist traditions and anarchist politics were subsumed in a new hybrid society. The practices of strictly accounting for money, no reelection for union leaders, and workers' self-management eventually succumbed to the pressures of the Mexican government and the national union. But during the process the workers demonstrated the depth and strength of their culture. When primitive conditions and then strikes caused extreme hardship, the workers of Poza Rica responded to the challenge by creating mutual aid societies in order to rescue those who were in the direst need. At Orizaba a remarkably similar pattern prevailed with the addition of extended family networks that provided material and emotional support. In the Mexican-American locales mutual aid and networks based on points of origin and compadrazgo have once again combined to help people adjust to new surroundings and challenges.

In Mexico, modern ideologies, including nationalism, emerged as products of the new experiences and the competition between the state and the foreign owners. Olvera Rivera argues that nationalism was not a powerful initiator of the workers' struggles with the foreign-owned oil companies during the 1920s and 1930s, but that once those confrontations were under way the workers responded readily to nationalistic appeals from the government.

The government's agrarian reform program, especially the large-scale land reallocations of the 1930s, ensured communal survival in the countryside. At the same time the Cárdenas administration's support of new union locals and strikes gave organized labor a place in national politics and provided the basis for the long-standing voting loyalties of the urban working class. Despite the fact that the PRI has frequently used corrupt electoral tactics to guarantee its hegemony, Mexican political stability is largely rooted in its appreciation of the cultural, political, and economic expectations of the working-class. While the present regime has not enabled rural and urban workers to prosper, their strategies and practices of mutual aid, cooperative endeavors, and union militancy are alive and well. Ironically, the government's failures have contributed to the sizable emigration of Mexicans to the United States and the creation of a new dynamic, the Mexican-American working class.[16]

An intensifying Mexican emigration to Texas after 1900 rapidly transformed the labor and ethnic balance of the state. Prior to the twentieth century, migrant labor had supplemented an indigenous and segregated minority work force in Texas. A racially defined work force similar to the conditions in Arizona noted by Ríos Bustamante prevailed in agriculture, mining, and railroads. During the Great Depression the political leaders of the state blamed the Mexican population for the economic hardships. The resulting wave of deportations included many people of Mexican heritage who held American citizenship. The rapid expansion of the economy during World War II and the resulting manpower shortages created sudden prosperity for the Mexican Americans in the state despite the persistent practice of discrimination. The labor shortages in agriculture led to the adoption of the Bracero (contract labor) Program with its notorious abuses. After the war, increased educational opportunity, easy horizontal mobility, and the steady expansion of the economy continued to erode the failed apartheid of the Rio Grande Valley, but discrimination persisted. By 1950 the American G.I. Forum and other Mexican-American organizations were demanding changes in civil and voting rights. These reforms have resulted in more political representation while leaving Mexican Americans as the lowest-paid identifiable workers' group in the state.

Ríos Bustamante demonstrates how the Arizona mining industry provided an important base for the economic survival of the Mexican-American working class there despite the systematic racial discrimination practiced by the leadership of companies such as Phelps Dodge. The mining boom of the late nineteenth century and the next few decades attracted large numbers of migrant Mexican workers escaping the threatening events of the revolution. Many of them gained union experience from the unrest that developed among the miners of Sonora before 1910. Others joined the Industrial Workers of the World and the Western Federation of Miners. Both of these unions made radical demands on employers, but some of the most powerful figures on Wall Street and the most influential men in Washington owned these companies. For example, Cleveland Dodge of Phelps Dodge sat on the board of directors of the National City Bank of New York, the world's largest bank, and was President Woodrow Wilson's best and oldest friend. Ríos Bustamante tells in depth how the companies led by America's most notable citizens practiced systematic and almost inhuman apartheid, and how the Mexican workers adapted and survived through mutual support and hard work.

Mexican workers began to migrate to the United States in increasing numbers early in the revolutionary period. Chicago was an important destination even then. In recent decades that flow has turned into a flood: contemporary Chicago claims a Mexican population of about 750,000. Necoechea Gracia explains that the migrants sought employment in the stockyards and slaughterhouses, but that the primary early employers of Mexican labor were the steel mills. He shows how the companies attempted to redefine the strong familial and mutual aid propensities brought by the Mexicans from their homeland. Moreover, he describes how the companies attempted to replace their "solidarity" with new loyalties to their places of employment. Insurance plans and other fringe benefits have done much to obviate the need for self-help organizations among the Mexican workers. Racial discrimination practiced by Anglo capitalists and American Federation of Labor leaders alike excluded many from union jobs and prevented the organization of locals for Mexicans. As a result, the workers had to organize on their own. They demonstrated their historical consciousness when they called themselves the Gran Círculo de Obreros Libres of South Chicago. They took the name of the most militant union in Mexican history, the syndicate at Río Blanco whose members rose up in 1907.

The Mexicans in Texas maintained an important demographic presence after the state joined in union with the United States. The founders of San Antonio and inhabitants of the Rio Grande Valley maintained a distinct culture throughout the rest of the nineteenth century. The agricultural working class followed the harvests across the center and eastern part of the state, and even further north, each year. Enduring economic privation and racial bias, Mexican workers in communities as diverse as San Antonio and Crystal City formed self-help mutualist societies for the maintenance of children, health care, housing, and employment. They formed cooperatives in the large cities. During the course of the twentieth century they have experienced eras of economic advancement during World Wars I and II and repression during the Great Depression of the 1930s. The conditions created by World War II especially benefited Mexican workers in San Antonio because of imposed federal rules that restricted employment discrimination on military bases, in contrast to the blatant racism found in the oil industry around Houston. Through it all the Mexicans evolved into a more complex and assertive society.

Weber relates a history of struggle and survival for the Mexican Americans of California. They began to go to California in large numbers at the same time that they began the great rural to urban migrations in Mexico, in the early twentieth century. Once in the Golden State they immediately encountered racial discrimination in employment, housing, and human services. They fell back on their own resources in order to defend themselves against hunger, illness, and unemployment. Infused by a continuing flow of new migrants, they formed self-help and cultural self-defense entities at the same time as did their compatriots in Mexico. Weber underscores one of the fundamental points of this book: that the nature of today's Mexican-American political movements is rooted in the 140 years of Mexican experience with mutualist societies, cooperatives, unions, and *sociedades de resistencia*. She concludes that transnational migrants are continuing to have an important effect on both sides of the border.

Notes

1. For examples of this work see Gregg Andrews, *Shoulder to Shoulder? The American Federation of Labor, the United States, and the Mexican Revolution, 1910–1924* (Berkeley: University of California Press, 1991); Paul Friedrich, *Agrarian Revolt in a Mexican Village* (Englewood Cliffs, NJ: Prentice-Hall, 1970); and Norman Caulfield, "Conflict and Accommodation: Mexican Labor and the State in the Twentieth Century" (Ph.D. diss., University of Houston, 1990).

2. For representative works see Robert R. Alvarez, *Familia: Migration and Adaptation in Baja and Alta California, 1800–1975* (Berkeley: University of California Press, 1987); Arnoldo de León, *The Tejano Community, 1836–1900* (Albuquerque: University of New Mexico Press, 1982); Mario T. García, *Desert Immigrants: The Mexicans of El Paso, 1880–1920* (New Haven, CT: Yale University Press, 1981); Richard A. García, *Rise of the Mexican-American Middle Class, San Antonio, 1929–1941* (College Station: Texas A & M University Press, 1991); Richard Griswold del Castillo, *La Familia: Chicano Families in the Urban Southwest, 1848 to the Present* (South Bend, IN: University of Notre Dame Press, 1984); Oscar J. Martínez, *Border Boom Town: Ciudad Juarez Since 1848* (Austin: University of Texas Press, 1975); David Montejano, *Anglos and Mexicans in the Making of Texas, 1836–1986* (Austin: University of Texas Press, 1986); Ricardo Romo, *East Los Angeles: History of a Barrio* (Austin: University of Texas Press, 1983); and Emilio Zamora, *The World of the Mexican Worker in Texas* (College Station: Texas A&M University Press, 1993).

3. Rene Millon, *Urbanization at Teotihuacán*, 2 vols. (Austin: University of Texas Press, 1976).

4. *El Seminario Artistico* (México), June 29, 1844; Rosendo Rojas Coria, *Tratado del cooperativismo mexicano* (México: Fondo de Cultura Nacional, 1952), 82–95, 183.

5. *El Seminario de la Industria Mexicana* (México), June 15, 1841.

6. See John M. Hart, *Anarchism and the Mexican Working Class, 1860–1931* (Austin: University of Texas Press, 1978).

7. Manuel Díaz Ramírez, *Apuntes sobre el movimiento obrero-campesino de méxico* (México: Ediciones de Cultura Popular, 1974), 52.

8. For mutualist societies established during the 1860s, 1870s, and 1880s see *El Socialista* (México), *El Hijo del Trabajo* (México), and *La Convención Radical* (México).

9. Hart, *Anarchism*, 1–103; Rojas Coria, *Cooperativismo*, 115–284. For the quotations see almost any issue of *El Hijo del Trabajo* or *El Socialista*.

10. Rojas Coria, *Cooperativismo*, 119.

11. Ibid., 194, 239–52; Hart, *Anarchism*, 50–82; Julio Bracho, *De los gremios al sindicalismo: Genealogia corporativa*, Instituto de Investigaciones Sociales (México: UNAM, 1980), 1–100. For the quote describing Carmen see Rojas Coria, *Cooperativismo*, 213.

12. *Tercer Congreso Catolico y Primer Eucaristico, celebrado en esta ciudad de Guadalajara, en octubre de 1906* (Guadalajara: El Regional, 1908).

13. For an emphasis on the workers' identification with liberalism and nationalism in this period see Rodney Anderson, *Outcasts in Their Own Land: Mexican Industrial Workers, 1906–1911* (Dekalb: Northern Illinois University Press, 1976). For the effects of radicals, socialists, and anarchists see Hart, *Anarchism*.

14. For the role of labor during the Mexican revolution see Hart, *Revolutionary Mexico: The Coming and Process of the Mexican Revolution* (Berkeley: University of California Press, 1987); and Ramon Eduardo Ruiz, *Labor and the Ambivalent Revolutionaries: Mexico, 1911–1923* (Baltimore: Johns Hopkins University Press, 1976).

15. Rojas Coria, *Cooperativismo*, 300–301.

16. For a discussion of contemporary working-class mutual aid practices and survival strategies see Claudio Lomnitz Adler, *Exits from the Labyrinth: Culture and Ideology in the Mexican National Space* (Berkeley: University of California Press, 1992).

CHAPTER TWO

Culture and Politics
Mexican Textile Workers in the Second Half of the Nineteenth Century

MARIO CAMARENA OCAMPO AND
SUSANA A. FERNÁNDEZ APANGO

During the second half of the nineteenth century, Mexican textile workers took part in numerous labor disputes that underscored their commitment and willingness to defend the freedoms they had enjoyed in their traditional way of life. The working class-factory owner confrontations that took place between 1865 and 1900 in the textile mills in the municipality of San Angel, southwest of Mexico City, are especially instructive. This essay will examine the political actions of the workers and the interactive influences of their traditions and the rising Liberal ideology of the time. It will explain the condition and experience of the workers and how Liberalism influenced the process of change.

A useful example of this interactive process took place in 1878. The workers at the spinning and textile mills of La Magdalena, La Abeja, and Tizapán, all located in the municipality of San Angel, went on strike. They complained that the factory owners, in demanding longer working hours and routines, "do not see us as Mexicans." The strikers demanded that they be accorded "the freedoms of artisans," and, quoting famed Liberal president Benito Juárez, asserted that "respect for the rights of others is peace." As Mexicans they placed their rights and expectations on a par with those of the emergent capitalist elite. They sought to exercise the same rights in the factories that they had enjoyed as industrial workers in the pre-factory artisanal workshops.[1]

A great number of workers and community citizens in the central valley of Mexico shared their concerns. The number of holidays and workdays and the conditions of labor were at stake. The people in the nearby towns of San Nicolás, La Magdalena, and San Bernabé sympathized with their demands, which they deemed to be "fair," that is, founded on the traditions of the artisans of the time and imbued with the Liberal ideas of the era. In taking political action at this point the workers were not motivated by a concept of class struggle or overt class consciousness even though their actions challenged what came to be the dominant practices in the emergent factory manufacturing system. They were defending an ancient system of rights and responsibilities that had pertained to the citizenry of Mexico for a long time.

The textile workers of the 1860s and 1870s were the first generation of factory employees in Mexico, and their behavior was still linked to that of their peasant and artisanal past. They brought deep concerns regarding identity such as kinship ties, customs, habitat, and trade into the factories. By the 1870s a small sector of the laborers was "second generation." These people were the offspring of the first workers and were more acclimated to factory rules. They accepted the work schedule, the norms that determined the relationships among them, and their wages. The adaptations made by the members of this growing group to factory conditions constituted the creation of a new way of life. Among the new elements was their rising sense of citizenship and its prerogatives. The indignation manifested during their struggles by terms such as "social justice" inevitably referred to their rights as Mexicans. They laid the foundation for the emergence of working-class culture. The speed of these changes depended not only on the way in which the workers assimilated the experience of the factory but also on their capacity to resist and fight. The transformation from pre-industrial laborers to workers can be seen by examining the first two generations.

Factories in a Rural Environment

The towns of La Magdalena, San Nicolás Totolapan, Tizapán, San Bernabé, San Jerónimo, Tlacopan, Santa Rosa, and Tetelpa comprised San Angel.[2] In 1854 the municipality had 6,383 inhabitants, most of whom were day laborers. Their settlements were linked by means of pathways and tracks. The workers sought employment on the haciendas, ranches, and mills. A minority were tradesmen and artisans such as blacksmiths, floriculturists, plowmen, stonecutters, carpenters, and shoemakers. In 1867 a railway finally connected the communities with the capital city.[3]

During the middle decades of the nineteenth century five large factories had been established in the municipality. In 1836 two textile plants—La Magdalena, which produced coarse cotton fabric, and El Aguila, which manufactured several types of wool—were built in the community of Contreras.[4] In 1843 two important spinning mills opened—La Hormiga, which produced cotton blankets at Tizapán; and El Batancito de Sierra, at the Barrio de Sierra, which wove fabric for undershirts. Seven years later, the factory of Santa Teresa opened in the town of San Jerónimo. It began as a paper mill, but toward the end of the century the owners turned to the manufacture of woolen cloth.[5] San Angel attracted the owners because it possessed the natural resources essential for the operation of the machines. In order to take advantage of waterpower the builders placed the factories close to the Magdalena River. The water and forest provided the humidity necessary for the weaving process. The towns in a sizable rural area were thus transformed into "manufacturers."[6]

Building these factories became possible thanks to heavy investments by foreign capital, usually represented by an entrepreneur-trader who had the mind of a usurer, behaved as a speculator, and used coercion against the labor force. Such was the nature of the textile bourgeoisie who emerged in Mexico during the second half of the nineteenth century. At the beginning of the century, water and steam engines supplied the power needed to revolutionize the manufacturing process and produce cloth at reduced prices. However, by the middle of the century, the modernization of the textile industry was interrupted. First, the large numbers of the population who lived on the margins of the monetary system limited the potential of the internal Mexican marketplace. The factories quickly saturated demand. Second, cotton prices rose, thus increasing the cost of production and then retail prices. The market contracted because of the combination of low buying power and higher prices. Most people barely earned enough to cover their elementary needs. The manufacturers were forced to store their output in warehouses.

During the 1860s and 1870s the entrepreneurs lengthened the workday from twelve to fourteen hours or more in order to protect their profits. They often adjusted wages downward. In that way the workers carried the burden caused by the rise in production costs and the limited markets. The workers resisted these moves, and frequent struggles ensued. The introduction of night-long shifts exacerbated their complaints.[7] In addition, the factory owners faced a sustained problem of labor shortages. Lacking an experienced work force and training infrastructure such as trade schools, they had to recruit, train, and maintain their employees. They needed cheap labor, but they had to compromise given the dearth of available workers. As a result, they used a form of coercion consistent with the imbalance of power between the rich and the poor, and the regional social setting.

Entrepreneurial Discipline: To Make "Honorable Men"

The employers adopted a paternalist system of controls over their employees, imposing strict regulations intended to keep them in the factories for longer periods of time and increase their output. In that way the issue of the number and length of shifts became of paramount importance to the emerging class of textile factory workers. In the eyes of the entrepreneurs, the workers who resisted these efforts were lazy, licentious, and unreliable. They abandoned their jobs too easily. Therefore, the capitalists attempted to convert them into "honorable men"—methodical, reserved, and less violent—through a new system of controls that joined the old order with the new. They combined the traditional corporal punishment of the hacendado with the new economic penalties, such as fines, layoffs, and dismissals, of the emergent industrial order. Nevertheless, in spite of strict authoritarian rules, the employers tempered them by establishing close personal links with the workers by means of compadrazgo, that is, those ties between the parents and the godparents of a child that were an important and enduring part of Mexican culture.

The design of the factories paralleled the hacienda, where there was no separation between the workplace and the big house (*casa grande*). The settlements of San Angel became factory towns. Surrounded by great walls or enclosed by rivers, they can be compared to prisons. The entrepreneurs attempted to govern the lives of the workers in an effort that could be felt in all spheres of life. Strict vigilance prevailed in the homes, schools, and churches. The owners also dominated local trade. They saw their factories as "islands of goodness" in the midst of a world inhabited by *leperillos* and *haraganes* (vulgar and lazy people); however, these islands were mere definitions, not the entire reality.[8]

The physical reality of the factories replicated the principal traits of hacienda society and rested on a four-centuries-old tradition. At La Magdalena an enormous brick wall surrounded the plant. As at many haciendas, the factory featured a big porch and windows and doors made of double layers of wood and glass with stone lintels. Behind the main facade there was a wide courtyard flanked by galleries in which the work areas and some workers' housing were located. The owners placed these buildings in accordance with the sequence of processing the goods. Two big chimneys towered over the structure, while a secondary courtyard was used for storing merchandise. The *tienda de raya* (company store) was in the northwestern corner of the facility, overlooking the street. The *casa grande*, where the managers usually lived, was placed on higher ground overlooking the whole installation. From the *casa grande* the workers' living rooms could be seen. In front of the factory to the right was the church of La Conchita, which featured the Virgin of Guadalupe, the patron saint of the textile workers.

Similar to life on the hacienda, workers encountered a variety of employment-related expenses. From their wages the owner deducted rent for their small houses, which were found both inside and outside the grounds.[9] The laborers were fined and charged for a number of reasons, including the breakdown of machines, production errors, lack of discipline, treatment of illnesses, attendance at school or church services, and food provisions given in advance. They were often paid with vouchers to be exchanged only at the *tienda de raya*. In addition, supervisors usually demanded a part of a worker's wage in order to ensure job security. While duplicating many of the most onerous aspects of hacienda life, the new order also suppressed some of the fringe benefits of the past. The bosses prohibited the breeding of pigs or the sale of milk so that the *tienda de raya* could monopolize the sale of staples. The entrepreneurs enforced the regulations, thus leaving the workers at their mercy. But appearances can be deceiving; beyond these conditions the workers contested the owners in seemingly endless conflict.[10]

Temporary Workers: Peasants and Artisans

The social origins and cultural backgrounds of the textile workers deeply influenced their behavior. Most of them had been agrarian laborers or artisans in the San Angel district, while only a few had migrated from other regions. Rather than being hostile to modern industry, many of the inhabitants of the area saw it as a part-time alternative to working in their own fields or those of the haciendas. They sought jobs in the factories when the need for labor in the fields decreased. At first, the men, women, and children in the nearby towns, of whom 95 percent were illiterate, covered the labor needs of the factory. The local work force included carpenters, blacksmiths, and laborers, who, lacking full-time employment or sufficient land, staffed the factories.[11]

Former peasants constituted the largest contingent among the new work force. Their traditions and expectations deeply influenced the running of the factory itself and led to constant tension between the laborers and the managers. The latter complained about absences on Mondays, during religious festivities, and in the sowing and harvest seasons. They also protested the consumption of pulque, an intoxicating beverage derived from the maguey plant, during working hours.

Meanwhile, the values and aspirations of the workers created even deeper divisions than the obvious complaints of the managers. The laborers thought about economics in terms of family well-being, which meant household income, clothing, housing, and food consumption. Many of these necessities could be obtained through traditional economic pursuits outside the factory. The workers also held a different conception of time, tied to the agricultural cycle, which left days if not weeks for actions to be taken. Their love for the land and nostalgia caused them to adapt their agrarian culture to the factory regime.

Their participation in kinship and communal activities also led to frictions with management. Many of the workers migrated from the same towns and entered the factory through the recommendation of another member of the family or the community. Thus, many factory workers represented an extended family or community network. Religious practices also competed with the owners' drive for efficency. The laborers judged much of their life in terms of religious faith, which helped them cope with everyday problems. When they left to work in the factory, they entrusted their lives to God;

and they asked favors of the Virgin of Guadalupe, whose image was placed in a shrine with candles in various parts of the factories. These religious feelings included the perpetuation of old practices such as the *limpias*, or ritual cleansings used to free one's self of evil spirits; the *mal de ojo*, or evil eye, for which the workers resorted to sorcerers when they wanted to direct it to the entrepreneurs and managers; and the celebration of saints' days, which led to absences and disruptions of the work schedule.[12]

The former artisans who entered the factories were diverse. Some came from abroad in order to teach their crafts to the new workers. In 1881, 66 percent of the workers at La Hormiga and 18 percent of those at La Magdalena who came from artisanal backgrounds had been born in Mexico City.[13] They introduced their own work ethic and hierarchies within and between trades inside the factories and taught industrial skills to those who had just come into the plants from the countryside. By organizing production, they determined the working rhythm of the departments and controlled discipline.[14] In addition, the plants near San Angel received workers from other factories, people who already had industrial experience. In the mid-1870s, for instance, those at La Magdalena came from the capital, Tulancingo, Texcoco, Querétaro, and Chalco, whereas those at La Hormiga came from Mexico City, Tlalpan, Coyoacán, Puebla, Guanajuato, Orizaba, Querétaro, and San Juan del Río.[15]

Many of these experienced and expert workers became leaders. Some were second-generation workers who, while better acclimated to factory life than the former peasants, accepted more of the mixture of values and ways of behaving because they had learned them from the examples of their parents. Wages were the link that united this second generation with the factories. Because they did not own the means of production, they depended absolutely on wages for survival. In contrast to the uninitiated, more of them sought longevity in the workplace. By the late nineteenth century a large number of people of the region depended on the factory—at La Magdalena full-time workers reached 31.5 percent of the work force, at Tizapán 50 percent, at San Antonio Otolapan 34 percent, and at San Jerónimo 35 percent. In less than one-half century the factories became more than centers of employment, they were crucial in the emergence of an altered way of life in which the workers and inhabitants of San Angel blended the new with the old.[16]

The experience of factory life promoted a sense of common interest among the workers. Together, they sought higher wages, job security, and better working and living conditions, yet they remained somewhat heterogeneous. For the less skilled there was little stability. Constant market fluctuations related to overproduction, the limited size of consumer demand, and the rising costs of raw materials frequently forced cutbacks, and those less skilled were the first to be laid off. Frequent fires and water shortages also caused layoffs. However, not all factory closings were temporary. The San Fernando mill closed permanently, forcing many of the workers to move to Juanacatlan, north of Tlalpan, in search of employment.[17]

Working-class mobility also affected factory life. The workers remained committed to agriculture for many years. Some labored in the factories only when there was no activity on the land. During the sowing, planting, and harvesting seasons even more abandoned their industrial jobs. Most of these worker-peasants were young single men. In 1870 at La Hormiga single males comprised 65.17 percent of the work force. La Magdalena was an exception; there, in 1873, married men made up 58.2 percent of the employees. But, overall, single men continued to be a majority as late as 1904.[18] They had many reasons for moving around—they changed jobs for better wages, more modern conveniences, and promotions in addition to the inability of some of them to adapt to factory work.

A substantial number of textile workers were not able to settle down and preferred to move from one place to another. They rejected the regime of long working hours, bad working conditions, and often violent and despotic treatment. When they tired of such abuses, they abandoned the place. However, there were others who tolerated them better and those who remained gradually became more sedentary. Through their collective experience these workers began to behave as a more cohesive class and tranformed the culture of the region.

Strikes also contributed to the textile industry's instability. At one point the workers at La Magdalena and La Fama Montañesa, both located in Tizapán, closed the factories, and more than seven hundred of them had to look for new jobs in Puebla, Río Frío, and Molino Viejo.[19] In 1873 the same problem occurred farther north at the shirt factory in Tepeji del Río. Here, as a result of a long labor struggle, some of the workers were reaccommodated in the San Angel factories. In 1877, three hundred families from the Hércules factory in Querétaro emigrated en masse to Tlalpan. Around one hundred workers from La Magdalena moved to Tenancingo, tried to found an agricultural colony, and finally went to work in the factory there.

From the 1860s onward, a small but growing nucleus remained in the factories full-time in return for a wage. At the beginning there were no workers over fifty years of age in the mills, but this situation was changing. By 1873 some were in their sixties, and by 1904 a sizable group was that age. Workers remained in place for longer periods of time. The second generation who emerged in the 1870s was born and grew up in the factory environment. Their parents, the first Mexican workers, left their offspring the inheritance of the factory way of life. Little by little, the second generation internalized the lessons to be learned from the capitalist division of labor and discipline as part of their natural order. They remained in place more out of necessity than for any other reason. Wages were their only means of support. That condition provided the material basis for the emergence of a working-class culture.[20]

Conflicts: Workers against Management

Several significant issues dominated the development of labor conflicts as the workers opposed disadvantageous changes. Strikes often resulted from the capitalists' push for longer workdays and work weeks and compressed earnings. In the early years preindustrial habits still defined the time spent, the acceptable level of work intensity, and wages. While these issues provided the material basis for conflict, at the same time there was a cultural crisis. New working and living conditions in which the workers surrendered their independence in the choice of housing, diet, recreation, and even political space continued as points of contention during the late nineteenth and early twentieth centuries.

As both sides gained strength the nature of the conflicts evolved. The workplace acquired a capitalist character based on the set work schedule, clear lines of authority, the juxtaposition of wealth and poverty, and the creation of a small permanent work force. But the workers also formed mutual aid societies and unions. Capital and labor fought over working conditions and wages, schedules, and citizenship rights and mobility. Both sides preferred direct negotiations without state mediation. The workers used strikes as their principal weapon against management, which resorted to lockouts and strikebreakers.

From 1856 to 1900 striking textile workers generally demanded more participation in determining work regulations, over which the owners attempted to maintain exclusivity. The first concern of the workers was to regulate the length of the working day, which usually extended from sixteen to eighteen hours. Ten strikes in the last forty-four years of the nineteenth century resulted from increases in the number of working hours and the imposition of "graveyard shifts." The struggle to suppress the graveyard shifts spread across the textile industry. During the strikes of 1877 in the San Fernando and La Fama Montañesa mills the workers demanded that time schedules be put in writing.[21]

For their part, the entrepreneurs fought against certain customs of the peasants and the artisans that sharply contradicted their drive for higher levels of output at minimal labor costs and maximum efficiency. These disputes underscored the different cultural spheres experienced by the two sides. The owners especially objected to *san lunes* (literally, Saint Monday). Many workers did not reappear on Mondays after what the owners called weekends of holiday revelry and drinking. In 1868 this conflict almost caused the total paralysis of the factories in the Valley of Mexico because the insistence on work on Mondays undermined an established artisanal practice. The entrepreneurs tried to promote punctuality by firing or dismissing workers who arrived late.[22] They also prohibited them from wearing the common clothes of the country people, a wide hat and *jorongo* (poncho), arguing that they were a hazard around machines.[23]

Other reasons for strikes during this period were the arbitrariness and abusive attitudes of owners, managers, and factory masters. In 1873 at Río Hondo, in the state of México, workers complained about the manager because he was too "proud, a tyrant, and interfered in their married lives." They did not understand that his mistreatment derived from the economic necessity to control their time and politically dominate them. They thought that it was the result of personal whim and that by changing the boss they would be able to solve the problem. Therefore, the aim of their struggle was to promote the defense of their interests by defending old practices and objecting to individual bosses for their insults. In this way they missed systemic issues.

A special set of arguments developed between the master artisans and the capitalists because the latter wanted to impose new standards for promotion. In doing so, the owners challenged the power and authority of the masters, diminished their authority, and overturned prerogatives inherited from the much older guild system. In spite of the fact that the companies underwent great change, both technical and administrative, modernization did not bring an immediate alteration in attitudes toward work. This process was slower; for a long time the masters tried to prevent the intrusion of the owners into matters that traditionally belonged to them. These included the training of apprentices, setting the pace of work, and overseeing quality. The entrepreneurs, nevertheless, pushed forward over time, reducing and gradually redefining the power of the masters within the productive process.[24]

Finally, there were also the struggles against economic exploitation, low and decreasing wages, fines, and kickbacks. Salary issues provoked sixteen strikes, or 39 percent of the total for the late nineteenth century. The strikes that revolved around purely economic issues may have been more numerous than this figure because those classified as regulatory usually related to the amount and manner of payments.[25] Thus, both economic and cultural conflicts affected relationships inside the factory. One could argue that at its deepest the dispute was cultural, a clash of two completely different worldviews. The workers tried to maintain those customs and habits that benefited them and opposed the pressures and loss of power entailed by the more modern system of factory production. The laborers and artisans confronted the modern entrepreneurs of the time, with each side advancing its own interests as understood in the context of its worldview.

Solidarity and Labor Identity

In the context of the organized labor movement the workers' "acts of solidarity" arose from the consciousness of being among their *companeros*, or fellows. This feeling of equality had its origins in shared traditions and in opposition to the rule of the entrepreneurs. Certain elements of identity and an old idea of reciprocity in the peasant communities and artisanal guilds led the workers to act together. Mostly because of their poverty, townspeople helped each other in hard times and crises, such as accidents, illness, and death. They sheltered the newcomers to the factory towns in their own houses until they could fend for themselves. The sense of solidarity was such that when a worker had a problem with the master or anyone else, his friends reacted as if all of them had suffered the attack. Thus, what was purely a business problem from the owner's standpoint often became a personal problem or conflict, a family issue, or a matter of concern for the whole town.

These notions of solidarity, reciprocity, and mutual help were based on the awareness of a way of life. Workers talked about their everyday difficulties; discourse was an essential way of transmitting their knowledge, their experience, and their history because most of them were illiterate. Words and facts emphasized the significance of individual identity, which arose from kinship bonds and from customs and traditions; those ties brought individuals together and created a sense of community. Their loyalty to these primary elements of character enabled them to adapt to the situation in the factories, where their opposition to the entrepreneurs endowed them with a class awareness.

Yet these communities were not homogeneous units. Wide social gaps were reflected in the occupations, power, and social prestige of certain individuals. A vertical social structure arose among the workers from this preexisting condition. The artisans formed a small but important group in the community and the factory. During the 1870s the second generation had the best-skilled jobs and commanded respect. They promoted a working-class culture and unions. Moreover, they enjoyed many advantages, which allowed them to act with some autonomy within the labor organizations, be it in technical or in personal matters. From this group also came those who promoted higher standards of performance and behavior and imposed discipline in the factory.[26]

The workers' admission to the factory was mediated by the masters, who recruited people for their respective departments. To know a master, or to have a friend who could recommend you to him, helped in obtaining a job, which otherwise was almost impossible. When an unknown person inquired into a job vacancy, the porter would answer, "You must not try here, this is a family place."[27] The surnames of the workers who resided in the factory compound's "living rooms" reflected this situation. Among the recurrent surnames were Sánchez and Soriano.[28] Also, if you came from the same place of origin, you found it easier to be admitted to a factory where fellow *vecinos* worked. For instance, the *vecinos* of San Nicolás Totolapan had, in the master who distributed the fabrics to be worked on each day, a key to enter La Magdalena. These circumstances allowed the continuity of artisanal authority, family cohesion, and friendship. Only relatives or those who came from the same region were taken on as auxiliaries by the masters, who refused to teach their trade to strangers. The newcomers had to go through a long and slow apprenticeship and adaptation to the factory. They were assigned to an experienced worker or to a master, who taught them the secrets of the trade. They then began to take over brief shifts for those who were absent.

The masters promoted an artisanal work ethic, both in the manner of working and in deportment during the workday. In that way the newcomers learned the factory system. In 1875 the masters of the Sociedades Mutualistas de Socorro y Ayuda Mútua (Societies for Mutual Help and Assistance) advised the laborers: "Work can improve your life. Work! But do not waste the fruits of your sweat in joyrides and sprees. We say, Do not drink, do not gamble, do not make use of the *san lunes*. Do not throw out the window the money that may give you the modest comforts of life and your children an education."[29]

The relationship established between the masters and their apprentices was both a result of the artisanal work ethic and of the kinship among them. These two became the ruling elements that ordered the social relationships inside the factory during this early phase of the Industrial Revolution in Mexico. They enjoyed a virtual teacher-student relationship: "Mister Marcelino Salas, in charge of cloth preparation, is a polite person who deals courteously with his operators; he is a good worker, a good teacher, and a practical man where his job is concerned."[30] Of master Simón Monroy it was said that he is "a machine carpenter, simple, kind, and courteous with all of those who need him; when a machine presents a difficult problem, he overcomes it with the determination and tenacity which characterizes him and all men of quality; he deals with each problem step by step on the basis of knowledge and forward thinking, that is, he uses experience founded on reason; he deserves the laurels of a hard-working and honest artisan."[31]

The master's position of authority was not restricted to the workplace. Frequently, masters led their communities; they took the initiative in organizing schools, national holidays, and cultural events, and they were the founders of the mutualist societies of the region. The rest of the community respected them. Thus, in 1871 the district council of San Angel elected Carmen Huerta as alderman of Contreras. Three years later the workers elected him as president of the Patriotic Junta. In 1884 he was a candidate for the post of colonel of the battalion of National Guards formed by the factory workers of the Federal District.[32]

Mutual Benefit Societies

The textile workers created a number of mutualist societies. In 1873 the labor force at the Contreras mill founded the Patriotic Junta of Contreras, with the masters occupying the leading positions. Rómulo García, a master, worked at El Aguila, where his uncle was the manager. García served as vice president of the Junta several times; a remarkable orator, he was featured at the parties and ceremonies of the mutualist society.[33] García also worked as a correspondent for the newspaper *El Socialista*. The members of the Junta elected Severiano García, a master of weaving and former artilleryman who had fought against the French invaders, to the positions of accountant, secretary, and first *vocal*.[34] He and several other veterans had founded the Junta. He promoted the idea of unionizing and mutual aid among all of the textile workers of the central valley of Mexico. The workers at El Aguila called him a "philanthropist and philosopher." Thus, the leaders of the Junta Patriótica de Contreras came from the distinguished workers, masters, and employees of the factory, people who had prestige within the community both by their place in the productive hierarchy and by their military service. These individuals distinguished themselves by acting as civil and patriotic authorities and by supporting the continuation of working-class practices and beliefs. They also helped develop fraternal relations between the textile workers and other artisans in the Valley of Mexico.

Nevertheless, the initial number of labor activists produced was relatively small. In 1872, when the first workers' central council in Mexico City, the Gran Círculo de Obreros, was established, it counted only seventy-one members. A year later, only thirty-one delegates from factories around Mexico City reelected the board of directors. The Gran Círculo included members from El Aguila and La Magdalena. In Contreras, which employed about five hundred workers, only seventy participated in the mutualist society and most of them came from the most distinguished members of the community, including artisans, masters, and war veterans.

Mutualist societies addressed concerns related to both the working and living conditions of the workers. Mutual aid was fundamental to all of them. By means of fee payments they created a fund for mutual assistance in case of illness, death, unemployment, or other crises, and they also gave each other moral and spiritual comfort. They promoted virtuous behavior and tried to restrain the vices of their members. They wanted to make the workers into good citizens capable of defending their interests against those of the capitalists. Moreover, they trusted that mutual assistance and cooperative stores would improve the living conditions of the workers and would have an overall positive effect on their social conditions.

In this sense, the mutualist societies did not threaten the capitalists, but they did not accept the labor hierarchies that the latter wanted to impose. Rather, they encouraged workers to take control of their lives and communities. The aim of the societies was not to destroy capital, but to look for a fairer way of life for all of the members, something that would give them a countervailing ethic, a feeling of equality with the capitalists.[35] Further, they hoped to challenge the owners by using education and civic training to convert the workers into good citizens. *El Socialista* pointed out the need for the workers to defend their interests not only against the capitalists but also against the government, by "training inside their own corporations in order to understand their rights and duties, to become morally aware of the importance of mutual respect, to become an example to others, to improve their working situation, and to completely abolish the degrading state in which they have remained for a long time, in relation to their capitalist bosses and even to their rulers."[36]

They emphasized that for mutualism to be achieved, it was necessary to elevate the "morals" of the artisans. Again and again they addressed the problem of drunkenness and its impact.[37] Members asked the Federal District Council to close the cantinas and *pulquerías* because many workers, instead of taking home their weekly wages, spent them in day-long sprees. Thus, they and their families, trapped in poverty, became even more miserable. Mutualists urged that workshops be installed in place of the cantinas and *pulquerías*. Some considered public dance halls corrupting places, full of vice.[38] Ultimately, the mutualist society members tried to

give the artisans greater mobility by socializing them. They knew
that a well-instructed people, in addition to knowing skills, rights,
and duties, would be less inclined to accept the owners' abuses.
The people thus would be able to elect their government representatives with less susceptiblity to demagogic politicians. The mutualists made a serious effort to create participatory citizens.[39]

Many artisanal and industrial groups organized mutualist societies and cooperatives, and some even tried to establish newspapers. During the 1870s they founded no less than twenty mutualist
societies with the aim of uniting the proletariat. Between 1870 and
1879 they founded ten "workers' newspapers" because they recognized that control of communications was essential to the working-
class cause. They created at least two more between 1880 and 1899,
seven during the revolution from 1910 to 1919, ten between 1920
and 1929, and twelve from 1930 to 1939.[40] The workers' press re-
currently pointed out that the future of the country depended on
public education: "The ignorant worker, because he starts to work
so early in life, has few opportunities for education; thus, it is not
his fault. But the rich man, he who does not know what work means,
he who has all the opportunities for education and profits from the
advantage given to him by wealth, is an infamous criminal who
deserves a very strict punishment . . . if he opposes instruction for
other human beings."[41]

Workers and Nationalism

Not only had Mexican workers undergone exploitation in foreign-
owned factories, but since 1862 they had also lived through the
French invasion and occupation of their country.[42] It is not surpris-
ing that strong nationalistic mottoes accompanied their opposition
to the entrepreneurs. This nationalistic sentiment, which became
blatant during the 1870s, led the textile workers to manifest their
support during the French occupation of the 1860s for President
Benito Juárez. To them the Mexican president meant "redemption,
liberty, and respect for human freedom. Invoking their Mexican
nationality, [they] claim their rights against the foreigners . . . sworn
enemies of the motherland and . . . owners of the factories."[43]

The demands for justice on the part of industrial workers during the second half of the nineteenth century and the first decade of
the twentieth were largely claims for the restoration of what they

considered to be their old rights. They took shelter in the historical causes of Padre Miguel Hidalgo y Costilla, the leader of the Independence Revolution in 1810, and of President Juárez against the foreign invaders who "exploited" the Mexican people. They identified these heroes with nationalism and patriotism, with the race to which they belonged. Thus, a textile union could exhort its members to be "dignified descendants of the indomitable race of Cuauhtémoc, Hidalgo, and Morelos [José María Morelos, another leader of the Independence Revolution] in their struggle against that which disturbs their way of life."[44]

Some weavers wrote in *El Socialista* that "it is an injustice to be considered a stranger in your own land," commenting on the fact that foreigners received higher salaries while Mexican workers earned miserable wages. Thus, the spinning workers at La Magdalena went on strike because the owners paid English masters five pesos and the Mexicans only ten reales (eight reales equaled one peso). To assert oneself as a Mexican meant to claim citizenship, an idea which the workers learned from nineteenth-century liberal ideology. They justified their struggle with the right to be treated as equals. *El Socialista* quoted their demands: "We are looking for the way which will best restore our rights."[45] In times of crisis the workers always expressed Liberal ideas along with their sometimes radical and nationalist arguments.

As a consequence, the celebration of national holidays became very significant for the workers. With a conscious use of the symbols of a heroic past, the celebrations contributed to making sense of everyday events. Music, parades, speeches, banquets, and a day off all became part of the ritual. The workers formed special committees in order to arrange a fiesta. Everyone took part—some obtained fireworks, while others prepared plenty of food and drink, and the community government usually helped with a sum of money. Mutualist leaders delivered speeches often critical of the gachupines (Spaniards) and other foreigners. The celebration ended with cannon shots. Thus, nationalism became interwoven with workers' mobilizations and the struggle against the capitalists. These elements helped to generate a common feeling of belonging among the working people and gave them a sense of identity both as members of the San Angel textile working class and as Mexicans.

Even when they fought with, and identified, national and foreign entrepreneurs as their enemies, however, the workers were not primarily concerned with anticapitalism. Rather, they focused on abuses and the rising Conservative forces operating under the motto of "Order and Progress," who essentially were challenging their right to organize. Aware of the political conflicts between Liberals and Conservatives, they tended to side with the Liberals, who offered them more freedom of choice. Their experiences as the first generation of industrial workers did not promote a sense of class distinction as much as it did a sense of unity as Mexican workers who had been deprived of the rights given to them by the Liberal Constitution of 1857. *El Socialista* captured a widely held sentiment when it declared: "Workers, take shelter in the principles of the 1857 Constitution in order to defend your rights first as Mexican citizens and then as workers."[46]

During the second half of the nineteenth century the emergent factory workers fought with indignation, unity, and national pride to achieve social justice. They framed their demands in terms of being Mexicans and not with a high degree of class awareness; after all, they were a new class. Fundamentally, the men and women who worked in factories considered themselves as Mexicans who worked rather than as Mexican workers. This perspective reflected their contact with their cultural heritage and guided their political attitudes and actions during the late nineteenth century and into the decade preceding the revolution of 1910.[47]

Notes

1. Cuauhtémoc Camarena O., "Las luchas de los trabajadores textiles: 1850–1907," in Leticia Reina, coord., *Las luchas populares en México en el siglo XIX* (México: CIESAS, Cuadernos de la Casa Chata, no. 90, 1983), 213–14.

2. See Francisco Fernández del Castillo, *Historia de San Angel* (México: Editorial Innovación, 1981), 239; and Antonio García Cubas, *Atlas geográfico y estadístico* (México: Imprenta de José Ma. Fernández de Lara, 1858).

3. Archivo Histórico del Ex-Ayuntamiento de la Ciudad de México (hereafter AHCM), Fondo San Angel, Estadísticas 1854, 1870, 1904, and 1913.

4. Archivo de Notarías, México, 1847, 42, Vol. 78, folios 261, 264.

5. AHCM, Fondo San Angel, Estadísticas, Box 1.

6. The Magdalena River served several factories near the Hacienda La Cañada. The river flowed past La Magdalena, El Aguila, Santa Teresa, La Hormiga, and Loreto and then into Lake Texcoco. See García Cubas, *Diccionario histórico, geográfico y estadístico* (México: Antigua Imprenta de las Escalerillas, 1896), II:321, and V:26; and Melesio Melitón Gracia García, *La Magdalena Contreras D. F., su historia* (Mexico: Tesorería del Departamento del Distrito Federal, 1979), 88.

7. The data in the AHCM, Fondo San Angel, show that there was dissension among the workers as a result of the wage reductions. See also Cuauhtémoc Camarena, "Las luchas," 211–301.

8. Dawn Keremitsis, *La industria textil mexicana en el siglo XIX* (México: SEP-Setentas, 1973), 64–67; *El Socialista* (México), January 25, 1874.

9. *El Socialista*, February 15, 1874.

10. Ibid., June 7, 1874.

11. AHCM, Fondo San Angel, Estadística, 1856, 1876, 1904, without box number.

12. San Angel was renowned as the "town of sorcerers." The population asked them for all kinds of herbal drinks either as remedies or for "evil" purposes.

13. According to Frederick J. Shaw, in 1849, 38 percent of the 120,000 adults in Mexico City lived in families in which artisans were the principal breadwinners. Of these, 70 percent were cobblers, tailors, carpenters, bricklayers, bakers, painters, weavers, and printers, and most lacked the capital to employ others. See Shaw, "The Artisan in Mexico City (1824–1853)," in Elsa Cecilia Frost et al., *El trabajo y los trabajadores en la historia de México* (México: Colegio de México, 1979), 399–418.

14. Ibid. There was a small contingent of eight workers from the United States who were qualified to operate the factories. AHCM, Fondo San Angel, Estadística, 1856, without box number.

15. Ibid., 1876, without box number.

16. Ibid., 1854 and 1913, without box number.

17. Bernardo García Díaz, "Migración y clase obrera en Orizaba," in *Historias* 19 (Revista de la Dirección de Estudios Históricos del Instituto Nacional de Antropología e Historia, México), (October–March 1988): 130. See also Cuauhtémoc Camarena, "Las luchas de los trabajadores textiles mexicanos: 1865 a 1907" (B.A. thesis in Social Anthropology, Escuela Nacional de Antropología e Historia, México, 1985), 177–80.

18. *El Siglo XIX* (México), August 15, September 2, 11, 12, October 31, December 7, 1868.

19. *El Tiempo* (México), October 15 and November 16, 1885; October 3, 1886.

20. AHCM, Fondo San Angel, Estadísticas 1871, 1873, and 1904.

21. The regulations in force between 1871 and 1878 stated: "1st. Working hours will be established by the factory managers. 2nd. By the very fact of going to work, workers accept the working conditions and hours established by management for each shift and work week. 3rd. The workers are required to work during holidays when requested. Whoever rejects these orders will be removed." *La Voz de México* (México), July 1, November 24, 1877; *El Pajaro Verde* (México), July 2, 6, 1877.

22. See AHCM, Fondo Tlalpan, Box 18, File 31, 1867.

23. Mario Camarena and Susana Fernández, "Un estudio de caso sobre el movimiento obrero: La industria textil en el Distrito Federal" (B.A. thesis, Escuela Nacional de Antropología e Historia, México, 1981), 89–90.

24. Entrepreneurs trying to regulate master artisans often caused conflicts with the workers because these actions were seen as an attack against the customs of the workers. *Historia Obrera* (México), no. 6 (1975): 2; *La Voz de México* (México), May 18, 1883.

25. For data on strikes between 1865 and 1883 see Alejandra Moreno Toscano, "Los trabajadores y el proyecto de industrialización, 1810–1867," in Enrique Florescano et al., *De la Colonia al Imperio* (México: Siglo XXI, 1980), 344–45; *La mujer y el movimiento obrero mexicano en el siglo XIX* (México: CEHSMO,

1975), 59, 184–87; Moisés González Navarro, "Las huelgas textiles en el porfiriato," in *Historia Mexicana* (México) 6, no. 2 (El Colegio de México, October–December 1956): 203–82; and Cuauhtémoc Camarena, "Las Luchas: 1850–1907": 173–310.

26. The Tlalpan textile factories' rule, in force since 1866, stated: "Since the master is responsible for the good operation of the machines and production, no worker can use them without the authorization of the person in charge, nor can he use the tools to mend the machines." 1866 Reglamento, *El Socialista*, July 14, August 4, 1872.

27. Virve Piho, "La obrera textil," in *Acta Sociologica* 4, Series La Industria (México: Centro de Estudios del Desarrollo, Facultad de Ciencias Políticas y Sociales, UNAM, 1974), 40.

28. AHCM, Fondo San Angel, Estadisticas, 1871, without Box Number.

29. *El Socialista*, March 7, 1875.

30. Cuauhtémoc Camarena, "Las Luchas: 1850–1907": 156.

31. Ibid., 108.

32. *El Socialista*, August 31, 1884.

33. Ibid.; and February 16, 1873, September 27, 1874.

34. Carmen Huerta, a weaver at El Aguila, participated in the mutualist society; he characterized himself as a "distinguished worker." The members of the boards of directors from 1873 to 1878 were: Marcial Salazar, a textile worker from childhood and recognized as a master of his field; Doroteo Reza, a master in finishing who learned from his father; and Simón Monroy, a master lathe operator, famous for his "ability and kindness." *El Socialista*, March 1, 2, November 30, December 14, 1873.

35. "El mutualismo en el siglo XIX," in *Historia Obrero* (México) 3, no. 10 (October 1977); *El Socialista*, August 15, 1868.

36. Cromwell, "El Congreso Obrero," *El Socialista*, April 2, 1876.

37. "La paz pública" and "Las clases obreras," *El Socialista*, March 18, 1888.

38. "Las pulquerías," *El Socialista*, January 19, 1873; "Soneto," in "Variedades," *El Socialista*, April 6, 1873; "Los bailes públicos," *La Tribuna del Pueblo* (México), April 29, 1877; and Joaquín Flandes, "El obrero del Porvenir," *El Socialista*, February 23, 1873.

39. Antonio de P. Escárcega, "La regeneración del obrero por medio de la instrucción," *El Obrero Mexicano*, May 20, 1984.

40. Florence Toussaint Alcaraz, *Escenarios de la prensa en el porfiriato* (Colima: Universidad de Colima, n.d.), 75.

41. "La instrucción es el camino de la prosperidad," "Cuestiones sociales," "El trabajo II," *El Socialista*, September 3, 1871, February 5, 1872.

42. *El Socialista*, February 8, 1874; José María González, "Los obreros," and "El hijo del trabajo," *El Socialista*, August 19, 1877.

43. Several mutualist leaders, including the weavers Carmen Huerta and Severiano García, distinguished themselves in the fight against the invaders during the French intervention. During the war there were several guerrilla groups in the area, apparently formed by workers and supported by the inhabitants of the factory towns. See Cuauhtémoc Camarena, "Las luchas: 1865 a 1907," 152–53.

44. Rodney Anderson, "Los trabajadores mexicanos y la política de la Revolución, 1906–1911," in Leif Adleson et al., *Sabores y sinsabores de la Revolución Mexicana* (México: COMECSO, n.d.), 234.

45. *El Socialista*, February 19, 1874, September 26, 1875.

46. "A sacred codex has been published—the 1857 Constitution—in order to ensure our holy rights as Mexican citizens. Through the 1857 Constitution, whose second section of the 17th article has been constantly infringed, no one can use violence to demand their rights." Ibid., September 26, 1875.

47. Rodney Anderson, "Los trabajadores," 240.

CHAPTER THREE

The Formation of the Working Class in Orizaba*

BERNARDO GARCÍA DÍAZ

One of the most neglected issues within the historiography of the Mexican working class is its geographical, social, and cultural origins. As a result of the relative boom of labor studies during the 1970s and early 1980s, there are a number of essays on the history of the labor movement that focus on its most dramatic struggles and the most significant trade unions. Nevertheless, there are only a few studies offering an explanation of the complex process of class formation. As a matter of fact, there is a tendency to equate the history of the labor movement with the history of the working class. The objects of study are generally workers' organizations, with their ideologies and policies. These are essential dimensions of the working class, but not their roots.

The textile workers of the Valley of Orizaba are no exception. Most scholars writing on the working class there have researched the most famous episode in Orizaba working-class history, the so-called Río Blanco strike of January 7, 1907. But they have neglected issues such as the prevailing environment in the factory town at the turn of the century and how the working class there took shape. The present research is an inquiry into the social, cultural, and ethnic origins of the textile workers of Orizaba.

The boom of the textile industry in Orizaba began in the last decade of the nineteenth century and was linked to the wider expansion of industry in Mexico. During this period, which ended

*Translated by Nair M. Anaya Ferreira and John Mason Hart.

around 1904–05, an unprecedented number of stock companies were founded, mainly by Frenchmen. This step was successful not only because of the innovative spirit of the French merchants-turned-entrepreneurs but also as the result of objective conditions. The textile industry had become a safe and lucrative area of investment as a consequence of technological changes and the advantages provided by the regime of President Porfirio Díaz. The most significant governmental assistance came in the form of protective tariffs, which imposed a tax on imported texiles of 100 percent.

New technology created changes in the international trade conducted between Mexico and the metropolitan countries [that is, in the United States and the nations of Western Europe]. The latter began to emphasize the export of capital goods. At the same time the introduction of electricity in factory production allowed a move to high-speed bobbins, automatic looms, and printing machines.[1] In response to the changing conditions, modernization came to Orizaba. It began with the creation of the Compañía Industrial de Orizaba, or CIDOSA. In 1892 this company founded the Río Blanco factory, which became the biggest and most modern facility in the country. The owners also bought the factories of San Lorenzo, Los Cerritos, and Cocolapam, which they renovated, expanded, and integrated into the Río Blanco site. These factories came to constitute a cohesive unit of production. The first three centers specialized in weaving and spinning fabrics, and Río Blanco bleached and printed them.

In the years that followed, the foreign owners incorporated other factories into the group. Santa Gertrudis produced jute, and Mirafuentes, located in Nogales, served as a spinning mill. The process culminated with the creation of Santa Rosa, inaugurated in 1899 and also owned by French investors, grouped under the name of the Compañía Industrial Veracruzana, S.A., or CIVSA. The Santa Rosa factory grew to 1,400 looms, 40,183 bobbins, and four printers. The Río Blanco factory reached 1,650 looms and 2,000 bobbins. In 1905 about eighteen hundred workers operated the Santa Rosa, not including the foreign technicians.[2]

The foreign owners imported high-speed automatic looms and bobbins, which brought great savings, and printing machines, which gave better and more elaborate finishes to their fabrics. These machines were a novelty in Mexico at the time. By 1898 there were only twenty-seven in the entire Mexican textile industry. Along with new machinery, European technicians and fitters also came to the country to oversee operations. To run the turbines inside the industrial plants the technicians diverted part of the water flow of the Río Blanco with canals several miles long. They also helped to develop hydroelectric plants at the falls near Rincón Grande and Zoquitlán. The availability of electric power generated by the Río Blanco allowed the industry to expand on a large scale. The technicians introduced electric energy to the Mexican textile industry only a few years after the first use of electrical motors in 1893 at textile factories in the United States.

The factories in the Valley of Orizaba gained renown as the most modern in Mexico at the end of the nineteenth century. They deserved their reputation. Even after the modern plants at Metepec and Atlixco were opened, Orizaba continued to be considered the main textile center in the country. The decision to select Orizaba as a place to install large modern factories was not accidental. Circumstances converged to create a favorable environment there for the construction of textile plants. The valley enjoyed the presence of the Citlaltpetl watershed, which performed the role of water and energy distributor. The humidity of the climate also allowed the manufacture of fabrics with a finer texture and weave than those made in the relatively dry climate of the Mesa Central. In addition, the railway enabled the industrialists to exploit the geographic position of the district. It was located midway between the port of Veracruz, where cotton grew, and the populous Altiplano, the main point for consumption and the distribution center for the nation at large.

The Río Blanco Valley, however, suffered from an essential limitation. There were not enough local people to supply labor for modern industry. The two largest factories had been built on the almost uninhabited properties of two Indian villages removed from the valley floor in the nearby mountains. The owners of the San Lorenzo factory had to import a great number of weavers, as did the others. Where did the people who contributed to the manufacturing of fabrics come from?

The data of the 1892 electoral register of the municipality of Nogales identify 427 workers who worked mainly in San Lorenzo, and a smaller number who worked in the recently inaugurated Río Blanco factory.[3] Only 55 of these people were natives of the region: 30 were from Orizaba and 25 from Nogales. The rest of the workers were immigrants. Almost one-half of the total number of immigrant workers came from the state of Puebla, with 144 from the capital city, and 66 from elsewhere in the state. Mexico City served as the second largest source with 66. Other immigrant workers came from the states of Tlaxcala (27 workers) and Oaxaca (11), while smaller numbers were from Veracruz as well as from Hidalgo, Querétaro, and Guanajuato. Most immigrants were young. About 57 percent were single, while married couples and families comprised 26 percent. Another 14 percent of the workers were married but living alone. The average single male worker was twenty-four years old. Sixty-two percent of the population was between eighteen and thirty years of age. A large proportion of workers, 183 out of 427, or more than 42 percent, knew how to read and write.

The labor force underwent substantial modifications during the next decade when the two largest factories went into full production. A sample of 603 workers at the Santa Rosa factory, one-third of its total force, showed that the sources of immigration became more varied.[4] Puebla remained the main supplier of immigrants with 47 percent, while Oaxaca went from having insignificant numbers to taking second place with 23 percent. Mexico City and its surrounding textile area contributed 13 percent, followed by nearby Tlaxcala with 8 percent and Querétaro with 5 percent. Some immigrants also came from the states of Hidalgo, Michoacán, and Guanajuato.

The magnitude of the Oaxacan migration represented the most remarkable change. Less evident, but equally important, were the changes in the group from Puebla. In 1892, Puebla City provided 144 of the 210 immigrants from the state. During the next decade the capital provided only 41 workers, while 212 came from the surrounding areas. The decrease in migrant workers from Puebla City combined with the increase coming from the countryside of the state and that of Oaxaca, mainly from the Mixteca, to turn rural immigrants into a majority. The Valley of Mexico and Tlaxcala remained significant providers of immigrants but were less important than Puebla and Oaxaca. If we put all the immigrants within two categories, we find that those who came from places with a pre-existing textile industry amounted to 34 percent, while those from places with no industries of that kind totaled 66 percent. Even though this information is useful, it is not enough. In order to understand the formation of the working class in Orizaba we must learn who these immigrants were from Puebla, Oaxaca, Mexico City, Tlaxcala, and Querétaro.[5]

The Workers from Puebla

From colonial times, the city of Puebla specialized in producing cotton, silk, and wool fabrics. It also generated skilled and craft workers. Many sought new opportunities and migrated to other places over time. (Some went to Mexico City in the early nineteenth century where they formed a colony of textile craftsmen.[6]) Puebla's textile activities increased during the nineteenth century. After the middle of the century a process of self-reproduction took hold among the factory work force. People inherited their role in the trade. This development corresponded with the rise of a new textile industry, already mechanized, which emerged in the mid-1830s on the banks of the Atoyac River, close to Puebla. The Constancia factory, the first one in the country, opened in 1835. Thereafter, the textile industry gradually achieved hegemony after having developed alongside artisanal production. The ten mills that existed in 1843 were soon joined by many others. By 1877 the municipality featured twenty-one factories.[7]

Villages grew up around some of these factories, thus ensuring a stable supply of workers. The villages and nearby pueblos filled with working families who specialized in factory employment. The combined incomes of several family members compensated for the low individual wages offered. If women were marginal participants in the process in the Orizaba region, the high proportion of children entering the factories made up the shortfall. In 1878–79 one-fourth of the textile workers were children.[8]

During the period of maximum expansion of the country's textile industry, Puebla possessed a work force experienced in the most modern methods of production. This skilled proletariat was able to emigrate to other regions. Poblanos (natives of Puebla) often migrated in search of higher salaries. For instance, Dawn Keremitsis points out that during the 1880s, Puebla entrepreneurs offered a meager minimum wage of only 25 centavos, "one of the lowest of the country," whereas the minimum wage in Orizaba was 35 centavos.[9] Juan Carlos Grosso agrees, but he adds that unemployment plagued Puebla due to an inability to absorb a rapidly growing work force. Part of the problem stemmed from the rapid proletarianization of displaced peasants and craftsmen.[10]

The workers from Puebla did not come only from the state capital and nearby towns, however. People also migrated from the agricultural districts of Chalchicomula, Tecamachalco, and Tehuacán. The townspeople of San Andrés Chalchicomula, Tecamachalco, Tochtepec, Quacholac, Cañada Morelos, San José Ixtapan, San Agustín del Palmar, and many other places joined them. The commercialization and privatization of agriculture drove people from the countryside and into the factory towns. While many Pueblan workers went to Orizaba, others kept on moving to the lower elevations of the agricultural district of Córdova. There they worked on the haciendas and plantations of the tropical lowlands.[11] Some of these rural migrants came from mixed peasant and artisanal backgrounds. For instance, at the district of Tecamachalco, there was a tradition of wool weaving on hand looms that prepared the immigrants for textile factory labor.[12]

The Workers from Oaxaca

The Mixtec Indians arrived in Orizaba after walking across wide mountain ranges full of cactus. They largely came from the districts of Tepozcolula, Coixtlahuacan, Tlaxiaco, and Nochixtlán, in La Mixteca, as well as from the central valleys, from the city of Oaxaca and from some of the towns around Etla. Some even came from the sierra of Juárez.[13] The Oaxacans were the last group of immigrant labor to arrive in the Orizaba Valley, but by the first decade of the twentieth century they had become the second largest.

The migrating Mixtecs differed from the Nahua Indians of the sierra of Zongolica, who did not enter the factories. While the Nahuas lived in the mountains that surrounded the textile valley, the people from La Mixteca came from many kilometers away. These kilometers multiply when one considers the trek not in terms of distance-space but of distance-time. To reach Orizaba meant that someone starting from Santa Catarina Tayata, in the district of Tlaxiaco, faced an arduous journey lasting several days.[14]

The Mixtecs did not suffer from the expansion of the haciendas during the midnineteenth century to the same degree as did the inhabitants of central Mexico. Even so, the privatization of communal land took place. The process of privatization developed mainly as a result of the growth of commercial agriculture in the region. Even before 1856, disentailment was proposed in some areas of La Mixteca,[15] which caused some agricultural producers to abandon their way of life.

One element as significant as being disenfranchised of the land—or perhaps even more significant because of its permanence— was the prevailing poverty suffered by the Mixtecs in their natural environment. Living in a harsh region, they found few resources offered by the mountains. Even in the valleys, seasonal agriculture was difficult and variable, and rainfall sporadic. Hunger was the force that drove the dispersion out of La Mixteca. Fernando Braudel's words about the mountains could be applied to them: factories of men for alien employment.[16]

Temporary migrations of agricultural laborers toward the Gulf lands preceded the migration to Orizaba. Toward the end of the nineteenth century there were *engancheros* who went up to recruit work crews in the district of Huajuapan de León.[17] These labor recruiters acted as intermediaries for the foreigners who owned the tobacco farms of the region of San Andrés Tuxtla in Veracruz. They gave money to those who agreed to work for a six-month period picking the harvest. It may be that these workers were among those who later went to Orizaba.

As a result of the modernization of the textile industry, production became more complex and was subdivided into a larger number of simpler jobs.[18] If, on the one hand, it was necessary to contract experienced workers for highly qualified tasks, on the other, there was a whole range of jobs that did not require any kind of specialization. These could be handled by migrants coming directly from the countryside. This situation prevailed in the printing departments, both at the Río Blanco factory and at Santa Rosa. Alongside the skilled printers or dyers, groups of migrant workers performed easier manual jobs. In addition, the factories required crews of workers to carry out hard and disagreeable tasks. Once the laborers became familiar with the migration route from La Mixteca to Veracruz, they could try their luck in the Orizaba factories. There, the French entrepreneurs needed them as much as they did the expert weavers.

Factory work offered the Mixtecs an alternative. They did not have to suffer the usual coercive treatment nor remain on the farms for long periods. They could go to the factories for a few weeks and then return home. When they became tired or fed up either with factory discipline, which was new to them, or with the way of life, they could leave there as well. As a result they took a long time to settle permanently in the industrial region. In the late 1910s, during the first years of unionism, union militants had to endure their detachment. They were temporary workers, constantly

coming and going between the factory and their communities, and
they showed very little enthusiasm for the unionist cause.[19]

A growing number of the Mixtecs became familiar with specific jobs with certain departments and learned a variety of tasks.
Orizaba and its factories seemed to them a lesser form of oppres-
sion, even if it was stranger than farm work. Besides, with the successive arrival of friends and relatives, the Mixtecs developed forms
of solidarity that made life less difficult in that far-away land. Dis-
tances were shortened by the Mexican Southern Railway, which
brought migrants from the city of Oaxaca and from the district of
Etla in the central valley ever closer to Orizaba. The railroad began
operating in 1892 and tied the Antequera with the rest of the country. In Etla two small factories had been installed—San José, in
1875, and Vista Hermosa, in 1885—further acculturating the
Mixtecs to industrial life.[20]

The third Oaxacan region that provided immigrants was the sierra of Juárez. In Xia, in 1875, an English entrepreneur, Thomas
Grandinson, installed a textile factory in order to take advantage of
the water power of the region.[21] He opposed importing workers and
organized a labor force by recruiting people from the nearby sierra.
He succeeded in forging a work force of male and female employees; but when the factory closed, the workers from the sierra of
Juárez left to join other Oaxacans in Veracruz and Etla.[22]

The Workers from Mexico City

Many of the workers who went to Veracruz originally came from
Mexico City and from the neighboring regions of Tlalpan, Contreras,
San Angel, Miraflores, Tlalnepantla, and Toluca. This region experienced early textile factory construction and competed with Puebla
for hegemony. In a few years it had more textile workers than
Puebla. In 1877, for instance, fourteen factories employed 3,261
workers, while in Puebla there were only 2,760 workers.[23] Most of
the big factories were located in San Angel, Tlalpan, and Chalco.
The concentration of more than 3,000 workers in one area fostered
the development of working-class communication and solidarity.[24]

A reproduction of the labor force, similar to the process in
Puebla, took place. By 1870 textile masters began to emerge from
among the workers and artisans. They started in the textile rooms

during childhood, and with their acquired experience could substitute for the foreign masters and skilled workers. Technical schools had contributed to this process since 1830. But other significant moments occurred, such as regionwide labor management struggles and organizng efforts. Sometimes workers tried to organize themselves autonomously, as the experience of the "Las Fábricas Unidas" (the United Factories) shows. At other points they accepted the guidance of craftsmen such as those who organized the Gran Círculo de Obreros (Great Workers' Circle). Of the forty-one strikes in the textile industry that broke out in the country between 1850 and 1883, twenty-seven of them occurred in the state of México.[25] The greater Mexico City area was the center of the textile struggle in the early period of industrialization. The mutualist societies that were formed in the 1860s slowly became resistance groups. When the Gran Círculo was formed, textile workers joined it. By 1875, twelve of the twenty-eight affiliates of the Gran Círculo were comprised of textile workers at factories in the Valley of Mexico.

An even more significant experience on the long and difficult road to developing a heightened level of class consciousness was that of "Las Fábricas Unidas," which functioned as a kind of coordinator of the workers' organizations of the Valley of Mexico. This organization was more labor oriented than the Gran Círculo because the workers, rather than the craftsmen, managed it themselves. It overcame the local and isolated character of labor struggles and generated a network of solidarity at the factory level. In addition to mutualist societies and workers' organizations, the population of the Valley of Mexico came together because of the War of Intervention against the French. Some weavers became guerrilla fighters against Maximilian's empire and in favor of the Reform Laws and were later recognized as leaders of their communities.[26] In the years before the war a group of them went to Orizaba. The workers from central Mexico were characterized by their organizing experience and known for their combativeness. Considering the number of strikes and other working-class projects that they promoted, we must admit that they constituted one of the leading forces of the incipient industrial proletariat.

In the years immediately previous to the opening of the French-owned factories in Veracruz, a wave of entrepreneurial repression took place. In order to hinder the organization of workers, owners circulated lists of workers who were not to be accepted in any factory. Strikers and those who organized meetings were shot and working-class leaders jailed. The press correctly viewed the workers of Tlalpan as "shrewd, persistent, and stubborn."[27] Even though they suffered a bitter defeat in 1875, they still went on strike four times between 1876 and 1877. The authorities sent the workers' board of directors to prison in 1877. Among those who emigrated, these experienced militants and other fighters from the Valley of Anhuac impacted Orizaba in important ways.

Internal population shifts—up to now little researched—were related to the extent of labor agitation and organization that emerged at Orizaba. Undoubtedly, labor struggles there were the heirs of organizing experiences that had emerged and developed on the Altiplano in the decades previous to the establishment of a modern industry in Veracruz. These collective experiences fused in the fertile environment presented by the French companies in Orizaba.

The Workers from Tlaxcala

"I lived in Nogales. . . . As I was the eldest, I remember when we arrived there. My father worked in Nogales for a while. According to him, we went there because my grandparents had also gone there looking for jobs. My whole family already had the habit of going to Veracruz. They had tried some towns in Tlaxcala, but the pay was better in Veracruz; besides, everything moved. The thing was that sometimes, also, we sold, we took food; the fruit from here, meat, cheeses, in sum, many times we sold them among our relatives or *compadres*. There in the Blanco river we also had relatives who worked in the textile factories." This testimony, given by Gregorio Serrano, "peasant-worker" of Santa Inés Zacatelco, reveals some of the reasons that influenced the migration to Orizaba. He tells us not only about the search for work and better salaries but also of the particular habits of the workers of the south-central region of the state of Tlaxcala. They left their communities to look for work and tried their luck at the textile factories, often ending up going to Veracruz.[28]

The area was a good one for textile production. The Atoyac and Zahuapan rivers flowed through it, and during the nineteenth century the Interoceanic Railway and a sheep-breeding industry impacted on the region. The towns there became suitable places for the installation of textile factories, which used old technology and traditional production methods. With the construction of the new factories, a part-time proletariat emerged to combine its work in the fields with that in the factories. The search for additional income beyond agriculture—that is, as craftsmen, traveling merchants, muleteers, or "manufacturers"—was not new in the region.[29]

When the industrialization of Orizaba occurred, the town had been brought relatively close to outside markets due to the railroad. Going to work in the factories did not involve the same sense of great adventure, or even a drastic change in one's way of earning a living. What changed was that the area of action in which the peasant-workers found their livelihoods became larger. They found work not only in Orizaba but in other textile regions of Veracruz as well.[30] The fact that migrant workers stayed away from Tlaxcala for weeks or even months created a growing rift between industrial work and agricultural labor. Some immigrants from Tlaxcala eventually decided to work full-time in the factories of Orizaba.

The migrants from Tlaxcala came from an area with a long-standing experience of protest and struggle against the hacendados in the region. However, more unique was the recent expansion of a dissident religious movement in the region, Methodism.[31] Missionaries successfully propagated Methodism in southern Tlaxcala, and the migrant workers comprised a great part of its membership. They went from one place to another, spreading their creed. Apart from forming a mutualist-type solidarity, Methodism had an educational function among the Tlaxcalan workers. They organized civic-religious rites on February 5, March 21, May 5, September 11, and other fundamental dates of the Liberal calendar. By doing so, they exalted the figures of Juárez, Hidalgo, and Morelos and praised the virtues of Mexican liberalism. During these meetings, criticism of the regime of Porfirio Díaz arose. Workers discussed the gap between political realities and the democratic principles of the Liberal Constitution.

The distribution of Protestant newspapers, such as *El Abogado Cristiano Ilustrado*, combined with the activities and zeal of local propagandists who carried on an enthusiastic proselytizing effort. When they left for Orizaba, several Methodist families from Tlaxcala took part in the formation of a new congregation in Río Blanco, which joined immigrants from Miraflores, Chalco, and other regions where Methodism had spread. The Río Blanco congregation, led by José Rumbia, played a significant role at the turn of the century because it became the seat—under the influence of the

promoters of the Mexican Liberal Party—of the first militant workers' organization of the region, the Gran Círculo de Obreros Libres
(GCOL).[32]

The migrants from Querétaro came from the capital of the state
and from a town created around the Hércules textile factory, which
had been founded in the 1840s with machinery, craftsmen, and
skilled workers imported from France. The Frenchmen instructed
the Mexican workers, who later replaced them.[33] After several decades, workers began to leave Querétaro and go to places such as
Juanacatlán, Jalisco, Uruapan, Michoacán, Veracruz, and even to
the region of Atlixco, Puebla.[34]

The immigrants who filled the factories at Orizaba were varied
and heterogeneous and contributed to Orizaba's reputation as a land
of outsiders. This diversity confirmed a historic constant in the process of working-class formation. There were basically two kinds of
immigrants. The first group was made up of those for whom the
factories only represented a sporadic and temporary occupation,
one way among others to earn their living. They accepted factory
work for reasons of survival alone. These workers identified with
the agricultural communities, the rural family, and a life in the countryside to which they hoped to return. The second group was formed
by those who came from other textile regions and had already accepted the fact that factory work formed part of their destiny. Between the two there was a diversity of people in transition, such as
the peasant workers of the Altiplano.

Those who had accepted factory labor as a primary part of their
lives did not constitute a majority of the immigrants, but they filled
a fundamental role in helping the other workers to advance their
self-awareness as a class. They promoted resistance groups and led
the way in the labor struggles that followed in Orizaba. The arrival
of small, but cohesive, groups of workers who already had factory
experience elsewhere helped to shape the emerging Orizaban society. These workers formed a textile proletariat characterized by
mobility within a large textile corridor that ran from the Valley of
Mexico to Veracruz and that occasionally included the factories in
Querétaro, Jalisco, and Michoacán. Because they had no assets,
workers were dependent on the labor market of an industry characterized by instability.

They responded with mobility. This nomadic proletariat moved
through the textile regions, either in small groups made up of friends
or relatives or in whole collectivities. Forced to emigrate when fac-

tories closed, many individuals and families carried their few belongings with them when they left. In 1865 the strikers at San Ildefonso, in the state of México, were evicted by the owners and police and moved to the factory of La Colmena y Barrón. In 1868 there was an exodus of workers from Tlalpan, Contreras, and Tizapán to the textile region of Tlalnepantla. In the same year the strikers of La Magdalena, La Fama, and San Fernando migrated to Puebla. In 1873 the strikers at Tepeji del Rio in the state of Hidalgo moved to San Ildefonso. Two years later the strikers at La Fama and San Fernando, in Tlalpan, were refused readmittance when the strike ended and so left for the factories of San Angel and Tlalnepantla. In 1877 the families of three hundred strikers at the Hércules plant emigrated to La Fama. Two hundred workers and their families arrived from Jalisco in 1889 as part of an effort to break a strike at San Fernando in the Valley of Mexico. In 1893 workers from Puebla went to San Antonio Abad to break a strike.[35] In 1896, one hundred workers and their families traveled from San Fernando to Juanacatlán, Jalisco.[36] That migration remains alive, memorialized in the following *corrido*:

> San Fernando is closed
> The workers are already leaving
> They take the machinery
> They go to Juanacatlán.
> Conrado Carranza and others
> go to build the looms
> so that when people arrive
> they are all ready.
> Good-bye, pulquito
> cured with banana,
> we go to Jalisco
> to drink only tequila.[37]

Other worker contingents also came from Querétaro, Puebla, and from the region of Guadalajara. The mass migrations were frequent enough that few years could pass without witnessing one.

The life stories of these transient workers are difficult to follow. But, even so, through oral history it is possible to know something about them. One such case is that of Primitivo Soto, who was born in Puebla, moved to Nogales, where he worked as a weaver in 1904, and later moved to Contreras and San Angel.[38] Soon after a strike at the La Hormiga factory he had to go to La Carolina. Later he traveled to Metepec, Atlixco, where there were some vacancies after a strike. He then wandered through the factories of the municipality of Puebla to return finally to Orizaba, where he settled at the Santa Rosa factory.

Another story is that of Alberto Lara Rojano, a worker who survived the Río Blanco strike of January 7, 1907. Born in Miraflores, Chalco, he came from a family with a textile tradition: his maternal grandfather was a weaver, and his uncles were textile workers. A few months after Alberto was born, the family moved to Tlalpan, to the San Fernando factory, because his father followed his uncle, a starcher. When San Fernando closed, Alberto's father moved to Contreras and his uncle went to work in two factories in Uruapan, Michoacán—La Providencia and San Pedro. Later on, his uncles moved to Puebla and eventually reached Río Blanco, where his father contacted them in order to enter the loom department.[39]

Another case is that of Agustín Flores, a boy from San Salvador Tzompantepec in Tlaxcala, who entered the factory La Trinidad in Santa Cruz when he was not yet ten years old. Together with his brother, he moved on to Metepec, where an uncle helped them. His next stop was the factory La Carolina, in the Valley of Mexico, where he met some relatives. In 1911 he arrived at Río Blanco and settled there.[40] Our fourth case is Antioco Mosqueda, who came from Querétaro. He arrived at Santa Rosa in 1901 after working at the factory La Reforma, in Salvatierra. From the Valley of Orizaba he went back west to La Virgen in Tajimaroa and finally ended up in Orizaba in 1918.[41]

These small personal histories offer a glimpse into the lives of people who finally settled in Orizaba, and their stories demonstrate the larger process taking place. Even more numerous would be the tales of those who only stayed for a short time and did not settle there. For instance, at Santa Rosa the level of transient workers was very high between 1902 and 1906. Of the 1,348 workers there in 1901, only 14 percent were still there five years later.[42] While it is not clear where the overwhelming majority of workers went, what is clear is that the working class found it difficult to settle down. In contrast to the people who came to stay, there was a vigorous countermovement of those who moved on. During these years the valley seethed like an anthill, with a colored and fluctuating mass coming and going endlessly. Leticia Gamboa has remarked on that extreme mobility at Atlixco. In a study of the population formed by four hamlets of workers at the factories of El Volcán, El León, La Carolina, and El Carmen, Gamboa discovered that only 18 percent of the workers registered in 1905 had remained in 1909. In the particular case of El León, she noted that of the total number of workers present in 1899, when the factory opened, only 11 percent remained in 1905. Of those registered in 1905, only 14 percent remained in 1909 as the migratory nature of textile labor continued.[43]

Several factors contributed to this mobility. People who arrived straight from the fields often found it difficult to adapt to their new situation, and there was also a seasonal exchange between agriculture and industry. At the same time, the instability of those who were more closely integrated to the textile factories reflected the creation of unmet expectations and dissatisfaction. Mobility was a sign of the desire to improve living conditions and also reflected the occasional crises suffered by some factories. As working opportunities increased, qualified workers did not feel as obliged to adapt themselves to the first unsatisfactory job that they were offered. Thus, they moved on, hoping to find a better one at a higher salary. If they did not find a better job elsewhere, they either continued migrating or went back home. Despite their transient nature, these workers belonged to a generation more preoccupied with finding vacant jobs and creating resistance associations than with a desire to return to the fields.

The size of this group was much smaller than that of the seasonal workers or peasant-workers, and it decreased even more when compared to the purely agricultural workers or the artisans of the period. The permanently industrial work force lived side by side with workers who came directly from the fields and who saw the textile mills as a possibile vehicle for rehabilitating a semi-independent agricultural status that they hoped to regain. There were also those who combined agricultural and industrial activities, either as free peasants such as those from Tlaxcala, or as *peones*, or laborers, who took factory jobs during the off-season in agriculture.[44] These pioneering groups of the modern proletariat, though a minority of the social structure of the second half of the nineteenth century, were very responsive to labor agitation in periods of crisis and had the ability to widen their protests beyond their numbers. Workers organized themselves while comparing and exchanging experiences and ideas. They associated with artisans and often knew how to read and write. They even contributed to sustaining newspapers. Moreover, they were people who had developed their own political convictions, and they further developed them and acted upon them through their participation in labor associations.

Migratory workers contributed to the emergence of an industrial working class beginning in the 1860s. Their migrations show us groups of workers who neither returned to the countryside nor entered into artisanal activities. The appearance of the great factories in places such as Orizaba or Atlixco, and the modernization and expansion of others in the Valley of Mexico, consolidated these workers as a group. The industrial regions were the ones which finally defined the face of the proletariat—sharply, unmistakably, and even dramatically—in a still deeply agricultural Mexico. They constituted what became a free labor market, although traditional ties of kinship and regional bonds were important in gaining access to work in some factories. Contacts were especially important in the smaller plants, where personal ties were fundamental. In fact, migration, far from being an element of disorder, required a certain level of organization with regard to personal contacts. The contacts kept workers informed about job opportunities; and, in the case of Orizaba, the first workers to arrive created a flow of information back to their places of origin.

The railroad facilitated communications and contributed to the internal migrations of those years. It was not a coincidence that most of the migratory routes coincided with the railways. By means of its employees and passengers, the railway not only made the widening of opportunities possible, but also its speed helped to diminish the psychological costs of the separation from home and family.[45] Displacements caused migrations from tiny hamlets in the mountains, such as Santa Catarina Tayata, and from the factory towns of the Mesa Central, to Orizaba. People joined friends, relatives, and fellow workers from the same places of origin. The mobility mirrored family and regional networks, producing another kind of geography that emerged from market and economic changes. Moreover, it was a young working class, both biologically, because of its age, and socially, because of their recent pre-industrial past. But it also contained a second generation of textile workers, some of whom became skilled. By the early twentieth century, textile workers in Orizaba had been forming as a class for several decades based in part on their experiences in various regions of the country.

Those familiar with the incipient industrial environment at Orizaba were the ones who absorbed the newcomers and educated them about the factory world. They integrated the new arrivals by teaching them how to do tasks, and by showing them the manners of worker conduct through their everyday examples. They taught them the urban concept of time, reinforced by the factories' sirens. Some of these workers, influenced by the new labor discipline, assumed the role of promoting order among the immigrants.[46] They also contributed to the process of social definition and led the first workers' movements and organizations. If we observe the workers' struggles, we realize that not much time passed before some form of collective resistance was put into practice. In 1881, at San Lorenzo, strikes broke out the same year that the factory was inaugurated. The same thing happened in Santa Rosa in 1899, when the strike there was declared only a few months after the factory began operations. These first migrants were quickly familiarized with the modern forms of worker struggle. They did not have to wait long before collectively facing the entrepreneurs.

When the Great Circle of Free Workers (GCOL) was founded in 1906, union leaders decided to create branches throughout the Altiplano and even in Oaxaca. This early break with local boundaries had to do with the Magonist project of creating a national opposition to the Díaz regime. It also coincided with the bonds that the migrants held based on their roots. But at the same time, labor unity was an inheritance from the experiences gained by "Las Fabricas Unidas" and by the Gran Círculo, both of which had begun thirty-four years earlier in the Valley of Mexico. The fact that the Gran Círculo and the GCOL shared similar names is not a coincidence. The memory and tradition of the first organization was carried into the second, even though they corresponded to different historical moments of the working class.

During the nineteenth century the workers had been consciously carrying forward their memories of previous struggles, which helped create new workers' groups.[47] From 1865, when the first movements appeared, to the late nineteenth century, the greatest number of strikes broke out among the textile factories of the Valley of Mexico. That is also where the most relevant workers' organizations appeared. Nevertheless, in the 1880s the factories of Veracruz, some of them just recently inaugurated, had an important place. Between 1880 and 1889, Veracruz led the nation in labor unrest. At the turn of the century the eye of the storm had moved toward the Gulf of Mexico. In 1906–07 the workers of Orizaba created the Great Circle of Free Workers, which had a brief but dynamic existence. It helped in some sixteen strikes that broke out in the state in only two years.

The modernity of the French factories at Orizaba offered the material basis for the crystallization of the working class in a relatively short time. The great size of their operations allowed the concentration of large numbers of workers at a few sites. In these factories human relations were anonymous, and workers lacked any kind of personal or effective participation. Those conditions made class relations more evident as well as more important.

In Orizaba, modernization and the size of the factories combined to reinforce working-class agitation. The entrepreneurial spirit evidenced there was more modern than that of textile entrepreneurs elsewhere in Mexico, and it was mirrored in the relationships created with labor. The owners broke away from the traditional patriarchy where the entrepreneur was frequently physically present in order to emphasize his control. That tradition did not prevail in Orizaba, and the workers managed to shake off the social ordering which they had been subjected to in the more traditional factories and in the fields.

The freedoms of the pioneer inhabitants of the factory towns, even if constrained, were wider than those which usually existed at rural factories or in the countryside. Undoubtedly, the capacity of modern factories to integrate workers helped to accelerate the process of unification and the development of self-identity among textile workers in Orizaba. In other areas of Mexican textile production a proletariat had been developing by means of a slow metamorphosis which lasted decades. In Orizaba this process was completed in a few years' time due to the previous manufacturing experiences of many of the migrants and to the spectacular industrialization of the region.

The factories contributed to the creation of a stable group of workers. This group developed gradually at first and then became self-reproducing. At Santa Rosa, 347 workers stayed over from 1908–09, demonstrating how a group of formerly nomadic laborers found permanent homes in Orizaba. The workers who had been there for a time were prepared by the turn of the century to absorb the newcomers into the factory world. They helped apprentices in the workshops and socialized them in the new ways of living in an industrial setting. The ongoing introduction of new workers, typical of a developing working class, was fundamental for maintaining the continuity of the organizing process.

In spite of the modernity of the factory system at Orizaba, and of the factory's capacity to absorb a variety of workers, a modern working class was only partially formed. A good number of workers who came together in the valley constituted a group who did not want to be an industrial working class, at least not full-time. They found many obstacles to unity. The new work and the life that it presupposed were strange to them. Everything involved cultural shock, which they tolerated only because of economic necessity.

Because it was a class rich in contrasts but poor in homogeneity, the road to a collective awareness was an uphill one. It must not have been easy to live together and to create bonds of solidarity among groups with such different geographical, social, cultural, and even ethnic origins. There were strong cultural and social differences to deal with. Inside the factory, one could find an experienced worker dressed in cashmere and a felt hat, with a factory past and proud of his occupation. Alongside him a recent arrival from the fields could be found wearing sandals and cotton breeches. Their interrelationship was not always easy.

Informal groups and mutualist societies were the first signs of solidarity and a move to resolve internal conflicts. It was only at the next level of the process that the broader labor organizations intervened. By that time, the first organizers had already engaged in battles to obtain agreements allowing workers' groups. These groups went beyond the limited horizons of family and friends, and militants worked hard to bring together a work force with varied origins and expectations. For the foreign owners it was not easy to manage this multifaced proletariat. They had to deal with militants and confront a less predictable and more active proletariat. The emerging working class proved readily capable of rejecting labor administration.[48] In the organizational sense, it must be said that the worker movement in Orizaba emerged from the experiences of the second generation of textile workers, but it also descended directly from the protest and resistance of the newcomers in the factories. These elements fused into a potent force, and on January 7, 1907, the workers of Orizaba transcended trade-union demands and rebelled in an act that anticipated the revolution of 1910.

Notes

1. Dawn Keremitsis, *La industria textil mexicana en el siglo XIX* (México: SEP-Setentas, no. 67, 1973), 60–154.

2. Bernardo García D., *Un pueblo fabril del porfiriato: Santa Rosa, Veracruz* (México: SEP-Ochentas, no. 2, 1981), 11–29.

3. *Padron General del Censo de Población del Municipio de Nogales*, 1982, Municipal Archive of Nogales, Letter P, no. 6. The data in this register were

processed in computer by Edda Arrez Rebolledo and Marta Meza, who designed its organizing program.

4. Research treating the migration included the birth books in the Civil Registry Archive, Ciudad Mendoza. The parents and witnesses who took the children for registration between 1900 and 1908 were noted.

5. Some ideas developed in this essay were taken from the collective project *Formas y formación: Historia social de la clase obrera en México, 1880–1940,* by Leif Adelson, Mario Camarena, and Gerardo Necoechea. Another important source is Rolando Trempe, "Storia sociale e formazione della classe operaria in Francia," *Annali della Fondazione Lelio e Lisli Basso-Issaco,* Vol. 4 (Rome: Franco Angeli Editore, 1982).

6. Juan Carlos Grosso, *Estructura productiva y fuerza de trabajo: Puebla, 1830–1890* (Puebla: Cuadernos de la Casa Presno, no. 2), 31.

7. Leticia Gamboa Ojeda, *Los empresarios de ayer* (Puebla: UAP, 1985), 25–33.

8. For the issue of labor reproduction see Grosso, *Estructura.*

9. Keremitsis, *La industria textil,* 202.

10. Grosso, *Estructura,* 33–34.

11. Teodoro A. Dehesa, *Memoria general del estado de Veracruz, 1896–1898* (Xalapa: Gobierno del Estado, 1898), 21.

12. Grosso, *Estructura,* 30.

13. For the Oaxacan migration see the appendix in García, *Un pueblo fabril,* 158.

14. Timoteo Reyes Reyes and Bernardo García D., Programa de Historia Oral del Centro de Estudios Históricos (hereafter cited as PHO-CEH); and Valentina Espinoza, Melesia and García D., PHO-CEH.

15. See Francie R. Chassens, "Oaxaca: Del porfiriato a la revolución, 1902–1911," (Ph.D. diss. in Latin American Studies, UNAM, 1986), 73–83.

16. Fernando Braudel, *El Mediterraneo y el Mundo Mediterraneo en la epoca de Felipe II* (México: Fondo de Cultura Económica, Vol. 1, 1953), 148.

17. Archivo General de Oaxaca, Sección del Gobierno, Cartas, Legajo 96, Expediente 7, July 1903.

18. Cuauhtémoc Camarena Ocampo, "Las luchas de los trabajadores textiles mexicanos, 1865–1907" (B.A. thesis in Social Anthropology, ENAH, 1985), 60.

19. Francisco T. Olivares, and García D., PHO-CEH.

20. Chassens, "Oaxaca," 125.

21. Ibid., 126.

22. Arturo Hernández, and García D., PHO-CEH.

23. Moisés González Navarro, *Las huelgas textiles en el porfiriato* (Mexico, Cájica, 1970), 35–37.

24. The discussion of the Valley of Mexico is based on the excellent thesis by Cuauhtémoc Camarena, "Las luchas de los trabajadores textiles."

25. Cuauhtémoc Camarena, "Las luchas de los trabajadores textiles, 1850–1907," in *Las luchas populares en México en el siglo XIX,* coordinated by Leticia Reina (México: Casa Chata, no. 90, 1983). For the complex history of the Gran Círculo de Obreros Libres see Jose Villaseñor, *Orígenes del movimiento obrero mexicano. El Gran Círculo Obrero de México, 1870–1880* (México: Avances de Investigación 51, Cela, UNAM, 1982).

26. Cuauhtémoc Camarena, "Las luchas de los trabajadores" (Thesis), 131–40.

27. Ibid., 20.

28. Interview, Don Gregorio Serrano by Beatriz Cano, Mexico City, September 12, 1979.

29. Raymond Th. J. Buve, "Protesta de obreros y campesinos durante el porfiriato," *Boletín de Estudios Latinoamericanos* 12 (December 1972): 1–20.

30. Abel Juárez, "El trabajo en la hacienda de San José de los Molinos," *De los borbones a la revolución*, coordinated by Mario Cerruti (Mexico: COMECSO-GV Editores, UANL, 1986), 204–5.

31. For the expansion of Methodism in Tlaxcala see Jean Pierre Bastían, *Protestantismo y sociedad en México* (México: CUPSA, 1983); idem, *Itinerario de un intelectual menor de la revolución tlaxcalteca*; and José Rumbia Guzmán, "Pastór y maestro de la escuela metodista, 1865–1913" (unpublished typescript, 1986), 7–11.

32. *Río Blanco* (Río Blanco), 28 February, 13 March 1976; Bastían, *Itinerario*, 7–11.

33. Margarita García Luna, *El movimiento obrero en el Estado de México: Primeras fábricas, obreros y huelgas, 1830–1910* (Toluca: Universidad Autónoma del Estado de México, 1984), 23–24.

34. For Juanacatlán see Jorge Durand, *La ciudad invade al ejido: Proletarización, urbanización y lucha política en el cerro del judio, D.F.* (México: Ediciones de la Casa Chata, 1983), 131–32. For Tajimaroa see José Alfredo Uribe Salas, *La industria textil en Michoacán, 1840–1910* (Morelia: Departamento de , Investigaciones Históricas, Universidad Michoacana de San Nicolas de Hidalgo, 1983), 138.

35. Cuauhtémoc Camarena, "Las luchas de los trabajadores," 177.

36. Durand, *La ciudad invade*, 131–32.

37. Ibid.

38. Primitivo Soto and García D., PHO-CEH.

39. Alberto Lara Rojano and García D., PHO.

40. Agustín Flores Serrano and García D., CEH.

41. Carmelita Mosqueda and García D., PHO.

42. García D., *Un pueblo fabril*, 62–63.

43. Leticia Gamboa Ojeda, "Dos observaciones sobre la clase obrera textil de Atlixco a fines del porfiriato" (forthcoming), 10–14.

44. Luis G. Morales, "Los obreros de mayorazgo, 1912–1918" (B.A. thesis, Universidad Autónoma Metropolitana, 1981), 47–50. Morales found some cases of *peones* still in debt in the second decade of the century.

45. John H. Coatsworth, *El impacto económico de los ferrocarriles en el porfiriato* (México: ERA, 1984), 65–66. Bastían, *Itinerario*; Rumbia Guzmán, "Pastór y maestro," 7.

46. Bastían, *Itinerario*; Rumbia Guzmán, "Pastór y maestro," 7.

47. For this periodization I am indebted to Camarena, "Las luchas de los trabajadores," 90; and his B.A. thesis, "Las luchas."

48. For indiscipline see García D., *Un pueblo fabril*, 46–48.

CHAPTER FOUR

Gender, Labor, and Class Consciousness in the Mexican Textile Industry, 1880–1910*

CARMEN RAMOS ESCANDÓN

From the 1880s onward, the Mexican textile industry grew rapidly with increased capitalization and modernized productive facilities. At the same time, increased labor specialization allowed greater control of the process of production. For instance, the reopening of the factory of San Antonio Abad in Mexico City, which was proudly announced as the second most important factory in the Republic, was celebrated by the owners as a definitive event in the development of the industry.

The concentration of labor in a single place, however, brought up harsh criticism. J. Figueroa Domenech, in his 1899 guidebook to Mexico, declared that "the shift to a stock company and the increase in capital increased the firm's production, but this did not improve the quality of the items; these, in fact, according to people who know the subject, cannot compete with the prints and fabrics of other factories that may be smaller but are well-managed by their clever owners and not by pompous boards of directors."[1] The concentration of labor and productive facilities resulted from technological progress and increased capital investment. The process of mechanization concentrated the means of production in a single site and increased the volume of production. The aim was to produce merchandise as fast as possible, without interruptions and in endless amounts for a market that was constantly growing.

*Translated by Nair M. Anaya Ferreira and John Mason Hart.

The changes in the management and organization of the factory had implications for the workers employed there. The concentration of production in a single place and the precise division of workers' functions created a working class that had specific features. The differences among the workers were established in accordance with the roles that they performed. Thus, the various functions in the workplace impacted on the manner in which workers organized and the form that labor struggles took, including conflicts among particular groups of workers.

This essay analyzes the relationship between the formation of the textile working class and their demands and the division of labor within the factory from the perspective of women. It explores how technological advances and the specialization of work affected female workers and the ways in which gender influenced the formation of an explicitly feminine labor consciousness.

Gender, a By-Product of Labor

In the study of the differences between workers and their particular situation within the factory, the analysis of gender difference has been neglected until very recently.[2] If we consider gender as a social construct which establishes, reproduces, and consolidates the relationships between men and women, we are then referring to historically constructed variations and nuances, and to the spaces in which this takes place. From this perspective the factory becomes the space where the differences between male and female workers emerge—differences which are created as a result of the varied tasks performed by men and women in the industrial process.

Several factors are used in order to identify these differences between men and women as workers:

1) What is the feminine work space, either within the factory or in the relationship between factory, workshop, and housework?

2) What is the relationship between female work and the process of production as a whole? What roles do feminine work fill in the working process at the domestic workshop, in manufacturing, or in the factory? And what tasks are assigned to women in the division of labor in the factories?

3) Labor, social, and leadership relations within the factory raise another key question. To what extent does the hierarchical rela-

tionship between men and women reproduce itself in factory tasks? And how are gender relations structured by work relations? Are there specifically feminine labor demands? How are the demands "by women" articulated within the set of labor demands as a whole?

4) What kinds of demands do women make? If we suppose that the formation of gender conditions specific labor demands, we can analyze the relationship between gender and the larger labor movement in which these demands are expressed.

Background: The Place of Feminine Labor

The first evident change in the space and nature of feminine labor in textile production in Mexico was the Conquest itself. During the pre-Hispanic period the most extended form of textile work was that of Indian women who wove and spun cotton and ixtle fibers as part of their domestic labor. Miguel Othón de Mendizabal, writing in 1935, explained that:

> Weaving was performed, and continues to be performed today, by means of the waist loom. . . . Such a loom, more than an instrument, . . . , is a technological process. The sticks which form it vary in number and size according to the kind of weaving they are planned for. Two of them are for assembling, distributing, and knotting on them the threads of the warp, others are for separating and moving the warp by means of combs; others regulate the width of the weave, and others are for crossing the weft with a shuttle and tightening it. What is unique in this device is that the woman weaver forms a physical part of it, . . . because although the upper section of the warp is tied by means of loops to a tree or to the wooden posts of a hut, the instrument is put in tension and ready to be used by the weight of the woman, who has a textile or leather sash tightened to her hips and knotted in two loops that go out of the lower base of the weft. The physical relationship of the woman to the loom limited the width of the cloth to the capacity of the arms of the weaver. Consequently, the fabrics were woven to a maximum width of half a bowknot; its length varied according to the kind of work, although it was also limited so that it did not form a roll that was difficult to handle. The weaving, as all manufacturing, was the exclusive field of women.[3]

Thus, in indigenous tradition, weaving and spinning were part of the domestic tasks which a woman had to perform inside the house. With the Conquest, production of the cotton indigenous fabrics was not substantially modified in its technique and volume because the taxes imposed by the Spaniards, to a large extent, were paid in cloth. Nevertheless, the Conquest introduced a new element: the craftsman workshop, with a pedal loom, operated by men. Thus, a gendered form of textile production was born with a changed spatial location and technique.

The introduction of the pedal loom constituted, from the technological point of view, a true "industrial revolution." The worker used a fixed wooden loom of two and four pedals, with teasels, wheels, spools with julios, tabours, combs, and colillo shuttles.[4] The Indians and mestizos accepted the new technology without undue problems. From the point of view of the distribution of labor between men and women, the greatest revolution was in the fact that "men claimed exclusive use of the new device, relegating women—who had always been the only weavers—to other activities such as washing, thistling, reeling, and dyeing wool. Nevertheless, women continued to use in private their archaic loom . . . for the kinds of textiles that required a small width of the weft."[5]

In 1964, Jan Bazant wondered how and why the temporary work of the peasant and Indian woman was transformed into a permanent job for the urban, apparently mestizo, man. It seems that the process was drawn out with significant regional variations. It is possible to point out here only the general outline. The first Spanish craftshops emerged early in New Spain; they multiplied and grew even against the guild's attempts to limit them. With the name of *obrajes* they reached enormous proportions.[6]

Nevertheless, the establishment of the workshops did not mean the end of the female presence in textile activities. Quite the contrary was true; Indian and mestizo women were integrated into the production of the *obrajes*. They supplied yarn, spun, and wound the cotton thread that was handed to the shops to be woven at the pedal loom workshops, or was woven by the women weavers on their waist looms. Ever since the first years of the colony, it was common practice for Spaniards to bring together Indian weavers and to make them work in a craftshop. This practice was explicitly forbidden by the Crown in 1549, and all the *obrajes de encomienda* were declared illegal in 1621. However, by 1680 it was clear that this prohibition had not been followed and that women were still working in them. According to Richard Greenleaf, toward the end of the colonial period, the number of women employed at the *obrajes* surpassed that of men. Thus, for example, in 1799 the Chalco workshop employed 2,265 women and only 1,316 men.[7]

However, the *obrajes* formed by basically female labor were not exclusively controlled by Spanish males. Women also owned them, or else female organizations, such as the Carmelite nuns of Valladolid, who in 1799 controlled a workshop that employed 145 girls. This shop was a case of an *obraje* school. The nuns instructed the girls in Christian doctrine, reading and writing, and taught them textile skills.[8]

Thus, the first gender difference found in the industrial work force lies in the fact that Spanish or mestizo men had the exclusive use of the pedal looms, which prevailed at the *obrajes*. The Spaniards relegated women to the role of spinners, of simple suppliers of yarn. Once cotton production became market-oriented, however, the role of women changed substantially. With the introduction of the pedal loom, the weaving tasks were distributed according to gender. Although at the beginning both male and female weavers learned how to operate the pedal loom, production was gradually concentrated in the hands of men. According to Othón de Mendizabal, with the introduction of the pedal loom and the spinning wheel, exclusively operated by males, women stopped producing at the waist looms in order to concentrate on the production of yarn. In the royal edicts of 1530 and others it was ruled that "all women, Spanish and natives, are to become used to spinning linen, wool, and cotton and to make flannel cloths and canvas in their homes."[9]

With the introduction of the Spanish-type loom many women had to abandon the activity of weaving cotton fibers in order to concentrate on spinning. Thus, the spinners emerged. They were women who sold their products to merchants or contractors, who often supplied them with the raw materials for a home-based cottage industry. As Indian women changed from weavers to spinners, they went from being autonomous craftswomen, with production directed toward domestic consumption, to piece workers. This shift continued throughout the colonial period. The *obraje* represented the mature expression of the continuous appropriation of Indian women's work. When women did work at the *obrajes*, we can only speculate that their presence was due to the fact that they, or a male member of their family, especially the husband, had fallen into debt.[10]

The rise of the *obraje* modified the female space where work was carried out. Women weavers no longer produced exclusively for home consumption but for commerce. The role of women in the textile industry was even promoted by the Crown. In 1600 and 1783 the Spanish government ruled that "women are to work in weaving and lathing; the distribution of materials produced by their weaving and spinning should be facilitated."[11] The quality of their work and the Crown's pursuit of its interests led to women's weaving and spinning becoming activities directed toward trade rather than subsistence.

Thus, during the colonial period, the figure of the woman was clearly associated with the textile industry. She was the supplier of raw material for the *obrajes*. Regarding this phenomenon, Richard Salvucci speaks of the *cuadrillas de hilanderas* (crews of spinning women) who supplied yarn for the workshops, an activity common to other countries such as contemporary England.[12] The number of spinning women increased toward the end of the colonial period, especially where cotton was concerned. From the eighteenth century onward, the *obrajes* multiplied with the corollary expansion of cottage spinning, so that by the end of the colonial period the Crown believed that it was necessary to regulate cotton weavers.[13]

From Spinners to Weavers

During the colonial era, spinning women had managed to sustain themselves in spite of the competition presented by the importation of foreign yarns. However, by the early nineteenth century they were unable to compete with the machine-spun yarns. Although some of these women were hired by the new factories established around 1840, many were displaced. The new factories employed women and children, especially in those regions where the Indian tradition of spinning as part of female domestic tasks was weak.

Women in these new factories faced deep prejudices. Bad feelings stemmed from the inconvenience caused when women worked outside the house and continued to share the same premises with men. Their work outside the home required a redefiniton of household duties. However, some entrepreneurs, such as Esteban de Antuñano from Puebla, with a "modern spirit," defended their participation in the recently created factories.[14] In 1837 he published a pamphlet in which he strongly supported women's work.[15] For

Antuñano, it was preferable for women to work at the factories, with other members of the family, rather than to remain "doing nothing" at home.

It is interesting to point out that the attempt to incorporate women into textile factory labor purported to reproduce, within the factory itself, the family workshop model. The family was organized as a unit of production where work was hierarchically assigned according to gender and age. Therefore, according to this model, gender relationships would remain untouched at the new factory site. According to Antuñano's model, the craftshop moved to the factory to the extent that entire families, including women, became integrated within it. Thus, the hierarchical ordering of the home-based workshop was repeated in the factory. Work was assigned according to gender, emphasizing the ordering of task differentiation according to traditional male-female work.

It must be stressed that the notion of a factory with a labor force made up of members of a single family resembles more the traditional craftshop than the "modern industry" of which Antuñano felt so proud. Besides the evident paternalistic motivation of Antuñano, there was another, even stronger, incentive: the economic factor. Wages for women were lower that those for male workers in the textile factories. For Antuñano, another motivation could have been the influence of the English model. This entrepreneur from Puebla, aware of the abundance of female labor in the textile industry in England, could well have imagined that it was the presence of women that had caused the astounding success of English textiles. However, the process of modernization in the textile industry in Mexico varied precisely because women remained in the crafts sector. This situation hindered female incorporation into the factory system.[16]

In spite of the fact that the incorporation of women into the textile factories may have seemed an innovative feature in its time, Antuñano's motivation and his argument for its justification were very traditional indeed. Women had to work in the factories so as not to remain in idleness at home. The factory was understood as a space that reproduced the paternalistic domestic sphere. Thus, the factory repeated the hierarchical gender relations that shaped the domestic workshop. Those relations were based upon the inequality of tasks and rights within the family. In the factories, there was a paternal and familial surveillance while the female worker performed her tasks. Antuñano's idea reproduced the same hierarchical system in the factory that women were subjected to in their families.[17]

In spite of Antuñano's declaration in favor of the presence of women in the factories, in his own factory in Puebla—La Constancia —female workers comprised only 10 percent of the work force in 1840. But local conditions varied widely. In other regions, by contrast, women surpassed men as factory workers during the first half of the nineteenth century. Such was the case in Sonora, Querétaro, and Durango as well as at the modern plant of Cocolapan, in Veracruz;[18] and it was particularly true of the factory El Tunal, in Durango.[19] El Tunal purported to be a model of modern technology, yet a number of difficulties hindered its success: a flood, the death of one of the co-owners in a shipwreck, and the company overspent. Even so, the firm finally opened its doors in 1841. The labor force there was made up of 200 workers, "three-quarters of it being women and children." Thus, most of the female workers were "young women, very skilled in their occupation, who are not entirely happy with their situation and who, relegated inside a solitary place, have to make disadvantageous comparisons. However, this was overcome, as the best of them had their contracts renewed."[20]

According to José Fernando Ramírez, El Tunal was a factory where the entrepreneurs intended to incorporate women into factory work. The owners thought that contracting female workers for the new textile mills was best for their profitable operation since women lowered the cost of labor while ensuring a high quality of work. This policy favoring the contracting of women exemplified the modern criterion on which the textile sector was promoted. At that time in Mexico, it was considered a sign of modernity to incorporate women into the textile industry, following the English and American models, where the female presence was massive. Thus, the owners of El Tunal even hired American female workers: "Some young women were brought from the United States. They are true models of hard work and cleanliness and are valued because of their moderation, their behavior, and, above all, because of their conduct, which is above all suspicion. Thus, it was natural that their good qualities were transmitted to the people who worked hard under their guidance, so that in their departments rules a sense of order difficult to imagine."[21]

Although the owner of El Tunal favored the employment of women, in other parts of the country the number of female workers in textile factories was much lower. The survival of the domestic craftshops paralleled the establishment and growth of new factories. Their resilience explains the meager presence of women in the textile factories in Indian regions, where women continued to weave and spin for home consumption and in cottage industry. Therefore, regional variations explain the diversity in the rhythm and volume of women's participation in the textile industry. Based on statistical data about the textile factories during the nineteenth century, it can be stated that the regions where women prevailed numerically were those with lower indigenous populations. Indian women continued to work at home, carrying out their traditional roles as spinners who supplied the factories, or as weavers working at family looms.[22]

Types of Female Work

The kind of work performed by women in the factory was fundamental to the process of gender formation. The tasks carried out by men and women became specifically male or female ones. Thus, a gender differentiation arose that affected both the way of organizing work within the factory and, at times, the kinds of working demands made. In the specific case of women, it may be assumed that their role as members of a family community also influenced their work at the factory. The studies about contemporary roles of women as workers emphasize the notion that female labor was conditioned, most of the time, by the family situation of the woman. This factor goes through various stages. We know, for instance, that there were differences in job participation according to age, and the continuing role as a member of the family community. The position as a daughter, a wife, or a mother also determined the possibility of having access to a job and of retaining it.

A second conditioning factor was rooted in the kinds of activities that women performed while combining their domestic tasks with their working duties.[23] This factor brings us to the interconnected processes of gender and class formation and to see the extent to which the division of labor affects gender formation. Several questions arise: How did the experience of factory work modify gender relationships? How did men and women experience it? How did the shift from crafts work to factory work take place? And how did the role of women change in this kind of work?

This last question is significant where the step from artisan to factory worker is concerned. In those cases in which factory work follows crafts work, it is possible to wonder about the effects of integrating women into factory production. The specific approach of studying female labor can throw some light upon the ways in which the transformation from workshop to industry takes place. It helps explain the continuity, or lack of it, in the forms of production. Thus, it becomes necessary to ask how female labor became integrated into factory production, and how the latter's composition changed over time. This problem is inherent to the differences between the process of industrialization in the cities and in those countries which Eric Hobsbawm has called "second comers."[24]

Although the issue of industrialization or of protoindustrialization surpasses the limits of this chapter, a first approach to female work in the textile industry, from a gendered perspective, consists of noticing the changes that took place within the activities of production according to gender division.[25] In the long run, these shifts correspond to basic modifications in the forms of production.

If we consider the history of the industrial process at a global level, we know that from the seventeenth century onward, female participation in industry was crucial. The demand for yarn, required by burgeoning textile production, created the necessity for spinning women, whose work became essential to textile production. The impact of British industrialization on women textile workers has had contradictory interpretations. Alice Clark, for instance, maintains that the industrialization process of the early stage harmed women by forcing them to leave their homes, eroding their role within the household. On the other hand, Ivy Pinchbeck defended the idea that women, once they obtained a paid job outside the house, improved their economic position and increased their self-assertion.[26] This argument is basically repeated more than one hundred years later in the case of Latin America. In my view, this debate shows the central significance of the issue. It has become important again with the appearance of a mostly female labor force in the border region between Mexico and the United States.[27]

For the Mexican case in the nineteenth century, it can be generally said that the presence of women weavers in the craftshops did not fully disappear with the introduction of the first "factories." If entrepreneurs such as Antuñano had to insist at first upon the convenience of having women in the factories, this situation resulted

from variations of a temporal and regional kind, but above all because of the work process itself.

Temporal and Regional Variations

It is significant to point out that textile activities in Mexico became
male according to the degree in which the working process became
mechanized. Thus, the crews of spinning women in colonial times,
referred to by Salvucci, had almost disappeared by the late nineteenth century. In his study about Puebla, Guy Thomson states
that toward 1835 women dealt mainly with combing, beating, and
spinning cotton fiber, but by 1842 domestic spinning had been
almost totally replaced by spinning machines.[28] Nevertheless, the
common habit of women being more closely linked to spinning than
to weaving was reproduced in the textile factories. According to
Jorge Durán, the spinning and yarns factories preferred to have
women among their staff workers, whereas weaving and fabric
factory owners sought a mostly male work force. It seems that a
larger number of looms corresponded to a larger number of male
workers.[29] As a matter of fact, if this was the general tendency, the
logical result would be that the number of women would diminish
to the degree that the technical process increased within textile
production.

Although regional variations within the textile industry in
Mexico were related to the degree of industrial technology, there
were three distinct geographical regions. The first, and perhaps the
oldest, is the area of Puebla and Tlaxcala, which has well-known
features including continuous textile production from colonial times
and lavish Indian textile handicrafts made by women. This area is
traditionally identified with Indian cottage industry. By 1877 there
was no female labor force in the textile factories. Of the twenty-
one existing factories in Puebla, only one had twenty women,
50 percent of the total number of workers. Instead, the owner employed a large number of children to work there.[30]

The second region, that of Mexico City and the state of México,
had fourteen factories, some of which were the largest in the country. These had a widespread female presence. In some cases, such
as that of La Hormiga in Mexico City, or La Colmena in the adjacent state of México, the proportion of women was quite high. La
Hormiga had 100 women, 250 men, and 50 children, while in La

Colmena the proportion of women to men was 165 to 410, with 50 children. In the third region, the intermediate area of the country, that of the states of Hidalgo, Guanajuato, Veracruz, Tlaxcala, and Querétaro, the presence of women was also seen but to a lesser degree. In the states of Nuevo León, Michoacán, Colima, Durango, Sonora, Jalisco, Zacatecas, and Aguascalientes, female participation was minimal.

It can thus be said that of the ninety-eight factories mentioned in the 1877 register or census, only twenty-three had women workers; and of these, only six had a predominantly female labor force.[31] These data support the view that women constituted only 20 percent of the work force in the Mexican textile industry.[32] The British consul in Mexico City, Lionel Carden, agreed with this view when he stated that only 13 percent of the labor force of the textile industry were women, 12 percent children, and 75 percent men.[33] A similar remark was made by the traveler Mae Sayus, who, comparing the Mexican situation with that of Europe and the United States, stated that "there is a complete absence of women in the factories. The jobs that are done by women in the United States, France, and Germany are here performed by men."[34]

Generally, the observers of the time agreed that Mexican textile workers in the late nineteenth century differed from their American counterparts regarding female labor. The absence of women in the textile factories was basically due to the permanence of craftshops manufacturing for the local market. At the end of the century, female workers concentrated there and, for the most part, did not go to work at the modern textile mills. The tendency toward modernization also meant the eviction of the few women who had been present in manufacturing. As craftshops were replaced by factories, women were displaced.

The Work Process

Even though the female textile labor force was smaller than its male counterpart, it was central to Mexican working-class history. A reading of the Register of the Municipality of San Angel, in Mexico City, allows us to evaluate the inhabitants of the region and to deduce the number of women working there. The General Register of the workers and their families at La Hormiga lists 698 people.[35] Of these, 251 were factory workers, including 214 males, of whom

56 were single and 158 married. Their ages varied between 15 and 40 years. The male workers covered practically all of the trades of the factory, both in the textile process and in maintenance and security. They included bricklayers, laborers, carpenters, machinists, knotters, spinners, packers, combers, wickers, teamsters, winders, benders, paymasters, managers, and, of course, weavers.

Only 47 women were included in the General Register as factory workers. Their ages ran from 14 to 50 years, and their civil status was even more varied than that of the men. Whereas the males were classified only as married or single, the women were registered as maiden, single, married, and widowed. The fact that women were classified according to their marital status pointed to a clearly generic differentiation, illustrating the significance of gender in the productive process of the factory. The owners registered men and women according to their gender, but in the case of women they also classified them by marital status and age. Widows, married, and younger women could be expected to have greater domestic responsibilities than their single counterparts. Their status affected their employability. Women with familial responsibilities may have offered greater employment longevity.

Out of the 47 women workers, only 10 were maidens: the youngest was 13 years old and the oldest 22. Their occupations included one cleaner, three stretchers, three wickers, and one winder; two-thirds were weavers. Married women ranged from 24 to 40 years old; there were 13 of them: eight weavers, two stretchers, one *trocilera*, one wicker, and one winder. Only 12 female workers were single; their ages ranged from 20 to 40 years and they performed the following tasks: four weavers, three stretchers, one wicker, one *trocilera*, and three winders. Regarding the widows, their ages varied between 27 and 38 years, and there were only seven: three weavers, three stretchers, and one wicker.[36]

While women in the factories were a minority, they were concentrated in weaving, but they covered various other skills, including those of cleaners, wickers, and winders. Nevertheless, theirs were secondary tasks in the overall process. Women weavers were always third weavers, which meant that they were less specialized within the hierarchy established in the process of production. The activity of weaving was undoubtedly the most important of all and was concentrated on married women, adults between 20 and 40 years of age, working at their productive maturity. On the other hand, the fact that they were married surely gave them a certain stability in the factory, and it may even be supposed that they obtained their jobs precisely because they were married.

Nevertheless, the presence of women in other aspects of the productive process leads us to conclude that women were not only found in weaving, nor was the weaving section in the factory mostly female, as was the case in England and the United States. The survival of a strong artisanal sector meant that many women preferred to remain in the domestic crafts sector. Most of them chose to work as household spinners rather than textile workers. The female experience in the textile industry was closely related to spinning and yarns. Once the process of mechanization took place, the spinners did not necessarily become weavers to such an extent as to make women the majority of workers within the factory. The different kinds of fabrics manufactured—cotton, wool, and linen—may have made a difference in the number of women employed, but there are not enough regional studies to allow us to make such a determination.

It can be said that the process of industrialization in Mexico was distinct from the British and American experience. Where female participation is concerned, Mexico differed greatly in the pattern of employment that took place during the first half of the nineteenth century in England and the United States. This observation is significant because it leads us to appreciate the variables in the industrialization process between metropolitan and peripheral countries. In Mexico, the indigenous element, with its regional features, was definitive in determining the participation or nonparticipation of women in the factories.

Although women were not a majority inside the Mexican textile factories at the end of the nineteenth century, it is still important to take them into account in order to evaluate the construction of social relationships between men and women in the labor process. Women mostly appear in the lowest-paid jobs: they were cleaners, stretchers, wickers, weavers, and *trocileras*. Although most of the women who worked at the factory were weavers, their numbers in relation to male weavers was surprisingly unequal. Women constituted a small minority.

At the same time, where the gender hierarchy within the factory is concerned, it is not clear whether the women who appeared as weavers or with specific skills were heads of family or not. Savina and Antonia Martínez both worked for La Hormiga. The former, 20 years old and single, worked as a weaver. The latter, presumably her sister, was an 18-year-old maiden. Although the same surname indicates kinship, it is not clear whether they both were factory workers, or whether one worked at home, because only the occupation of the elder is evident.

Outside the Factory: Sewing Other People's Clothes

The relative scarcity of women in the Mexican textile factories does not undermine the important connection between female labor and the textile industry. Women seamstresses and assemblers became integrated into the textile sector as an indispensable labor force for assembling clothing. Tasks were performed by women outside the factory, in their houses or in workshops established exclusively for this purpose. These jobs were paid by the piece, not by the hour.

The tradition in which women sewed other people's clothes was well known by at least the early nineteenth century. Seamstresses made garments at their own homes or they visited the houses of the bourgeoisie, where their jobs consisted of mending the family's garments. In 1854, *Los mexicanos pintados por sí mismos* minutely described this kind of seamstress:

> Whether the poor seamstress was the daughter of a retired captain or of a public-school teacher, or of a nobody, this does not matter: most of the time nobody speaks of her origins, nor of her etymology, nor of her roots, in sum, to say once and for all, she is a kind of anonymous being who does not know her father, because nobody knows who he was, not even the priest who baptized her. . . . There is an endless number of girls of all the classes of society who, condemned to misery, try to get, with their manual labor, a sad meal, and only find, after long drudgery, a miserable refuge against hunger and infamy.[37]

Seamstresses who worked at other people's houses were replaced by those working by the piece, once the sewing machine changed the relationship of these women with their job by making them proletarians. The difference between them was determined by whether or not they had a sewing machine.

Less independent seamstresses faced a new kind of exploitation: the owners of the machines gave them garments to be joined and assembled, which had to be sewn at the recently installed workshops where the women gathered. Their working days were not subject to set hours, nor did they enjoy complimentary perks. The work continued until the productive needs were met. In fact, the working and living conditions of the seamstresses were terrible, and newspaper editorials asking for their improvement were frequent.

In 1876, *El Socialista* complained that "the owners of the sewing machines take the best part, because the unfortunate seamstress has to work long hours in order to manage a stingy salary."[38] Seamstresses' wages ranged from twelve reales to one peso in 1880, but by 1884 their salaries were so low that the Mexican Philanthropic Society established sewing rooms where the seamstresses had free access to the machines. In spite of the fact that this access allowed them to hire their labor independently and to select a workshop of their choice, their wages still were so low that they had to work twelve hours in order to earn fifty centavos per day.[39]

These piece workers were also called *obreras de la munición* (ammunition workers) because one of their most frequent jobs was that of assembling army uniforms. In June 1889 the government paid for the work by the piece at a rate set according to the complexity of the task. Nevertheless, the contractors did not respect these prices. Perhaps because there was a surplus of workers, apart from the authorized contractors, subcontractors appeared and charged the women for getting them work, thus lowering their already meager salaries even more. In 1901 the seamstresses earned only thirty centavos for a twelve–hour work day.[40] In the following year the Sociedad Fraternal de Costureras (Fraternal Society of Seamstresses) took advantage of a gathering for the celebration of the birthday of Porfirio Díaz to complain about their terrible working conditions.[41]

The Demands of Women Workers and Their Organizations

The presence of female workers in the textile factories was made known in the 1865 labor conflict at the factories of San Ildefonso and La Colmena near Mexico City. Textile workers began to organize at that time in order to protect their interests. In January the owners of San Ildefonso increased the workday for women from 5 o'clock in the morning to 6:45 in the evening. Their time on the job remained one hour less than the male workers, because the manager admitted that they needed to leave earlier to attend to their domestic duties at home. Women, however, insisted that their domestic duties required even more time than they were being given.[42]

The incorporation of petitions addressing the specific needs of women in the textile industry continued to be part of the wider demands presented by the working class. In 1876 the manifesto calling for a workers' congress to convene included a demand for the improvement of the working conditions of women.[43] The same concerns appeared again in the strikes at Río Blanco in 1898, and in 1906, when the first national textile organization, the Great Circle of Free Workers (GCOL), was created. The textile workers articulated their platform at a national level, and it represented the specific concerns of their guild. If it is true that there were no women on the board of the Great Circle of Free Workers, they still made their presence known through wage demands. Female labor was differentiated, and they specifically called for a different salary from that of men and children. Until then, female workers had received the same pay as children, and, although the salaries varied according to the region, wages for women generally were about one-third that of men.[44]

For the first time the Great Circle promoted an explicit policy of salaries for men and for women, thereby placing a higher value on the latter's work in the factories.[45] Still, the wage difference was based on gender, not on the kind of work performed; and women earned, just because they were women, a lower salary than their male colleagues who were doing the same job. The growing awareness of the difference between male and female workers was evident in the content of their demands and organizations.

A general aspect in which gender contributes to our knowledge of working-class formation refers to the role of women in workers' organizations. It is important to point out that the way in which men and women participated in labor struggles could be radically different. But let it suffice here to analyze two distinct manners of labor organizing. The first is a labor organization made up exclusively of female membership, the Hijas del Anáhuac (Daughters of Anáhuac), which was bound to the Mexican Liberal Party. It was formed in 1907 with women who worked in the spinning, weaving, and cap-manufacturing factories to the south of Mexico City: La Abeja, La Hormiga, and Santa Teresa. The gatherings, which brought together more than three hundred women, took place on Sunday afternoons in the house of the sisters Catalina and Carmen Frias. While the Daughters of Anáhuac followed the guidelines of the Mexican Liberal Party, it made specific demands for the improvement of the working and living conditions of women workers. What is interesting about the Daughters of Anáhuac is that its project went beyond mere working demands and comprised an entire program of social improvement that included the protection of the Indian race, the establishment of prisons dedicated to rehabilitation, severe punishments for corrupt civil servants, and salary increases for teachers.

From the perspective of gender relations, the most significant aspect of the program was the demand to "suppress the restrictions that public life and public peace impose upon the freedom of speech and press." This demand illustrated the need for a freer attitude toward women. The other demand directly linked to gender relations was that of "establishing civil equality for all the children of the same father, suppressing the law which established the differences between legitimate and illegitimate children." This aspect of the recognition of the rights of illegitimate children particularly affected women workers in a society in which single mothers prevailed.[46]

The program of the Daughters of Anáhuac and the kind of participation that it advocated evidently surpass mere unionist or worker concerns of the female textile workers and show its wider interest in national politics and social problems. Thus, the "female manufacturers" of the turn of the century demonstrated their capacity to organize at a national level and their ability to include gender problems in their demands for social reform.

The second example of female labor organizing was the Río Blanco strike.[47] This action was a spontaneous one in which women, in their traditional roles as housewives, played a crucial role. The confrontation between the constituted power and the workers of the Mexican textile industry, at the factory of Río Blanco in January 1907, showed that gender relationships took part in the struggle itself. Female intervention was fundamental in the struggle between workers and authorities: "At five o'clock in the morning, the factories' sirens called to work. But no worker went inside. At the gates of the factory of Río Blanco, workers Isabel de Pensamiento, Carmen Cruz, and Dolores Larios headed a group of women which formed the First Collision Brigade and which had as their only weapons old and hard bits of bread and tortillas, ready to be thrown against any strikebreaker who dared to enter the site."[48] Women totally abandoned their passive role and gave a new dimension to their domestic role by transforming food into weapons to attack the strikebreakers. The presence of women in the first row also had symbolic value: the intimidation of dissident workers. Women represented another form of political presence. Based upon their traditional role as suppliers of the family, they legitimated their presence at the factory.

It was precisely when the conflict reached its peak that the once-passive women rose to become assailants. It was they who, enraged, attacked the *tienda de raya* (company store), a symbol of their difficult everyday survival. Another reading from the perspective of gender of this episode is the fact that the duration of the conflict took it away from the public-political domain, and its intensification occurred at the moment when the struggle had an impact upon what was traditionally the female domain of the home. Thus, one can speculate to what degree women, taking a protagonistic and aggressive part in the movement, broke the parameters of acceptable behavior, at least according to the ideological discourse of the period. Although women were a minority presence in the Mexican textile industry in the late nineteenth century, the distribution of tasks within the factory, as well as the forms of political organization and the content of the labor and social demands that they created, points toward a process of gender differentiation between men and women. That differentiation still affects women workers today on both sides of the border.

Notes

1. J. Figueroa Domenech, *Guía general descriptiva de la República Mexicana* (México: Ramon S. N. Araluce, 1899), 188.

2. I use the concept of gender in the way employed by Joan Scott: as a process that reproduces the social relationships between the sexes. See Scott, "El género, una categoría útil para el análisis historico," in James Amelang and Mary Nash, comps., *Historia y genero: Las Mujeres en la Europa moderna y contemporanea* (Valencia: Ediciones Alfonso el Maganim, 1984), 23–58. See also Joan Scott, "El problema de la invisibilidad," in Carmen Ramos Escandón, comp., *Género e historia* (México: Instituto Mora/Universidad Autónoma Metropolitana, 1992), 38–65; idem, "Gender: A Useful Category of Historical Analysis," *The American Historical Review* 91 (December 1986): 1053–75; and idem, "The Problem of Invisibility," in S. Jay Kleinberg, ed., *Retrieving Women's History* (Paris: UNESCO, 1988), 5–29.

3. Miguel Othón de Mendizabal, "Las artes textiles en México," in *Obras completas*, Vol. 6 (México: n.p., 1946–47), 284; and idem, "Historia social y económica de México. Siete conferencias," in "La organización y división del trabajo," in *Cuadernos Americanos* 1 (México): 1942.

4. Othón de Mendizabal, "La evolución de la industria textíl," in *Obras completas*, Vol. 3 (México: n.p., 1946–47), 344.

5. Ibid.

6. See Richard Salvucci, *Textiles and Capitalism in Mexico: An Economic History of the Obrajes, 1549–1840* (Princeton: Princeton University Press, 1987).

7. Richard Greenleaf, "The *Obraje* in the Late Mexican Colony," *The Americas* 3 (October 1967): 227–50.

8. Ibid., 241.

9. Manuel Miño Grijalva, "Obrajes y tejedores en Nueva Espana" (Ph.D. diss., Centro de Estudios Históricos, E1 Colegio de México, 1984), 53; see also idem, *La protoindustria colonial hispanoamericana* (México: FCE, 1993).

10. Margaret Villanueva, "From Calpixtli to Corregidor," *Latin American Perspectives* 12 (Winter 1985): 17–40; idem, "Autos y diligencias en orden a la vista de los obrajes y haciendas de la jurisdicción de la villa de Cuyoacán, 1660. Mandamientos sobre índios en los obrajes," *Boletín del Archivo General de la Nación* 11, no. 1 (January–March 1940): 28.

11. Miño Grijalva, "La política textil en México y Peru en la epoca colonial: Nuevas consideraciones," *Historia Mexicana* 38 (October–December 1988): 307.

12. Salvucci, *Textiles*. For the English case see Alice Clark, *The Working Life of Women in the Seventeenth Century* (New York: Augustus M. Kelley, 1968).

13. Miño Grijalva, "Obrajes," 7; Guy Thompson, *Puebla de Los Angeles: Industry and Society in a Mexican City* (Boulder: Westview Press, 1989).

14. The term "factory" is used here in the sense given to it during the nineteenth century. In contemporary historiography the term "protoindustrialization" is used to analyze the transition from small-scale manufacturing to factories.

15. Esteban de Antuñano, *Ventajas políticas, civiles y domésticas que por afar ocupación a las mujeres en las fábricas modernas que se estan levantando en México deben recibirse* (Puebla: Oficina del Hospital de San Pedro, 1837), 6.

16. See Stephen Haber, *Industry and Underdevelopment* (Stanford: Stanford University Press, 1989).

17. Antuñano, *Ventajas*, 4.

18. Robert Sandoval Zarauz, "La industria textil mexicana," in Luis Barjau, ed., *Estadísticas económicas del siglo XIX* (México: Instituto Nacional de Antropología e Historia, 1976).

19. José Fernando Ramírez, "Fábrica de Tejidos del Tunal o sea apuntes para la historia de la industria mexicana seguidos de algunas observaciones sobre la posibilidad de conciliar sus intereses con los de la agricultura," *El Museo Mexicano* 1 (México) (1843): 120–40.

20. Ibid., 123.

21. Ibid.

22. Sandoval Zarauz, "La industria textil"; Juan Felipe Leal, *Del estado liberal a los inicios de la dictadura porfirista* (México: Siglo XXI, 1980).

23. For a contemporary view of this issue see Elizabeth Jelin and María del Carmen Feijoo, *El ser y el deber ser de las mujeres* (México: El Colegio de México, 1986).

24. Eric Hobsbawm, "First comers y second comers," in Cafagna et al., *Industrialización y desarrollo* (Madrid: Alberto Corazín, 1974), 47–73. For protoindustrialization in Mexico see Manuel Miño Grijalva, "Proto-industria colonial," *Historia Mexicana* 38, no. 4 (October–December 1989): 793–818; and idem, *La protoindustria*, passim.

25. Louise Tilly and Joan Scott point out that in the French and British cases, changes in the mode of production did not necessarily transform the work of women, although industrialization brought a series of demographic, economic, and organizational changes in the family. See Louise Tilly, *Women, Work, and Family* (New York: Holt, Rinehart, and Winston, 1978), 227.

26. See Clark, *The Working Life of Women*; and Ivy Pinchbeck, *Women Workers and the Industrial Revolution, 1750–1850* (London: G. Routledge and Sons, 1930).

27. See Susan Tiano, "Women and Industrial Development in Latin America," *Latin American Research Review* 21, no. 3 (1986): 157–70. Regarding female labor in the Mexico-United States border area see Alberto Dávila and Rogelio Saenz, "The Effect of Maquiladora Employment on the Monthly Flow of Mexican Undocumented Migration to the U.S., 1978–1982," *International Migration Review* 42, no. 1 (1990): 96–107; John Reichtert and Douglas Massey, "History and Trends in the U.S. Border Migration from a Mexican Town," *International Migration Review* 14, no. 4 (1980): 475–91; Michael Seligson and Edward J. Williams, *Maquiladoras and Migration: Workers in the Mexican-U.S. Border Industrialization Program* (Austin: University of Texas Press, 1983); Susan Tiano, "El programa mexicano de las maquiladoras: Una respuesta a las necesidades de la industria norteamericana," *Aztlán*, 14, no. 1 (Spring 1983): 201–8; and Alejandro Mungaray, "Division internacional del trabajo y automatización en la produción: El futuro de las maquiladoras," *Investigación Económica* 164 (México) (April–June 1983): 231–53.

28. Guy Thomson, "The Cotton Textile Industry in Puebla during the Eighteenth and Early Nineteenth Centuries," in Nils Jacobsen and Hans Jurgen Puhle, eds., *The Economies of Mexico and Peru during the Late Colonial Period, 1760–1810* (Berlin: Colloquium Verlag, 1986), 188, 170.

29. Jorge Durán, "Las pioneras del género" (Colegio de Jalisco, manuscript), 6.

30. Carmen Ramos Escandón, "Mujeres trabajadoras en el México Porfiriano, 1876–1911," *Revista Europea de Estudios Latinoamericanos y del Caribe* 48 (June 1990): 36; Juan Felipe Leal and Joseph Woldenberg, "Del estado liberal a los inicios de la dictadura porfirista," in *La clase obrera en la historia de México* (México: IIS/UNAM, 1981), 46; Ana María Hernández, "La mujer mexicana en el industria textil" (unpublished, 1940), 14.

31. Leal and Woldenberg, "Del estado liberal," 48–49.

32. See Dawn Keremitsis, *La industria textil mexicana* (México: SEP, 1979); and idem, *The Cotton Textile Industry in the Porfiriato: Mexico, 1870–1910* (New York: Garland, 1987), 196.

33. Lionel Carden, "Report on the Cotton Manufacturing Industry in Mexico," *British Diplomatic and Consular Reports*, Miscellaneous Series, no. 453 (London: Foreign Office, 1898), 10.

34. *El Economista Mexicano* 36 (México), 380.

35. Padrón General de los Trabajadores de la Fábrica de la Hormiga y de las familias de los trabajadores, Archivo Histórico de la Ciudad de México, Registers, Box 3, File 27, 10 pages.

36. Ibid.

37. José María Covarrubias, *Los mexicanos pintados por sí mismos* (México: Imprenta de Murguía y Cía., 1854), 45.

38. *El Socialista* (México), June 11, 1876.

39."En favór de las costureras pobres," *La Convención Nacional Obrera* (México), May 27, 1894.

40. "Nuevo esquilmo a las obreras de la munición," ibid., February 27, 1901; "Las costureras de la munición," Ibid., March 3, 1901.

41. Moisés González Navarro, "El porfiriato, Vida social," in *La historia moderna de México*, vol. 4, ed. Daniel Cosio Villegas (México: Editorial Hermes, 1957), 20–37.

42. John M. Hart, "Working-Class Women in Nineteenth-Century Mexico," in *Mexican Women in the U.S.: Struggles Past and Present*, ed. Magdalene Mora and Adelaida del Castillo (Los Angeles: Chicano Studies Center, UCLA, 1980), 152.

43. Hernández, "La mujer mexicana," 17.

44. Keremitsis, *The Cotton Textile Industry*, 188.

45. Hernández, "La mujer mexicana," 25.

46. Carmen Ramos Escandón, "Señoritas porfirianas: Mujer e ideología en el México progresista, 1880–1910," in *Presencia y transparencia: La mujer en la historia de México*, ed. Ramos Escandón (México: El Colegio de México, 1987), 143–62.

47. For a reconstruction of events see Bernardo García Martínez, *Santa Rosa y Río Blanco* (Jalapa: Archivo General del Estado de Veracruz, 1989); Carmen Ramos Escandón, "La política obrera del Estado mexicano: De Díaz a Madero. El cave de los trabajadores textiles," in *Mexican Studies/Estudios Mexicanos* 3, no. 1 (Winter 1987): 19–48; Rodney Anderson, *Outcasts in Their Own Land: Mexican Industrial Workers, 1906–1911* (De Kalb: Northern Illinois University Press, 1976); and Salvador Hernandez, *Magonismo y el movimiento obrero en México: Cananea y Río Blanco* (México: UNAM, Centro de Estudios Latinoamericanos, 1977).

48. Hernández, "La mujer mexicana," 31.

CHAPTER FIVE

Syndicalism and Citizenship
Postrevolutionary Worker Mobilizations in Veracruz

Elizabeth Jean Norvell

In the early 1920s, in the aftermath of the Mexican Revolution, the workers at the port of Veracruz organized and challenged the capitalist elites of the city over working conditions, private property, wages, and political power. A sense of empowerment grew among these men and women and thus allowed them to act as a class in order to influence their city's politics and culture. During this period, the already heterogeneous society of the port city rapidly stratified along class lines. The work force, made up of a wide variety of skilled and unskilled workers, artisans, the underemployed, and those in the informal economy (most notably prostitutes), held divergent ideas. Yet, together, they demonstrated their class unity to the city's elites. Throughout the early 1920s community and familial relations proved important in maintaining workers' solidarity, but the key to the success of this movement was the belief in their rights as citizens of Veracruz and their mutual respect for differing points of view.

The formation of the working class in Veracruz can be traced back to the modernization projects introduced during the dictatorship of Porfirio Díaz, who dominated Mexico from 1876 to 1910. The rapid growth of railroads and industry led to increased trade between Mexico and international markets. As the country's main commercial port, Veracruz underwent tremendous expansion as a wave of immigrants from both Mexico and abroad doubled the city's population between 1884 and 1910. The population grew from 24,000 to 50,000.

The arrival of entrepreneurs and workers in the port helped to form the base for the capitalist and working classes of the postrevolutionary era. Wealthy entrepreneurs and companies from the United States and Europe, particularly from Spain, invested in large, capital-intensive port enterprises such as shipping, brokerage firms, and urban real estate. In Veracruz these immigrants became a powerful elite, a capitalist class. Many middle-class Spaniards also arrived in the port with the idea of making it their home. They invested in a wide range of businesses, including grocery and fabric stores, bakeries, wineshops, restaurants, and small factories that produced goods such as shoes and pasta. This group formed a "traditional" middle class of small property owners and merchants distinct from the elite capitalists who invested on a larger scale in the "modern" sectors. Similarly, the workers who entered the new enterprises and who toiled in the maritime trades became a powerful group because they moved the bulk of the nation's seaborne imports and exports. The skilled artisans and workers who found employment with the small property owners formed a middle sector of the working class. At the bottom of the social ladder were the city's poorest, least skilled, and most marginalized workers.[1]

Throughout the late nineteenth and early twentieth centuries the immigrants developed a way of life and a culture based on their past customs as well as on the socioeconomic and climatic circumstances of the city. Due to the tropical heat, which suffocates the area at least six months of the year, social life flourished in the cool of the mornings and evenings. In the mornings, Porteños met for coffee and conversation at cafés, while in the evenings they listened to music and danced under the tropical moon. The Spanish immigrants brought fashionable dances such as the tango and the fox-trot, and held exclusive affairs attended by the upper classes.

Meanwhile, the workers, fortified by immigrants from the Gulf Coast regions of Mexico and Cuba, developed their own culture based on the cuisine, music, and pastimes of the Caribbean. Most notably, the port's popular classes danced the seductive *danzón*, introduced by Cuban immigrants, on a nightly basis in working-class housing complexes known as patios. Thus, while music, dances, and festivities came to represent a single port life-style, two distinct cultures based on class were developing within it. During the postrevolutionary labor movement, local class conflict was often played out on this cultural terrain as workers asserted their own customs and beliefs in the city's public places in order to influence the definition of port society and citizenship.[2]

As the Porfiriato turned into revolution in 1910, the Veracruz workers mobilized, organized, and educated themselves in preparation for the triumph of the popular classes. As they did so, their differing work experiences led to two distinct types of radicalism and militancy: one based on anarcho-syndicalist principles of direct action and distrust of the state; and the other on multiple action, which included direct action and political participation. The combination of these differing perspectives and the idea of the victory of the entire Mexican pueblo over those who had attempted to conquer it for hundreds of years fueled the citywide labor movement of the early 1920s.

In 1906, Porfirio Díaz had authorized the formation of the Compañía Terminal de Veracruz, S.A., a British firm that had been granted a ninety-nine-year concession for the hauling, loading, and storage of all import-export goods that passed through the port. In order to increase efficiency, the company installed hydraulic cranes and extended railroad tracks to meet the ships at the docks. At the same time, the shipping companies speeded up the loading and unloading of cargo aboard ship. They separated workers between those who worked on deck (the stevedores) and those who toiled below (the *jornaleros*, or day laborers), and then granted supervisory power to a select few foremen who maintained a brisk work rhythm. While the workers below passed cargo—some pieces weighing up to one hundred kilos—along human chains from the storage holds deep within the ship along narrow corridors until it reached the deck, the stevedores ran the cranes that lifted the cargo from the deck of the ship to the edge of the dock and back again.[3]

The rationalization of work processes that took place within the maritime industry during the Porfiriato had important effects on the organization, ideology, and militancy of the dock workers. It alienated maritime workers from their employers, thus causing them to form one of the city's first unions, the Union of Stevedores and Laborers of the Port of Veracruz. It also instilled within the men a sense of discipline, which aided them in leading the citywide offensive against the capitalist classes. Further, the maritime workers' experiences within the economy's most modern sector demonstrated to them the economic importance of their work as the movers of commerce. This realization later led them to seek power within the postrevolutionary state.

Unlike the maritime workers, the artisans and laborers of the middle sector were not accustomed to strict work or organizational discipline. Anarchist ideas such as the value of individual liberty within communal settings of mutual aid appealed to these workers, whose liberties were at risk due to increased industrialization and whose relations with employers stemmed from the guild system. The addition of anarcho-syndicalist tactics of direct action, strikes, and sabotage offered this group of workers new means to preserve old ways and to make new demands.

In 1912 labor leaders such as Pedro Junco Rojo of the carpenters' guild and Narciso Faixat of the bakers' union founded a local chapter of the Casa del Obrero Mundial (House of the World Worker). Through the Casa, these leaders began to reach out to the city's most dispossessed citizens. An economic slowdown from 1910 to 1919, due to the revolution and World War I, decreased employment opportunities and worsened the plight of poor workers. Many from this marginalized group were women, often from the countryside, left to fend for themselves through prostitution after the loss of husbands and fathers to revolutionary battles.[4] Anarchist leaders held public meetings in patios and public parks to educate this class of workers with anarcho-syndicalist ideas such as the uselessness and immorality of seeking government assistance in arbitration with the capitalist classes. They encouraged the use of direct action, general strikes, and public demonstrations. At this time, the middle-sector workers made two important contributions to the future labor movement. First, they helped to radicalize the women who would later become the movement's most zealous participants; and second, they created links between the middle and lower working classes that would later prove critical in maintaining working-class solidarity.

By 1916 many of the port's workers consistently demonstrated militancy and loyalty to anarchist principles. Others, mostly maritime workers and leaders, had formed close ties with the Constitutionalist government of Venustiano Carranza, which had begun to suppress anarchists in Mexico City.[5] In the years following the revolution, the workers' new political involvement combined with anarcho-syndicalist tactics and ideology. As workers-turned-politicians endowed the working classes with new political power, anarchists maintained a radical dialogue among workers and critically scrutinized those in positions of authority. This mix of forces created a dynamic and controversial atmosphere to which all the main groups of workers contributed. Key to the cohesion of this movement were ideas of citizenship, unity of purpose, and respect for differences of opinion.

Veracruz's postrevolutionary working classes can be divided into three categories. One group, the politically and economically influential maritime workers, formed the League of Workers of the Maritime Zone of the Port of Veracruz in 1920 and affiliated with the Regional Confederation of Mexican Workers (CROM). The membership of the more broadly based Renters' Syndicate comprised a second element. Its membership cut across all sectors of the working classes, but the most militant participants were women who adhered strictly to anarcho-syndicalist principles. The third, more disparate group encompassed the variety of workers who toiled in the city's local, nonexport-import economy. The majority of them affiliated with the Local Federation of Veracruz Workers (FLTV), a chapter of the General Confederation of Workers (CGT). The members founded the FLTV on anarchist ideology, but their tactics proved moderate compared to those of the Renters' Syndicate.[6]

The first workers to assert themselves in Veracruz after the revolution were those involved in the maritime trades. By virtue of their economic power, experience in unionization, and relations with the revolutionary state, these workers entered the political arena as a means of furthering their working-class goals. By early 1920, with the close of the revolution and the end of World War I, commercial trade increased rapidly while a shortage of male labor created an opportunity for maritime workers to make demands of their employers. On February 21, 1920, delegates from the stevedores and day laborers, bargemen, crane operators, freight inspectors, cart drivers, and the Compañía Terminal employees met to form the League of Maritime Workers of the Port of Veracruz. One month later, the Union of Mariners and Fire Stokers of the Gulf of Mexico joined the League, adding to its strength.

Stevedore Rafael García had been selected president of the League at its foundation. Three months later he was also named president of the Union of Stevedores and Laborers, at which time he led the maritime workers into direct confrontation with their employers. The first dispute came in March 1920 in opposition to a registration procedure imposed by the Compañía Terminal after a series of robberies on the docks and in the warehouses. The workers viewed the company's insistence that each one sign in and out of each dock and warehouse as a violation of their constitutional rights. On April 1, one hundred workers walked off the job in protest, and on April 12 a district judge found the registration unconstitutional, giving the League a major victory over a powerful company.

The maritime workers soon began to request and receive more from capital, with the exception of the Compañía Terminal. In May 1920 the Union of Stevedores and Day Laborers formed a commission to request a 100 percent wage increase from all shipping companies. By early July each of the firms, except the Compañía Terminal, had agreed to raise wages. Further, the company announced that it did not recognize the union. The intransigence of the Compañía Terminal led to the general strike of 1920, which began on July 15 as a well-coordinated effort between the League of Maritime Workers and the railroad workers of the FFCC Mexicano. Both dock and railway workers sought wage increases and union recognition. Together they had the power to bring commerce to a halt in the port and to keep goods from reaching Mexico City. By July 22 the strike had spread. Not only had all work on the docks stopped, but streetcar workers, electricians, bakers, and tobacco workers also walked off their jobs in support of the strikers.[7]

The general strike of 1920 presented Rafael García and the League with the opportunity to prove themselves as powers in the port city and to change popular perceptions of what and who constituted local authority. As president of the strike committee, García directed well-organized brigades of workers who, in the first few days of the strike, patrolled the docks and warehouses to ensure that all activity had ceased. As the strike expanded, the worker vigilantes monitored all the city streets and refused to allow anyone to carry anything, whether by cart or by hand. In order to transport an item, written permission was needed from García. On one occasion, a commission of workers argued with a shop owner and with the police. The merchant was attempting to move bolts of cloth from his store to another and the strikers were demanding that the goods remain in place. The strikers insisted that García was the only person capable of resolving the issue, arguing that, "for now," in Veracruz, the only authority was "Negro García." In the end, the commission spent the night in front of the shop to be sure that the bolts of cloth were not transported.

The fact that García, a working-class Negro, had the social potency to empower workers to bring about a citywide crisis indicated that a change in Veracruz's political structure was occurring. The influence of the traditional ruling class, made up of rich, fair-skinned merchants of European descent, could no longer dominate the city as it had in the prerevolutionary era. In fact, the middle classes were willing to recognize the maritime workers' power and to use their influence to urge foreign capital to do the same rather than continue to lose money in a drawn-out strike.

On the morning of July 23 local merchants assembled in such great numbers that the Chamber of Commerce building could not hold them all, and they were forced to find a larger area. The president of the Chamber began the meeting by stating that its purpose was not simply to find a solution to the immediate problem of the stoppage of commerce. He added that the merchants must find a way to pressure the Compañía Terminal into coming to a "good arrangement" with the maritime workers so that such strikes would not occur again soon. The merchants decided to request the assistance of the customs administrator and the municipal president in setting up a meeting between the merchants and the strike committee.

Later that afternoon, García and the strike committee met with the Chamber of Commerce leaders. He explained that the Compañía Terminal workers had been requesting salary increases for some time; and since their requests had been ignored, the workers decided to declare a strike, as was their right. García continued, arguing that since the merchants would not have been interested in the betterment of the workers, they decided that a general strike was necessary for the attainment of their goals. At this time, the secretary for the Chamber of Commerce declared that claim untrue, that the local merchants would have supported the workers from the beginning and that they had worked for days to get the Compañía Terminal to accede to the demands for increased wages.

Whether or not the merchants would have supported the workers from the beginning, they clearly understood the extent of working-class power by the end of the strike and accepted the necessity of dealing with the demands of local workers. Further, the pressure that the merchants exerted on the Compañía Terminal seems to have paid off. On the following day the strikers accepted a 50 percent wage increase offered by the company. Further, they had proven themselves both capable local authorities and

influential actors in civic negotiation. In the following weeks, many of the unions that had struck in sympathy with the maritime workers also received 50 percent wage increases.[8]

García and his fellow stevedores used their newfound public recognition as a means to political power and began to reshape traditional ideas regarding port society. In 1921 he and his colleagues, as members of the Workers' Party (Partido de Trabajo), won a local election and seized the municipal government from the merchants who had traditionally dominated it. Throughout the campaign, García referred to the city's capitalist classes as "the shameless ones" who had socialized and done business with the "gringos" during the 1914 U.S. occupation of Veracruz. He called into question the patriotism of the capitalist classes and presented the working classes as the "real Porteños."

On January 1, 1922, in the Teatro Principal, amid red and black flags, García and his colleagues took their oaths of office. In his inauguration speech, García proclaimed that the workers' participation in politics had been a "spark" sent forth from the revolution and that this election demonstrated that Veracruzanos were "not a conquered people." By expropriating the words "Porteño" and "Veracruzano" (two customary terms for someone who lives in the port of Veracruz) to describe the popular classes in comparison with the capitalist "traitors" who fraternized with gringos during the revolution, García began to redefine the meaning of port citizenship. This new, popular ideology portrayed respectable Veracruzanos as nationalistic working people who would not tolerate domination by capitalists whose allegiance to money superseded their loyalty to country.

The maritime workers did not limit their influence within the city to the realm of the political. As Veracruzanos, their cultural power was equally important to them. On May Day in 1923 the League of Maritime Workers laid the first stone of the future Casa Obrera (Workers' Center), a social hall. By its completion in 1925 the Casa Obrera would take up an entire block in the center of the city. At the ceremony, José A. Cárdenas, a representative of the League, stated that the purpose of this "temple of work" was not politics, but simple pleasure. With the placement of their social hall in the center of city life, the maritime workers expressed to port society their right to enjoy a Porteño life-style full of dance and diversion.

As the maritime workers pursued cultural influence, they challenged the capitalist classes over the use of city space. One example demonstrates the intricacies of this cultural class conflict and negotiation. In February 1923 the League wanted to hold a benefit dance for a group of recently arrived workers from Puebla in the social hall where the Unión de Mejoras Materiales, a merchant association, usually held dances each weekend. The Unión refused to allow the League to hold its dance in the hall but donated two hundred pesos to the workers' fund and conceded to the League the right to use, for one time only, the bullring "Villa del Mar" for a bullfight to benefit the new workers.[9] Recognizing the maritime workers' social position, the Unión was willing to negotiate the issue with them and even make significant concessions. The workers, however, would not strike up the *danzón* in their social hall. The place of dance was sacred in port culture, and that particular social hall was elite terrain. The Unión, however, found an acceptable solution in the bullring, where it was customary for elites and the popular classes to attend functions together. Meanwhile, the workers obtained an acceptable site for their fund-raiser and two hundred pesos as consolation for not receiving their first choice.

Throughout the early 1920s the maritime workers continued to fight for union recognition, all-union work forces, and collective contracts. At times, they utilized strikes, but often they relied on the use of the boycott against companies resistant to their demands. Through the League of Maritime Workers' organizational ties within the port as well as with other ports, most notably Progreso and Campeche, the stevedores were able to pressure a single company for which they refused to work while continuing to work for others. All maritime workers, at all levels of the production process, were affiliated with the League, which maintained relations with organizations in other ports. They therefore had the power to halt all phases of a company's operations. In late 1922 the League won boycotts against the El Aguila petroleum company, the Compañía Terminal, and the Ward Line shipping company over issues of union recognition, the right of union workers to be supervised only by other union members, and the reinstatement of workers unjustly fired. Clearly, the maritime workers enjoyed power within the capitalist system, while others did not. As they would soon discover, however, they were just one facet of a potent working-class community in Veracruz.

García vowed always to remember his working-class roots at his inauguration as the mayor of Veracruz, yet he belonged to the most economically and politically powerful sector of the city's working classes. For this reason, although he wanted to believe that he could act on behalf of all the port's workers, he soon learned that he did not comprehend the motivations, ideas, and struggles of its poorest ones. Further, he soon realized that in order to avoid local crises, he, like the capitalist classes, would have to allow those below his social and political space to speak and act as port citizens.

Housing problems in Veracruz had been developing since before the revolution, when the port experienced rapid and massive immigration. During the revolution, a housing shortage allowed landlords, some of the port's wealthiest business people, to raise rents by 500 percent. By 1921 only 3.5 percent of the city's population owned their own home. The most severely affected by the housing situation were the women and children of the poorest classes, who often did not have a man of working age in the house. The issue, however, concerned and angered the entire working class, which was forced to pay excessive rents for unsanitary living conditions.[10]

On February 2, 1922, García attempted in vain to prevent an uprising among the renters by holding an organizing meeting in the public library. He had hoped to initiate a renters' union that would push the state government to enact a law regulating the cost of housing. Herón Proal attended the meeting, but when García refused to let him speak, he left without saying a word. On February 3, Proal sent out fliers calling for a rally that evening in the centrally located Juárez Park, where those in attendance agreed to meet on a nightly basis. By February 6 the Revolutionary Renters' Syndicate (Sindicato Revolucionario de Inquilinos) had chosen an executive committee, appointed Proal as president, and agreed not to deal with the authorities, to form recruitment committees, and to refuse to pay rent until landlords reduced rents to their 1910 levels, or 2 percent above the property value. García had failed to recognize that those most affected by the housing crisis, the city's poorest, were those most educated in anarcho-syndicalism. His initiative for a renters' law was quickly overshadowed by a massive rent strike.[11]

Proal took his ideas for a rent strike to the prostitutes on February 27. At the same time that the municipal government had been creating new regulations to control prostitution in saloons, Proal called a meeting of the prostitutes and addressed them as "dear *compañeras.*" On March 6, the same day that the first patio declared itself on strike, the prostitutes also announced their resistance by dragging onto the streets the tools of their trade—beds, mattresses, and chairs, all of which they were forced to rent in addition to rooms—and setting them aflame. The renters' strike had begun and quickly spread. By March 12, sixty-one patios were on strike, by March 13 more than one hundred, and so the numbers grew day by day.[12]

On the night of March 12 the Renters' Syndicate held its first public demonstration, which set the tone for the nightly, public, and at times confrontational, appearances in Juárez Park. At 8:00 P.M., men, women, and children began arriving in the park. By 8:30, a large number of demonstrators had gathered, and Proal invited the crowd to march through the streets with José Olmos, secretary of the Renters' Syndicate. The crowd followed Olmos, red flag in hand, through the streets to the offices of the city's most detested landlords, the Cangas. Orators there were interrupted with shouts of "Down with the bourgeoisie! Death to the exploiters of the people! Death to the Cangas!" The Renters set off firecrackers and marched to the central plaza.

Once there, they requested and received permission for Proal and his colleague, Porfirio Sosa, to speak from the balcony of the Hotel Diligencias. Sosa spoke of the power that the Renters possessed to free themselves from the bourgeoisie, while Proal bemoaned futile attempts by politicians to deal with the problems of the people. Later, the demonstrators took the march to the *zona de tolerancia.* Proal proclaimed the prostitutes "true heroines" who had initiated the renters' movement and asked the men to follow the women's example. While the crowd dispersed, Proal continued on to the Teatro Principal where, in order to expand the movement further, he stood perched on a chair orating as the audience filed out of the building after the evening performance.[13]

For two weeks the nightly rallies continued as the Renters complied with their commitment to stop paying rent, thereby creating a difficult situation for the new mayor, who faced pressure from the landlords. García soon announced that he would not attempt to halt evictions. In response, Proal publicly declared that the mayor's power had gone to his head and that he had renounced his origins. Proal explained that as a politician, García was obliged to uphold the laws that oppressed the masses.[14] The mayor was infuriated by Proal's pronouncements, and he prohibited the nightly demonstrations in Juárez Park. Proal and the Renters ignored the prohibition, and soon direct confrontation between García and the popular classes erupted over their right to speak and act publicly.

García ordered Proal's detention on the morning of March 22. The arrest took place in the central market at nine o'clock in the morning, just as the city's women were beginning to make their daily purchases. Within five minutes a crowd had gathered, the size of which prompted the police to call for reinforcements. The police escorted Proal to jail, with the crowd following behind. Once inside the jail, Proal faced García, who accused the anarchist of subversion and opportunism and demanded that he stop the nightly meetings. Proal replied that neither he nor the executive committee made up the movement, that the people who comprised the Renters' Syndicate would decide its future.

As García left the jail, a delegation of Renters went to his office and demanded to know the reasons for Proal's arrest. García responded by accusing the delegation members of betraying the working class. In the meantime, a crowd of almost one thousand people had gathered outside the jail as a contingent of maritime workers joined in after the end of their morning shift. The addition of the maritime workers, members of García's own union, demonstrated that the renters' movement was not made up of "a few opportunists," as the mayor had stated. The militancy of the workers as they attempted to force entry to the jail illustrated their insistence on the right to free speech in public places and class unity. As the crowd grew, the police inspector wanted nothing more than to be rid of Proal and his followers. García, therefore, ordered Proal taken away in a car, but when the car did not arrive, the police decided to use public transportation. While Proal waited with the police on the corner for the streetcar, the crowd saw him and charged. They swept him up on their shoulders and carried him away. En route to Juárez Park, a sympathizer loaned Proal his horse. The anarchist rode the rest of the way on horseback, red flag in hand, leading the masses to a triumphant public demonstration.[15]

Drama, frustration, and action were recurring themes throughout the renters' movement. The massive support for the Renters' strike as demonstrated by the numbers of workers that came to the defense of Proal that afternoon in March forced the local authorities to allow the Renters public space to meet and make their demands. The people's belief in their right to public discussion and protest was at least as powerful as their respect for García's authority. This lesson García painfully learned on the evening following Proal's arrest when a group of workers pelted him with rocks as he left a local theater. The next day, García asked for another meeting with Proal. This time he acted in a conciliatory manner, stating that he had only intended to speak with the leader, not to detain him for a prolonged period. He continued, saying that he had not rejected his origins, that he was "clearly of the people," and that he would permit the Renters' Syndicate to proceed with its nightly meetings in Juárez Park. He requested that its members maintain as much order as possible.[16]

One reason for the rapid success of the renters' movement was widespread support, including that of the maritime workers and artisans, for the rent strike. On May 19 the leaders and delegates from all of the unions affiliated with both the League and the FLTV agreed that their organizations would offer both moral and material support to the Revolutionary Renters' Syndicate. Further, they declared that membership in the League or the FLTV meant co-membership in the Renters' Syndicate.[17]

The everyday activities and direct action that made the renters' strike possible, however, were principally the work of women, many of them prostitutes, who formed their own group known as the Libertarian Women. Because of the socially unacceptable nature of their work, prostitutes paid almost double the rent charged to others who often had larger dwellings. Until the emergence of the renters' movement and the social support of Proal, prostitutes had little recourse for action against their landlords. Further, the renters' movement gave these women who were not even allowed into public dance halls the opportunity to demonstrate their self-respect and social worth to the community.[18]

The women upheld the Syndicate's key rule that "for solidarity, camaraderie, and humanity" every renter should assist any other renter in danger of being evicted "without pretext and without excuse," and to do so with self-righteous pride.[19] They blew police whistles to call other members to the assistance of renters in danger of eviction and aided the homeless in the occupation of vacant dwellings. Once the new "tenants" and their belongings were safely inside, they hung a sign at the door, "On Strike. We don't pay rent." The women also dealt with collectors, many of whom were also women, sent by the landlords to obtain payments from the strikers.

These collectors infuriated the women, who often used direct action tactics against them. On one occasion, a group of Libertarian Women sent a letter to a female collector requesting that she stop attempting to charge rents. When the collector retorted with offensive language, the women formed a committee to go to her house, pull her out the door, and parade her through the streets. At first the woman refused to go with the committee of about fifty people, but upon realizing the threatening nature of the crowd, she acquiesced. The Renters escorted her from the house through the center of the city, condemning her as loudly as possible until they reached the local. There, they warned her to stop attempting to charge rents or something more "serious" could happen.[20]

Through these acts in defense of the city's working-class homes and families, prostitutes found personal as well as social power. They did, after all, sell their bodies in order to feed and house the members of their own families too old or too young to work for themselves. Their cause had been one of family before the renters' movement had even begun. Like the maritime workers, the Renters also asserted themselves culturally within the city of Veracruz. Unlike the stevedores, however, the Renters did not solicit property rights from the city council to erect social halls, nor did they compete with the upper classes for rights to hold dances on elite terrain. Rather, they took over Juárez Park, located at the entrance to the main avenue running directly through the center of the city and right beside Liberty Park, where the upper classes tended to congregate.

In their raucous way each night the Renters celebrated the culture of the pueblo and their radical determination to liberate themselves from their landlords, who probably witnessed it all from the distance of the avenue separating the two parks. As the Renters arrived each night, they set off firecrackers, a customary way of announcing a fiesta in the pueblos. The men, women, and children who gathered together sang traditional local songs along with the "Internationale" late into the evening. They often held carnivals on the weekends, attended by members of all sectors of the working classes, where they listened to traditional Mexican music and enjoyed tamales, *tortas*, and local dishes. Even inside the city jail, the Renters rebelled by singing the "Internationale" late into the night. Both the politically and economically influential maritime workers and the militantly anarchist Renters had proven their strength and resolve within Veracruz as well-organized and disciplined workers' organizations. Between these two extremes was the vast majority of workers who toiled in the city's local economy: bakers, restaurant workers, corn grinders, streetcar workers, electricians, et al. This part of the working class represented a complex middle sector of workers and artisans. They both maintained civil relations with employers not that better off than themselves and were becoming increasingly alienated from the capitalist classes as the society stratified.

The heterogeneity of this sector of the working class made it difficult to organize along modern syndicalist lines. Some of the more radical workers believed in the necessity of tactics such as strikes and sabotage. Others, less alienated from their employers, were unsure or even opposed to the use of such extreme methods in dealing with them. As noted, in 1919 the middle sector had organized along trade union lines, formed the FLTV, and in 1922 affiliated with the Mexico City-based CGT, which had been founded in 1921 on anarcho-syndicalist guidelines.[21]

The FLTV's leadership rigidly considered the membership's differing points of view as a lack of class consciousness. An examination of the role of the FLTV in Veracruz's postrevolutionary labor movement, however, elucidates the importance of heterogeneity in holding the citywide movement together despite radical differences in opinion and ideology, particularly between the maritime workers and the Renters.

A review of the crisis of 1923, in which the FLTV unions organized a citywide walkout in solidarity with striking electrical workers, its cultural activities, and relations with the League and the Renters' Syndicate illustrates the main characteristics of all sectors of Veracruz's working classes as well as the pivotal role of the FLTV in maintaining working-class unity. In early July 1923, the electrical workers went on strike against the Light and Power Company over the issues of union recognition, a collective contract, the eight-hour day, and a 50 percent wage increase. On August 7 they signed a collective agreement with the company that granted them union recognition and the eight-hour day, but the company held firm against a wage hike. The electricians, therefore, continued the walkout. On August 13 the FLTV announced its support of the electricians and pledged a sympathy strike if a resolution were not forthcoming within five days.[22] On August 17 the state Arbitration

Board declared the strike illegal and ordered the electricians to return to work. They refused, and on August 20 a general strike encompassed the city.

On August 19 the FLTV union members had met to choose a strike committee and police force. The strategy of the strikers was similar to that employed by the maritime workers in the strike of 1920: to stop the flow of goods into and out of the port so that the local capitalist class would pressure the Light and Power Company to concede a wage increase. This time, however, the League would not participate. Although it morally supported the electrical workers, an issue much more important to the League's power within the transport industry was at stake and kept them from striking. The League had been fighting with the Confederation of Societies of Railroad Workers of the Mexican Republic for some time, had recently helped create the Veracruz Port Railroad Workers' Union on syndicalist lines, and wanted all of the railroad workers in the port to join that union.

The Confederation workers refused to be absorbed by the new union or the League and had decided to strike over the issue just as the strike of 1923 was beginning. Concerned with maintaining and fortifying its power, the League decided that it would be more prudent to deal with the issue of the railway workers than to strike in solidarity with the electricians.[23] Without the support of the maritime workers, it would be impossible to halt completely the flow of goods through the port, making it difficult to put pressure on the local bourgeoisie. In the final analysis, the leadership of the League was more concerned with the power of its organization than with a wage increase for the electricians.

At the other extreme, the Libertarian Women took direct action in solidarity with their "brothers" the electricians. Operating under the assumption that the strike would not succeed if the bourgeoisie continued to eat, the women began a campaign to syndicalize the servants and cooks employed by the upper classes. On August 21 they began by attempting to convince the servants, most of whom were young women and girls, to join the striking men and refuse to work for their employers. When the servants did not respond to the idea of syndicalism, the women's tactics became more aggressive. On August 22 they entered the markets early in the morning in order to meet the servants as they made their daily purchases. Upon confronting them, the women seized their baskets of food and demanded, with threats of physical violence, that the servants follow them to the Renters' Syndicate local. Later in the morning the servants were transferred to the Restaurant Workers' Union local where they signed papers agreeing to syndicalize and join the strike in exchange for their freedom. The women accompanied the servants back to the houses where they worked and explained to their employers that the servants were now part of a union, that they were to receive one day of rest per week, and that they were obliged to attend all union meetings and events.[24] The collaboration between the women of the Renters' Syndicate and the Restaurant Workers' Union is interesting in light of the fact that even Proal distanced himself from the actions of the women, saying that they did not act on his behalf. Neither did the strike committee condone the actions, yet clearly elements within the Restaurant Workers' Union, part of the FLTV, advocated such tactics.

Indeed, throughout the seven-day strike, the FLTV was forced to deal with its own diversity. By the second or third day the strike committee had managed to stop street traffic, but its members found it difficult to enforce the closing of all restaurants and grocery stores as well as to discipline the entire rank and file. The electricians continued with the walkout, sabotaged the power lines, and had little trouble persuading their "brothers" the streetcar workers to stop work.

The bakers used violent tactics in defense of the general strike. In one incident, a group of bakers entered the Café Parroquia armed with large sticks. They demanded that the owner close the café and that the employees stop work. When the owner refused, the strikers overturned tables, broke dishes, and wreaked havoc until he closed.[25] The strike committee found it much more difficult to compel the corn grinders and carters to stop work. Although both groups were unionized, many corn grinders and carters were self-employed or worked for owners who hired only one or two people, making their relations with these employers distinct from those of the electricians and streetcar workers, both employed by a large foreign company.

These differences in militancy presented a problem for the FLTV strike committee, particularly as negotiations between electricians and the Light and Power Company dragged on. In order to continue the strike, the committee had to negotiate with various FLTV members as well as with the small shop owners who sold goods to the working classes. Despite the efforts of the Libertarian Women to distribute food, the workers suffered more than the upper classes due to food shortages. On August 23, three days after the strike began, the committee agreed that corn grinders could work two hours per day, while grocery stores were allowed to remain open until noon. The committee warned, however, that if store owners attempted to raise prices, they would be "severely punished." Further, the committee made a distinction between corn and other basic foodstuffs consumed by the popular classes, and bread, considered a luxury item for the upper classes. The strike committee agreed that cafés could operate within fixed hours, thus allowing the port's citizenry their daily hours of coffee and conversation. Yet the committee cautioned café owners that any attempt to sell bread would result in the destruction of their tables and chairs.[26] Thus, the strike committee was able to negotiate between the middle sectors of both workers and owners, preserving the strike while articulating working-class values and fostering a broadening of the rights of citizenship.

On August 27 the strike ended with the Arbitration Board ruling that the walkout was illegal. Nevertheless, on the evening of August 27, the church bells rang while the workers set off firecrackers and fired gunshots to celebrate their efforts and the end of the strike. Although the FLTV leadership lamented the "lack of solidarity" among many workers, its ability to negotiate among various workers and shop owners kept the strike alive throughout the long negotiations between the electricians and the Light and Power Company. The FLTV promoted understanding and citizenship among the middle and working classes.

The FLTV kept open the lines of communication and understanding between the most powerful, well-off workers and the most dispossessed. The FLTV and its member unions corresponded with both the Maritime League and the Renters' Syndicate on a regular basis. It kept current on the League's executive committee changes, strikes, and boycotts. In early October 1923, during the League's dispute with the railroad workers, the Restaurant Workers' Union invited both organizations to a meeting in the public library.[27] Similarly, the FLTV circulated the Renters' Syndicate's newspaper, *Guillotine*, and supported it morally and organizationally as the authorities turned to violent repression.

The FLTV's cultural activities reached out to all sectors of the working classes, affirmed revolutionary ideals, and encouraged solidarity. Through their artistic group the FLTV put on revolutionary plays that brought together the entire working-class community and reminded the workers of the ideals of the Mexican Revolution and the plight of the poor. One of the FLTV's biggest productions took place upon the visit of Enrique Flores Magón to the port in 1923. To celebrate his arrival, the FLTV's theater group presented Ricardo Flores Magón's *Tierra y Libertad*, a play that portrayed Mexican revolutionary nationalism interacting with the family and community. Those institutions hold Mexicans together and constitute the basis for revolution. Although the injustices of landowners and capitalists tear at it, the family remains together, with each member making sacrifices for its preservation even when that requires taking up arms.[28]

Their production of another Flores Magón play, *Verdugos y Víctimas*, featured a dialogue between the prostitutes and the rest of the working-class community. In this play, female characters discuss their reasons for turning to prostitution. They explain that their husbands, fathers, brothers, and uncles had died fighting against the rural revolutionary forces, the Villistas and Zapatistas, and that they were left with the responsibility of feeding children and older members of their families. This play criticizes the urban working classes for not supporting their "brothers and sisters" in the countryside.[29] Although perhaps more radical in ideology than many of the port's most powerful union leaders, these plays were written by a national hero among all the popular classes and thus enjoyed wide attendance. Moreover, children's choirs sang local songs at each performance, providing an air of communal solidarity and a sense of family and community.[30]

Understanding and communications between sectors of the working classes became crucial to keeping the labor movement intact at times of tension between the Renters' Syndicate and the local, state, and federal authorities. In early July 1922 the federal army and municipal police used a split among the Renters' Syndicate leaders to attack it and arrest Proal and about fifty men and ninety women. Several were wounded or killed during the assault. In the organizational disarray that resulted, the FLTV stepped in to keep the Syndicate together. By early October the FLTV had convinced the League to join it in forming a Committee for the Prisoners to fight for the release of all incarcerated Renters. On October 11 the Committee sent a telegram to President Obregón demanding their release.[31]

By November 1 friction had developed between the League and the FLTV, which wanted to take a radical, direct-action approach to freeing the prisoners. The League disagreed, stating that the issue was a "judicial" one.[32] On the following day an incident between the police and the protesting Renters could have led to serious conflict among the working-class groups. However, the FLTV mediated between the League and the angry Renters.

On November 2, the Day of the Dead, the Renters' Syndicate organized a march to the local cemetery to honor its comrades killed in the violence of early July. On the road to the cemetery, the police began to follow them. Resenting their presence, the Renters shouted insults at the officers. Violence ensued, leaving one Renter dead. This incident outraged the working-class community and led to a citywide work stoppage and a demonstration initiated by the League. In order to avoid disorder, the League took it upon itself to lead the demonstration. On November 3, three thousand of the city's workers from the Maritime League, the FLTV, and the Renters' Syndicate formed a procession behind the red and black coffin of the slain Renter and marched from the center of the city to the highway leading to the cemetery. After the burial, the workers returned in silence to the center of Veracruz where they had planned a rally and speeches. As they passed the central plaza, the Renters suggested that the speakers use a balcony of the Hotel Diligencias. The League members, however, marching in front, ignored the Renters and led the demonstration to Vásquez Park, also located in the center but not as prominently as the Hotel Diligencias. Both the speakers from the League and the FLTV called for calm and measured action; indeed, those who spoke for the Renters did so in subdued tones. The League's patronizing attitude toward the marchers, however, infuriated the Renters. As the crowd dispersed, they returned to their local where they verbally attacked the League for not allowing the pueblo to speak freely.[33]

The fact that the Renters returned to their local rather than air their grievances in public indicates that, even when angry with the League, some form of working-class solidarity existed between them. Further, the Renters' hesitancy to criticize the FLTV illustrates that they realized the value of their relationship. It also suggests that had the FLTV not been present at the demonstration, conflict between the Renters and the League might have erupted. Although the Renters' resentment of the League ran high that day, the efforts exerted by the FLTV, the support that it had lent the Renters (which included the Committee for the Prisoners) helped to bridge the gap between the powerful Maritime League and the anarchistic Renters. The FLTV held the city's labor movement together at a critical moment in a show of strength and solidarity before both the capitalist classes and the local authorities.

In conclusion, throughout the early 1920s, following the Mexican Revolution, a unified and mobilized working class in the port of Veracruz created a citywide labor movement, yet various segments constituted that working class. Shared concepts of family, community, and citizenship functioned as common threads to overcome differences in economic and social background, ideology, and militancy within one tapestry that was the working class of the port of Veracruz. For this group, the idea of family manifested itself in the responsibility that each person felt for the well-being of family members, especially those unable to provide for themselves. The idea of community respected each individual within it. When the police killed a Renter on the way to the cemetery on the Day of the Dead, all of the workers stopped for a day of mourning and protest. Furthermore, all of these workers took pride in calling themselves Veracruzanos and presented themselves as the "real Porteños" through their cultural activities.

Although family and community relations affirmed unity, the idea of citizenship and respect for the rights of workers to express themselves were central to the labor movement. The public nature of daily life in the city caused each of the groups to take their struggle to the streets, parks, and central plaza. Moreover, their right to do so seems to have been respected by much of the middle classes. Without this respect for open, polemical discussion among the citizenry, such a dynamic citywide labor movement could not have taken place.

The military took note of the importance to the labor movement of public discussion. On the day of Proal's arrest in March 1922, the local police seemed almost dismayed at the fact that the army detained him for nothing more than public discourse. The police did not use violence against the crowd attempting to break Proal out of jail, but instead negotiated with it. When federal forces began to work in conjunction with the local police, however, the most militant anarchists were killed and imprisoned, thus stifling the freedom of the citizens to express themselves. On November 3, 1922, when the League of Maritime Workers and the FLTV both encouraged the Renters not to use hostile language in their speeches, they feared the consequences of another confrontation between the Renters, the military, and local police. They did not want to see more of their fellow workers killed or imprisoned.

Despite violent censorship, however, events such as May Day in 1923 demonstrated to the city and its authorities that the working class constituted a proud community. As union members marched down the Avenida de la Independencia, they trumpeted their pride on banners. The Philharmonic Union chose, "Honor Art"; the Women's Syndicate of Corn Grinders, "For the Cause of the Organized Worker . . . For Women's Rights"; the Restaurant Workers, "Union and Work"; the Union of Railroad Workers, "Honor and Glory to Those Who Die for a Steadfast Ideal" and "Long Live Socialism"; the FLTV, "Health and Libertarian Communism"; the League of Maritime Workers, "Union Makes Strength"; and the Renters' Syndicate carried a red flag that simply proclaimed, "Anarchism." The workers of Veracruz united to confront the abuses of the ruling classes in a society of extreme inequality. They succeeded in breaking the monopoly on power of the old elites by using the lessons of citizens' rights, unity, and struggle learned during the revolution.

Notes

1. The discussion of late nineteenth- and early twentieth-century modernization and immigration in the port was taken from Bernardo García Díaz and Laura Zevallos Ortiz, *Veracruz: Imagenes de su historia* (Veracruz: Archivo General del Estado de Veracruz, 1993).

2. The term "patio" refers to housing which included apartments surrounding a common area where one found the bathroom, water spigot, and washboard. Workers gathered nightly in the common area to chat, listen to music, and, with the rise of the labor movement, organize collective action. See García Díaz and Ortiz, *Veracruz*; and Isabel Muñoz Herranz, "El arte musical (1920–1924) como expresión de la vida en el puerto de Veracruz" (M.A. thesis, Universidad Cristóbal Colón, Veracruz, 1992), for popular culture in the port in the late nineteenth and early twentieth centuries,

3. Rafael García Auli, *La unión de estibadores y jornaleros del puerto de Veracruz: Ante el movimiento obrero nacional e internacional de 1909–1977* (n.p., 1977).

4. Octavio García Mundo, *El movimiento inquilinario de Veracruz, 1922* (México: SEP-setentas, 1976), 27–28.

5. See John M. Hart, *Anarchism and the Mexican Working Class, 1860–1931* (Austin: University of Texas Press, 1978). The Casa del Obrero Mundial, an anarcho-syndicalist organization during the revolution, founded chapters throughout the country. The Casa combined the anarchist ideas of communal living and union power to be gained by direct actions such as strikes and sabotage.

6. The Spanish titles are the Liga de Trabajadores de la Zona Marítima del Puerto de Veracruz, of the Confederación Regional de Obreros Mexicanos; the Sindicato Revolucionario de Inquilinos; and the Federación Local de Trabajadores de Veracruz, of the Confederación General de Trabajadores.

7. *El Dictamen* (Veracruz), February 21—22, March 20, April 2, April 13, May 25, July 14, July 22, 1920. In 1923 the League included the Unión de Estibadores y Jornaleros, Carretilleros del Puerto, Lancheros del Puerto, Trabajadores de la Compañía Terminal, Marineros y Fogoneros del Golfo de México, Checadores del Puerto, Grueros del Puerto, Calafates y Carpinteros Navales, Empleados de Veracruz, Ferrocarrileros del Puerto, Empleados del Departamento de Tráfico, Liga de Oficiales Navales, and Empleados y Trabajadores de Compañías Petroleras.

8. Ibid., July 23–24, 1920. The railroad strikers of the FFCC Mexicano accepted a 50 percent wage increase a few days before the Compañía Terminal made the same offer to the maritime workers. That probably influenced the company, although local merchants pressured the firm to offer a raise.

9. Ibid., January 2, May 2, 1922; February 1, 1923.

10. García Mundo, *El movimiento*, 19.

11. *El Dictamen*, February 3, 4, 6, 1922; García Mundo, *El movimiento*, 71–72.

12. *El Dictamen*, February 28, March 7, 1922; García Mundo, *El movimiento*, 84–87.

13. *El Dictamen*, March 13, 1922.

14. Ibid., March 21, 1922.

15. Ibid., March 23, 1922; see also García Mundo, *El movimiento*, 96–99.

16. *El Dictamen*, March 24, 1922.

17. Archivo General de la Nación (hereafter AGN), Ramo Obregon/Calles, Expediente, 407-V-17. The Liga de Trabajadores de la Zona Marítima informed President Obregón of their and the FLTV's support for the Renters' Syndicate, but if anything should happen to the Syndicate's leadership they were ready to take over.

18. García Mundo, *El movimiento*, 68–69.

19. *El Dictamen*, March 12, 1922.

20. Ibid., March 1922–December 1923, passim.

21. Rafael García, *Las luchas proletarias en Veracruz: Historia e autocrítica*; *El Dictamen*, April 3, 1922.

22. *El Dictamen*, August 14, 1923.

23. Ibid., August 20, 1923. See also María Rosa Landa Ortega, "Los primeros años de la organización y luchas de los electricistas y tranviarios en Veracruz, 1915–1928" (Thesis, Universidad Veracruzana, Xalapa, Veracruz, 1989).

24. *El Dictamen*, August 22, 23, 1923.

25. Ibid., August 22, 1923.

26. Ibid., August 24, 1923.

27. Archivo Sindical del Puerto de Veracruz (hereafter ASP), MCMA. 1923, 237/Un.

28. MCMA, 1923, 235/Fed., August 2, 1923, ASP. *Tierra y Libertad* portrayed officials as stooges of the rich and without patriotism while it showed the pueblo as dedicated to family, community, and love of the land, expressing true patriotism. In scenes of rebellion and defiance, Flores Magón states that men, women, children, and old people represent the entire pueblo.

29. MCMA, 1923, 149/Un., May 23, 1923, ASP.

30. Correspondence in the ASP shows that the FLTV sold tickets to the Renters' Syndicate and League. Other FLTV plays included *Pan del Pobre, Maldita Sea la Ley*, and *Regeneración*.

31. Exp. 407-V-17, Anexo I, Ramo Obregón/Calles, AGN.

32. *El Dictamen*, November 2, 1922.

33. Ibid., November 3, 1922.

CHAPTER SIX

Identity, Culture, and Workers' Autonomy
The Petroleum Workers of Poza Rica in the 1930s*

ALBERTO OLVERA RIVERA

Discovered in 1929, Poza Rica was the last oil field developed before the nationalization of the petroleum industry. The field started production in 1932. The historical circumstances encountered by the local working class differed significantly from those experienced earlier in the century by the oil workers at Tampico to the north and Minatitlán to the south. After coming together from diverse regions and with varied backgrounds, the workers at Poza Rica developed a remarkable degree of self-sufficiency and political autonomy. During the mid-1930s, however, a political confrontation between the Mexican government and foreign interests led to the nationalization of the oil industry. At that moment nationwide labor syndicates also took shape. These outside forces transcended the workers' more localized priorities and experience.

During their first few years, however, the oil workers at Poza Rica underwent a remarkable evolution that reflected their diverse origins and their collective on-scene experience. Some of them came from the mountains of the Huasteca. A few did not speak Spanish. Inexperienced, they came into the camp as outsiders recruited by labor contractors. Once there they mixed with the more experienced and skilled workers. Some of the more seasoned ones practiced trades and had participated in labor-organizing struggles at the older

*Translated by Nair M. Anaya Ferreira and John Mason Hart.

oil camps before their arrival. Former artisans comprised a third group of workers. Skilled in metal working, mechanical trades, and related fields, they formed an important component of the new work force.

Many of the older workers already carried anarcho-syndicalist ideas regarding self-management, workers' power, and self-help with them. They saw themselves as an autonomous class vis-à-vis their employers and the managers. Their experience in the labor struggles at Tampico and the fields to the south helped them to transcend their heterogenous social origins and varied cultural backgrounds. The Poza Rica work force came together because of its status in the oil industry. Its members quickly found that cooperation was an important tool in their competition with employers and in their efforts to survive the harsh conditions that they encountered. As a result they overcame their separate identities rooted in racial and ethnic backgrounds, the propensities to form exclusive guilds for the protection of a few, and localism. They created a homogenized working-class culture. Their union became a major force in daily life, filled a political vacuum, and helped to synthesize many fragmented cultures into one. All this happened very quickly, at a pace never before experienced in the oil fields.

Then, in 1938, the nationalization of the oil industry suddenly altered the social and political situation of the workers at Poza Rica. When the government gave them symbolic control of the industry, the clear differentiations between them, the company, and the national union were erased. The workers' sense of identity, based on the difference between labor and capital, lost its clarity. The local union began to interact with politicians and to depend on government largesse. The aim of this chapter is to deal with the early period between 1932 and 1938 in which the oil proletariat at Poza Rica constituted itself socially and adopted the symbols and beliefs that formed its sense of identity. Because of limited space we will not study the postnationalization era and the decline of workers' autonomy but, rather, the formative process of that sense of autonomy and their self-support practices.

The Process of Working-Class Formation

The formation of the working class and new working-class groups is a continuing process comprised of three major factors: 1) the cultural and political adaptations made by their predecessors; 2) the material changes that arise from capital accumulation; and 3) the relationship of the workers to the state. However, this formative experience does not operate on an accumulative basis. What is achieved in one era can be lost in another, with advances followed by setbacks. This is especially true in countries where the state is the main economic and political player, and where the working class fails to reach a high level of organizational and political independence. In the case of Mexico, the working class in general failed in its struggle to achieve autonomous ways of communicating and taking strategic actions.

The Mexican working class largely took shape during the rise of modern capitalism in the last third of the nineteenth century. That is when the railroads were built, the textile industry came to the fore, and other modern industries appeared. During the first decade of the twentieth century, the oil and sugarcane industries developed and became highly significant because they created industrial enclaves closely linked to the world market.[1] From a technical and materialist point of view the working class took its original shape during the expansive phase of the world economy, which predominated toward the end of the reign of Porfirio Díaz. The industries that were formed, such as textiles, sugar mills, breweries, and oil refineries, and the job skills that were created during that period continued to prevail until the end of World War II. The principal Mexican oil refineries remained those that had been built at the turn of the century: Minatitlán in the south, and Ciudad Madero near Tampico in the north. The manner of transport, and of extracting and pumping crude oil, also remained unchanged.

Nevertheless, in the political and institutional arenas the Mexican Revolution of 1910 constituted a defining moment for workers as a whole, and its effects were gradually consolidated until the end of the era of President Lázaro Cárdenas in 1940. Before the revolution, workers' resistance acted for the most part in a juridical and institutional vacuum under identities based on primary solidarities: regional bonds, ethnicity, and guilds. After the revolution there was a long period in which state officials built institutions that mediated the conflicts between workers and employers. They normalized and recognized unions, collective bargaining, and arbitration while the rights bestowed upon the workers by the Constitution of 1917 gradually materialized. The settlements of endless conflicts between workers and capitalists and the workers and the state characterized this process.

In 1924 the first union earned official recognition from an oil company. The Workers' and Employees' Union of the "El Aguila" Oil Company (Sindicato de Obreros y Empleados de la Compañía Mexicana de Petróleo "El Aguila"), located at the refinery in Ciudad Madero, signed a collective bargaining contract. The agreement came after long years of intense worker-capitalist confrontations compounded by the vacillations of the government in the implementation of its labor policy.[2]

The earlier uncertainties ended in 1931 when the president of Mexico promulgated the federal labor code, the Ley del Trabajo. At that point trade unionism became an accepted and permanent institution in society. A second generation of Mexican workers had gone through the process of class formation in the new industries and were now to be accounted for in the political life of the country. The unions represented their interests while a juridical apparatus guaranteed, in theory, the rights won during the revolution and enshrined in the constitution.

This process, however, had an enormous political cost for the working class. Indeed, independent and radical trade unions, almost all of them with anarcho-syndicalist connections—those that had begun the struggle for workers' rights—were considered dysfunctional by the politicians in view of their need to integrate the working class and the new regime. Thus, between 1915 and 1930 the government officials and union members engaged in a struggle that ended in the early 1930s with the defeat of the anarchist-inspired workers' movement. In spite of those setbacks the ideological and independent cultural propensities of the anarcho-syndicalists prevailed for a number of years, especially in the textile and oil industries. Thus, a new political phase in working-class history began. The Communists failed to marshal significant support; and during the Cárdenas era a new working-class leadership, loyal to the government and integrated with it, seized control of organized labor. They did so through the creation of the Confederation of Mexican Workers (Confederación de Trabajadores de México, or CTM).

In the case of the oil workers' unions, this process coincided with a terrible crisis in the industry as a whole—a crisis that reduced its production by almost 70 percent between 1921 and 1930. Entire oil fields closed, exploration dropped to a minimum, and jobs at the refineries were reduced. The union members found their room for maneuvering circumscribed. The crisis created internal divisions, mainly between the large workers' organizations of Ciudad Madero and Minatitlán. The political fragmentation of the unions was only overcome in 1935 when the government helped to create a national syndicate, the Mexican Oil Workers' Union (Sindicato de Trabajadores Petroleros de la República Mexicana, or STPRM).

The political incorporation of the working class into the government was not achieved, however, without resistance. In fact, it took President Miguel Alemán, who served from 1946 to 1952, to eliminate the independent leadership of the trade unions and create a state-dominated political structure for the workers. The president crowned this achievement with the elimination of the Lombardist or radical wing of the CTM. In 1949 the government began a three-year campaign against the Communists who were already isolated and other radicals in the union leadership, leading to their expulsion from the unions. The stage was then set for *charrismo sindical*—that is, a state-controlled union movement with politician leaders loyal to the government.[3]

The government's consolidation of control over the oil industry coincided with the crisis in production and the nationalization. The economic emergency and ensuing confrontation with foreign powers aided the government in wearing down the workers, who fought long and hard for their independence. The once-autonomous syndicates fell under the control of the government and the tyranny of caciques. The long period of state domination of the unions in the petroleum industry began at the same time as it did in the other sectors of the economy.[4]

The 1930s were a transitional period between the end of one era of Mexican industrialization and the beginning of another. In the new epoch the old industries that had dominated the economy— oil, mining, textiles, and railroads—gradually lost their primacy to the emergent automotive, metallurgical, electronic, and capital goods producers. The specific case on which we are focused, that of the petroleum workers at Poza Rica between 1932 and 1938, brings the workers of the older industries into the national unions of the new era. The experience of the Poza Rica oil workers demonstrates how the merger of the anarcho-syndicalist working-class orientation of the 1920s and the new nationalism of the 1930s took place. The anarcho-syndicalists carried a political discourse with an orientation toward workers' self-management and socialism. However, the workers' nationalism intensified and transcended anarcho-syndicalism during the struggle between the Mexican state and the foreign companies.

Poza Rica and Its Significance for the Mexican Oil Industry

Poza Rica was born as an exception to the prevailing forces in the national oil industry during the early 1930s. While oil output fell drastically from 1923 onward and a number of smaller companies went bankrupt, El Aguila developed new fields including Poza Rica. Undoubtedly, El Aguila's importance as the country's largest oil firm was reinforced by its status as a subsidiary of the powerful multinational Royal Dutch Shell. It operated the three most important refineries in Mexico at Minatitlán and Ciudad Madero near the Gulf Coast, and Acapotzalco near Mexico City. These great resources gave El Aguila the ability to risk the development of new fields where other oil companies could not. In addition, its large investment in refineries gave it a further incentive to develop national production while surpluses could be exported to Europe, where the company's sales network was extensive.

In the face of declining production in the Golden Lane, or Faja de Oro, and the exhaustion of the field at Palma Sola the company's owners decided to explore the intermediate area lying between the older northern and southern zones of production.[5] The workers drilled several wells in a narrow strip extending eighty kilometers from Palma Sola to Tuxpan. In doing so they employed the most advanced technology of the time, drilling holes some two thousand meters in depth, more than double the depths reached previously. Between 1926 and 1929 the crews methodically drilled the wells called Mecatepec 1 and Poza Rica 2. In 1930 oil gushed from the latter site, thus confirming the potential of the new area. The Kilometer 52 sign on the railroad line from Tuxpan, at a place called Poza Rica, marked the center of the new field. Poza Rica 2 dazzled the oilmen with an output of 100,000 barrels per day. Its volume even exceeded the fabled but exhausted wells in the Faja de Oro.[6]

By 1932 the new field had been brought into production largely by the efforts of the workers from Palma Sola, using the equipment they brought with them.[7] Nevertheless, the construction of the new camp required more workers than were available at Palma Sola. The rich new field required the drilling of several wells at a time, large storage tanks, rail lines leading to the wells, pipelines, and separation batteries.[8] The population of the camp grew rapidly. In 1934 there were 380 permanent workers and more than 500 temporary ones.[9] In 1936 the number of long-term employees had grown to 680 while the transient workers totaled some 1,000.[10] Thereafter, the number of workers continued to grow.

Poza Rica was an isolated place inhabited by a few Totonac Indian families. A tropical area, several streams and the Cazones River had kept it isolated. The El Aguila owners obtained twenty-five-year leases of adjacent lands and ordered the construction of workshops, offices, living quarters, and support facilities. A community of temporary buildings took shape. All of the edifices as well as the rail lines could be readily dismantled and moved, a necessity given the uncertain future of the oil fields. Even the houses of management personnel were modular constructions made from wood and raised on platforms in anticipation of flooding. Metal sheets comprised the walls and roofs of the workshops. Given the provisional character of the camp the company did not insure the facilities. The workers at Poza Rica would have to improvise their own way of life.

The Composition of the Work Force

When veteran and new workers arrived at Poza Rica, they found most of the equipment, aside from the high-tech exploratory rigs, substantially the same as that used at the turn of the century. The technicians had made some adaptations, the motors were more powerful, the drills were harder and more precise, the pumps operated more efficiently, and the separators worked better, but the overall character of oil field work had not changed. The petroleum workers performed highly varied tasks in dispersed locales. Six areas of work specializations shaped their experience:

1) construction of infrastructure, including railways, roads, pipelines, drilling rigs, and buildings. In this sector of work, tasks were explicitly divided, but skill levels were relatively low;
2) well drilling, the fundamental occupation in which the crew chief required an extremely high level of skill and experience;

3) repair and maintenance of machinery, for which skill levels ranged from craftsmen down to the basics in the repair of tools, machines, and electrical components. Repair crews maintained a variety of installations including the firehouse, roads, and walkways;

4) surveillance and control of volatile moving fluids, whose specializations included oil and gas pumping and transmission lines as well as oil processing in the refineries;

5) administrative work, which called for accounting skills; and

6) exploration, which required a highly developed command of technology including measuring instruments.[11]

The spatial dispersion and material experience of the oil workers from camps to the wide variety of tasks that they performed created a highly specialized working class, one that could have been highly fractured. The widely separated personnel found it difficult to see the larger picture of the productive process or to develop a range of intimate relationships with the other workers. However, the union would serve as their most important source of collective identity and largely overcame the conditions pointing toward fractality that included not only the dispersal of the workers and their skill levels but also their diverse backgrounds. The trained workers came from two distinct backgrounds. The first group originated in Palma Sola: they were administrators, production foremen, drill operators, welders, mechanics, and pipe fitters together with their apprentices. These 152 men had lived in almost total isolation for years at an abandoned hacienda without conveniences or sources of entertainment. The second group consisted of unemployed petroleum workers who had lost their jobs with the smaller companies that had closed during the prolonged depression and the crisis of 1929 that afflicted the industry. They had become part of an enormous class of largely unskilled workers that roamed the oil-producing region looking for employment. The majority of this group came to Poza Rica by way of Tampico having been forwarded to the new field by the administrators at El Aguila's headquarters.[12]

The seasoned workers who arrived from outside the district brought distinct backgrounds and political conceptions with them. The railroad workers remembered their early union struggles, just as the oil workers did. The latter group had experienced fierce confrontations with the foreign-owned oil companies since the mid-1920s. They remembered the outcomes: union recognition, the signing of collective bargaining contracts, and the establishment of ties with the government, but also rejection and repression.[13] This situation held true for other workers from Tamaulipas and Veracruz as well, who in one way or another had found themselves caught up in political conflicts associated with the birth of the Partido Nacional Revolucionario (PNR) and the elimination of radical alternatives. This experience pertained specifically to the workers from the El Mante sugar mill in Tamaulipas and the rural schoolteachers from the Huasteca Veracruzana.[14]

Their prior political and union-organizing experience would be decisive in enabling the Poza Rica oil workers to avoid some mistakes, but at the same time they confronted the intrusion of an urban-industrial culture that greatly differed from the rural world to which they were accustomed. It should be noted that the majority of the skilled workers identified themselves by trade, say, as solderers and machinists rather than by social class. Their pride as individual craftsmen still prevailed despite their recognition that organization as a union served their interests. They felt a sense of superiority to the unskilled laborers.

A large number of campesino youths lacking industrial skills and organizing experience joined the mix of workers at Poza Rica. There were, however, substantial differences among them. Those who came from the northern district of the Huasteca between Tampico and Tuxpan had at least witnessed the earlier oil boom carried through by the American companies there. They already spoke Spanish and could readily integrate. They carried a system of mutual support that depended on members of their extended family, and that background opened them up to the acceptance of other forms of solidarity, including mutual assistance and survival in a new setting.

In contrast, the majority of campesinos from the neighboring Sierra de Papantla, the north of Puebla, and from Hidalgo knew nothing of such matters and in some cases did not even speak Spanish. These workers, often recruited by labor contractors, found unskilled low-paying jobs. The company put them to work in maintenance, painting buildings and keeping roads clear. They had less job mobility because of their lack of experience and language skills. Among the Native Americans, ethnicity counted for very little. They depended on the labor contractors for jobs and adopted the mutual aid strategies such as shared housing that generally pertained to the very poor.

For the workers from the countryside, their arrival in the industrial world meant a new capitalist regime where the time clock regulated life. The work went on regardless of the weather, and infractions of the rules meant punishment. They learned the rules from the former artisans in the skilled jobs and from supervisors who had a very strict sense of duty. The foreign employees were few in number and tended to be remote from the unskilled workers. The inexperienced workers adapted to industrial discipline rapidly; there was no time to waste. The overall situation led to formal hierarchies in the labor force based on work performance.[15]

The relationships between experienced workers, those with skills, and the new unskilled employees are typical of any industry that has reached a certain level of maturity extending across two or more generations of workers. At Poza Rica the relationships took shape almost immediately. The contrasting cultures based on origin, varied skills, and the dictatorial behavior of the labor bosses deeply impacted the transition from the timeless individualism of the farmer to the time- and class-based experience of the workers, but the new workers either had to adjust quickly to a new way of life or give up their jobs.[16]

Despite the differences among the workers, they shared a common objective: to secure higher levels of income. Some hoped to emigrate to a city later on, while others wanted to return home in relative affluence. But for the most part they thought in the short term. A rough atmosphere characterized the petroleum camps. Bars, whorehouses, and outdoor sports dominated leisure time. The Church was an important aspect of life elsewhere, but not at Poza Rica; in the oil fields, religion was less important. Moreover, the oil workers' life-style was very expensive. The workers made their own "petroleum culture" as they went along. They created a more attractive way of life despite the hard work, scarce resources, unhealthy conditions, and isolation.

An army of musicians, waiters, waitresses, bartenders, prostitutes, and performers made up a labor force separate from the oil workers. From their numbers a female work force emerged. In this situation the women lacked a basis for mutual support and lived in a state of marginality dependent on the labor contractors. The employers and clients both denied dignity to the prostitutes and waitresses.[17]

The idea of worker well-being, job security, and more ample conveniences, however, became something more than a dream. The knowledge that Poza Rica was the most important petroleum field in the nation and that they were producing great wealth gave workers a sense that being a *petrolero* was important. A sense of pride arose. The workers overcame their differences and developed a strong sense of community. They formed a syndicate to face common problems because of their common experience as workers.[18]

The Oil Workers' Syndicate and Collective Identity

The insecurity of their work, the arbitrary nature of their employers, the deplorable living conditions, and a sense of defenselessness, combined with the knowledge of those who understood their rights, constituted the basis for labor unrest. This response was a predictable one during a period in national history when labor organizations elsewhere had already initiated a series of large working-class mobilizations.[19] Lacking job security and isolated between their old way of life and the new one, the petroleum workers had no choice other than to organize for self-defense. They needed a collective bargaining contract that guaranteed jobs. The prior existence of the Sindicato de Obreros y Empleados de la Compañía Mexicana de Petróleo "El Aguila," which served the workers at the Ciudad Madero refinery and the administrative employees in Tampico, helped the union organizers at Poza Rica. Instead of forming a new syndicate, with all of the problems that presented, they could simply join the older union and sign the prevailing contract, which had taken some ten years of strikes and confrontations to obtain. The company administrators at Poza Rica supported the idea.

On July 9, 1934, after a small group of organizers had done their work,[20] the transmission line workers called a meeting attended by some 300 of the 1,000 workers in the camp and formed a local of the El Aguila union.[21] The men elected their officers from the local organizers, who had called the meeting with a delegation from the Tampico union headquarters attending as observers. Thereafter, the workers held regular Thursday meetings, at first in front of a rooming house and later in a building offered to them by the company. The meetings gradually increased in importance until they were the principal event of community life. Workers learned how to speak in public. Speakers taught points of labor law, disseminated petroleum industry news, and discussed local problems and regional issues. The workers quickly appreciated the idea of solidarity with others during conflicts with management. Inequalities of education and background still held them back, but little by little a common language took shape and filled the political and cultural void that had existed.[22]

The appearance of the syndicate constituted a decisive moment in the rise of a community of interests among the workers and of political cohesion. The union supplied the forum for the creation of a symbolic universe that enabled the workers to reevaluate their position and recognize the power possible through unity. As the center of community life in Poza Rica, the union held art shows and other social activities. In addition to resolving labor and housing problems it opened a school attended by workers in which employees of the company served as teachers. Finally, consistent with the artisanal tradition, the union provided mutual aid assistance during illness and personal calamities. In effect, the Poza Rica union assumed the role and responsibilities that had taken many years to develop in the earlier petroleum-producing areas, thanks to the leadership offered by the union officials from Tampico who had stayed on to help get things started and to the critical mass of local workers with union experience and the skills needed to make the project work.

The quick adhesion of the skilled workers to the syndicate also helped to get it started. The conflict between the Cárdenas government and the foreign oil companies in 1937 and 1938 helped enlistments. The middle-level workers feared that they might lose their jobs and provided a ready source of sophisticated union leadership. Their knowledge and the information that they provided during the ensuing confrontations proved of decisive value during 1937 and 1938.

Some middle-status workers also worked with a small number of Communist militants. They held joint meetings in the local Masonic Lodge, which turned into a seedbed for union leaders and organizers after 1936. The political pluralism of this group and the presence of other leaders reinforced the already strong leadership for the local union. They held general assemblies and took open votes. In that way, as the result of local conditions and the convictions of the people, the struggle for syndicate power was conducted democratically during the first years of organizing.

Because the syndicate legally represented the workers with El Aguila and then successfully expanded its power to include agreements with the labor contractors, all of the workers in the Poza Rica area were obliged to join. The union also monopolized public life. It began to organize the ceremonies and rituals that celebrated political figures and historic events. A working-class culture emerged. The unionists discussed local and national problems, political issues, and nationalism, and created their own revolutionary mythology. The thin ties between the local school and the maturing union became strained. The schoolteachers and the workers offered competing versions of *fiestas patrias*. The syndicate itself had become a teacher of morals, history, and culture in the community.

The creation of a sense of national identity paralleled that of class consciousness. Both undertakings came about by oral means, given that the majority of workers were functionally illiterate. They repeated new semiotic formulas such as "working class," "proletariat," "brothers," "class solidarity," "nation," and "imperialism." The fact that educational services developed in Poza Rica at the same time that the "socialist education" program was being promoted by the Cárdenas government helped spread the new terminology among the teachers and students. Meanwhile, the doctrine continued to be spread in the union's public meeting halls. The rise of working-class nationalism at Poza Rica stemmed from local conditions and coincided with the national campaign mounted by Cárdenas. But, despite the fact that they were confronted with a foreign-owned company in the case of El Aguila, the workers at Poza Rica did not view the company with any more hostility than any other capitalist firm. In the early 1930s the defense of labor interests did not contain any greater level of nationalism than a concern for working-class redemption. For this reason, class consciousness dominated the thinking of union members.

In addition, national affirmation was an educational project and did not necessarily mean a rejection of foreigners.[23] The symbolic references to national history, such as the Independence War of 1810–1821 and the popular struggle against the French intervention of the 1860s, did not lead to widespread animosity or criticism of the oil companies for their multinational character. In the case of Poza Rica, the worker-owner conflict that led to nationalization of the foreign-owned properties was, more than anything else, a labor struggle. It became a matter of national pride when the foreign companies attacked the decision of the Mexican Supreme Court in favor of the unions in March 1938.[24]

The union exercised a very strict sense of public morals derived from the anarcho-syndicalist ideology of public service without personal gain and no reelection of leaders. The syndicate members did not exhibit a xenophobic nationalism toward the company; instead, they respected their bosses for the high quality of their work. The union officers changed completely each year, while even small expenditures were publicly posted and the wide participation by the membership left little space for clientelist practices or the concentration of power.[25] Furthermore, a rare circumstance contributed to the open and democratic practices. The most politically sophisticated workers (and there were many of them) belonged to several distinct parties and differed in ideology as Communists, nationalists, anarchists, social democrats, and syndicalists. Even more, the membership of many of them in the Masonic Lodge Fe, Luz y Verdad gave them a sense of being moral guides that compounded their sense of responsibility as skilled workers. Role, status, personal pride, and prestige came together to create a group of workers dedicated to union democracy. Some members were more important than others, but personal differences compounded the diversity. Public conviction and the competition between groups at Poza Rica created a unique circumstance that prevented the formation of local *cacicazgos* that plagued unions elsewhere.[26]

In August 1935 the government, after a long and arduous campaign, succeeded in recruiting the petroleum workers into the STPRM. The government sought to create a national workers' organization to help it confront the foreign oil companies. The unionists' democratic precepts shaped the delegations that Poza Rica sent to national meetings, and members often paid their own way.[27] As the Poza Rica workers joined the new union they were thrown into the middle of a historic struggle for power between the workers, the government, and the companies. The new national union leaders demanded a nationwide contract.[28] Nevertheless, at the first national convention of the new union held in 1936, the Poza Rica delegation requested its own representation at the negotiations.[29]

That request was reasonable given that Poza Rica had become the third largest work center in the industry. With 680 union members it trailed only the refineries at Ciudad Madero and Minatitlán in size. But the leaders of the national union did not grant the local legal standing until 1937, and ultimately they deemed it to not have special standing or rights.[30] When the Poza Rica leaders initiated their own negotiations for a new contract with the El Aguila management, they forced the national syndicate officials to recognize them or lose face. At that point the Poza Ricans thought that the age-old problems of unequal housing, equipment, and salaries between themselves and the workers at Ciudad Madero would be resolved.[31] But in May 1937 the situation changed. The union leadership in Mexico City launched a nationwide walkout in order to force the companies to sign a collective bargaining contract that had been in dispute for six months. Between May 28 and June 8 the striking oil workers paralyzed transportation and slowed industrial production throughout the nation.[32] At that point the government pressured the workers to end the strike because of the damage being done to the economy and suggested that the union take the case to arbitration and the courts. The syndicate leaders immediately agreed.[33]

Nevertheless, at Poza Rica the crisis deepened. El Aguila refused to accept either the terms offered at the national level or the authority of the new union.[34] The company management went further, reducing the allowances that it paid to workers for housing and fringe benefits. They argued that no collective bargaining contract was in effect. The Poza Rica workers decided to strike on their own accord. The national union, however, opposed unilateral action at the local level regardless of the provocation, especially since Poza Rica produced some 50 percent of the national oil output.

In spite of the pressure, the Poza Rica workers persisted in striking and shut down the refineries for fifty-seven days. The El Aguila owners deliberately stalled on resolving the conflict in order to create a nationwide oil shortage and force the government to move against the Poza Rica workers. The company officials expected to turn public opinion against the strikers. Instead, the confrontation united the workers and the public against the company. They believed that their survival depended on mutual support. In addition, the fight brought the surrounding community into virtually universal support for the strikers. The Poza Ricans enjoyed the backing of the store, cantina, and restaurant owners, and even the health-care givers, who suspended their bills until the strike was over.[35] In addition to the creation of solidarity the Poza Rica workers went further: they decided that they did not need the company and could maintain the wells, pumping stations, separators, and pipelines by themselves. Refusing to accept the supervision of company management, they established committees that supervised and carried out the essential functions in the spirit of workers' self-management. At the same time they set aside 40 percent of the salaries earned and contributed one peso daily to each of the workers on strike.[36]

The Poza Rica workers kept up with the progress (or lack of same) in the negotiations through the head strike committee in Tampico, while at Poza Rica they were in permanent assembly with the meeting hall kept open around the clock. They discussed the strategies of the company, the government, and the national union. They gained a practical education in which the company pursued selfish interests versus theirs; the government revealed ambivalence, at first encouraging them and then pressuring them to end the strike; and the national union leaders revealed their concerns about power, discipline, and control of the workers.[37]

The strike ended on September 15, 1937, with El Aguila agreeing to most of the workers' demands, although some points remained unsettled because they were linked to the still-ongoing national dispute. The Poza Rica workers basically settled their strike because of the company's concessions and the government's concern about an oil shortage, and, to a lesser degree, because the national union, concerned about its lack of control over the locals, wanted them to settle as well. The national media had ganged up on the strikers, blaming them for gasoline shortages and calling them incorrigible radicals who put their personal interests above those of the nation.[38]

El Aguila awarded them their back salaries. The workers accepted the final agreement that their leaders had signed in Tampico, but only provisionally because a number of job descriptions and security issues remained unresolved. The workers recognized that reasons of state had taken precedence over their own interests. They hoped that the national union would carry the fight forward and win the needed concessions from the companies.[39]

Upon settling the strike, the Poza Rica workers decided to take over a small cooperative store that had been opened in 1935 by some of the urban immigrants who were dissatisfied with the meager offerings in the company outlet. Each of them had contributed fifty pesos as a membership fee to get it started and bought goods at cost. They already had two years of experience in running the store when the strike began. During the fifty-seven-day shutdown the cooperative sold its goods on credit to the strikers and assumed an enormous debt which it could not pay.[40] Recognizing its importance in providing staples obtained from local producers, the union members decided to buy the cooperative once the strike ended.

Using the buildup of back salary, they paid off the stockholders and redeemed the debts. The union now owned the cooperative, which became the most important store in Poza Rica. In 1937 the union members elected the first store directorate for a one-year term.[41]

From the beginning, in 1930, the experienced workers, who later became advocates for the union, were the decisive force among the workers at Poza Rica. If El Aguila controlled the productive process, then the syndicate controlled access to work.[42] The union carefully monitored the company's compliance with the terms of the collective bargaining contract, especially in regard to salaries, thus bringing to an end the traditional despotism of the *patrón*.[43] Competing with the regular school, the workers established a night school in order to carry forward a resolution passed in 1936 that all those who could not read and write would receive six months of free instruction. If for any reason a worker rejected the instruction, he would be suspended from the union. This policy was almost impossible to implement, however, because a majority of the illiterate workers chose not to go to school. Nevertheless, a significant number, especially young women and older children, learned how to read at the night school.[44] The syndicate then undertook the encouragement of culture: ceremonies to celebrate national holidays including the anniversaries of Independence, the Revolution, Labor Day, and the day on which the local was founded. It also organized the distribution of housing, provided food staples through the cooperative, and showed movies.

All of these activities did not question the discretion and power exercised by the company in the production of petroleum. The Poza Rica workers, however, were the first to suggest the possibility that they could assume control of production. Although they did not challenge the hierarchical order at the time, they did believe that the capitalists were not needed. This self-confidence soon became essential after the nationalization of the oil industry, when these same workers had to take over control of production and faced a terrible scarcity of spare parts because of the international boycott against the oil industry.

During this historically important episode the Poza Rica labor force took workers' self-management very seriously. They named their department chiefs, sometimes overruling the superintendents and union leaders, and gave full rein to the utopian notions of work for everyone and a guaranteed standard of living. Even the officials, in their version of the nationalization, which described the takeover of petroleum production only as the "economic independence of Mexico," recognized that event as the result of the actions taken by the petroleum workers.

When the situation became difficult because of the international boycott against Mexico, the workers made use of their artisanal experience and new nationalistic zeal, fabricated their own materials, and accepted wage cuts. Hence, in 1939, when the government decided to bring the entire petroleum industry under its control, the workers initially resisted because they could not conceive of the nation's interests being separate from their own. During the strike the Poza Rica unionists suggested the expropriation of the oil field and the creation of a workers' cooperative to President Cárdenas.[45] In 1938 a new phase of struggle had begun, a confrontation in which the state defeated the drive for collective class interest and working-class autonomy, subsuming it in the concern for national interest. The state officials sought to make the government the sole legitimate political representation of the nation. The great paradox of the nationalization crisis of 1938 was that while it demonstrated the creative capacity of the workers, the state functionaries managed to deprive them of autonomy and subordinate them to government authority. But that is another story.

Conclusion

The Poza Rica petroleum workers developed as a group during the era of foreign oil company hegemony and as such developed a specific group identity vis-à-vis management and the state. After the labor-versus-management and productivity crises began, the actions taken by the Cárdenas regime had a dramatic impact. The interests of national and local, foreign and Mexican, and class and state forces, as well as the local trade union versus the national, all came into play. In the latter case the institutionalization of unions played a major part. During the 1930s relations between the state and the working class changed. New symbols replaced those created during the earlier phase of petroleum industry syndicalism, essentially those of state-encouraged nationalism.

The Poza Rica case, like so many other enclave economies, shows that the proletariat became the active force in what was a vacant sociopolitical space but within the context of systemic factors. The workers applied mutual aid in order to survive the difficult early years. Later, as the context changed, the national state and local unions came together as enlarged entities at the center. The international factors relating to the government and the foreign oil companies also helped define the outcomes. The dynamics of local and national interests and those of class appear as levels of reality understood by the local workers according to their experience and logic. During the process, conditions changed rapidly, and in the end new forms of identity emerged that had been unthinkable in earlier periods.

The actions of the local workers show an adaptability to unique challenges and demonstrate that union practices and political learning do not follow universal topologies. Rather, they depend to a considerable extent on the characteristics of the local people involved and on the public conditions created during the process of struggle. In Poza Rica the greatest local differences from the general pattern in Mexico are found in the varied nature of the immigrant workers, the unique conditions that they encountered, and the fact that in their union no member assumed strongman status or even dominated the public forums. They conducted a true process of deliberation and decision. In the small world of the petroleum camps the density of life reduced to a minimum the private experiences of the individual while that density maximized each individual's public involvement. That process enabled the group to have the maximum historical impact.

The systemic factors mentioned above merged with the facts of local life and created the workers' identity that emerged. It had a strong element of autonomy, which fused at different points in their experience and political development with anarcho-syndicalism, communism, and nationalism. The national situation favored the rapid formation and synthesis of a collective workers' identity and sense of autonomy. The institutionalization of union life began with clear democratic, participatory, and autonomist principles. The workers at Poza Rica "skipped stages in their development" as a class and developed a unique approach to problem solving that resulted from their own special experience. In that way they epitomized the heroic spirit of the era and were better able to resist the discipline that the state officials so successfully imposed on other unions during the 1940s. The Poza Rica workers stood out for their independence of mind and action against state hegemony and the controls over them sought by national union officials long after other workers' groups had submitted. It was not until the 1950s that they surrendered to the greater power of outsiders.

Notes

1. Carmen Blazquez and Alberto Olvera, "El desarrollo industrial de Veracruz, Siglos XIX y XX," *Historia y desarrollo industrial de México* (México: CONCAMIN, 1988).

2. See Leif Adelson, "Historia social de los obreros industriales de Tampico, 1906–1919" (Ph.D. diss. in History, El Colegio de México, 1982); and Mirna Benítez, "La organización sindical de los trabajadores petroleros en la Huasteca Veracruzana, 1917–1931," *Anuario V* (Jalapa: Universidad Veracruzana, Centro de Investigaciones Históricas, 1988).

3. See Blanca Torres, *Historia de la Revolución Mexicana: Período 1940–1952* (México: El Colegio de México, 1984).

4. See Javier Aguilar, ed., *Los sindicatos nacionales: Petroleros* (México: A. G. Editores, 1986).

5. The Faja de Oro, or gold strip, was a narrow piece of land that covered forty-five miles in the middle of the Huasteca Veracruzana. It had several huge oil deposits at a low depth. Its wealth turned Mexico into the second largest oil producer in the world in the early 1920s. However, the irrational and primitive exploration of those fields led to their quick exhaustion.

6. *El Petróleo en México* (México: Gobierno de México, 1939), chap. 1.

7. Sinesio Capitanachi, *Palma Sola, Furbero y Poza Rica* (Xalapa: Editora del Gobierno del Estado, 1984).

8. The separation batteries were small industrial facilities where oil was separated from gas.

9. Permanently based workers are those who enjoy job security. Their dismissal involves serious costs for the firms because the workers gain three months' severance pay for each year worked. As employees they receive subsidies for house rentals, health-care services, etc. By contrast, when the contracts of temporary workers expire, the firm has no responsibility. This difference led trade unionists to fight for the permanent status of as many workers as possible.

10. See Capitanachi, *Palma Sola*.

11. Alberto Olvera, "Los trabajadores ante la nacionalización petrolera: El caso de Poza Rica," *Anuario V*, 1988.

12. Author's interview with Heriberto Martínez, Poza Rica, July 1984.

13. Leif Adelson, "Coyuntura y conciencia: Factores convergentes en la creación de los sindicatos petroleros de Tampico durante la decada de los veinte," in E. Frost and J. Zoraida, eds., *El trabajo y los trabajadores en la historia de México* (México: El Colegio de México, 1979).

14. Author's interview with Martínez; author's interview with Emilio Gallardo, Poza Rica, July 1984.

15. Leopoldo Alafita, "La administración privada de las empresas petroleras, 1880–1937," *Anuario V*, 1988.

16. Unfair supervisors often made arbitrary promotions. The union maintained a roster intended to force the recognition of seniority.

17. Interview with Patricia Cullar by Evangelina García de Tapia, Poza Rica, June 23, 1987.

18. Alberto Olvera, "Orígen social, condiciones de vida y organización sindical de los trabajadores petroleros de Poza Rica," *Anuario V*, 1986.

19. See Arturo Anguiano, *El estado y la política obrera del cardenismo* (México: Era, 1975); and Joe C. Ashby, *Organized Labor and the Mexican Revolution under Lázaro Cárdenas* (Chapel Hill: University of North Carolina Press, 1963).

20. Many accounts regarding the bravery and heroism of the founders of the trade union are narrated by the senior workers of Poza Rica.

21. Olvera, "Orígen social."

22. Ibid.

23. The Archive of the 30th Section of the Sindicato de Trabajadores Petroleros de la Républica Mexicana (hereafter, STPRM), Poza Rica branch, has a complete collection of the meeting proceedings from its founding until 1940. This collection, unique in oil industry unionism in Mexico, contains discourse and union practices.

24. The Poza Rica proceedings and the unionists interviewed did not reflect an early nationalist discourse against the firm but, rather, a unionist one. A nationalistic tinge appeared after nationalization had taken place. See Alberto Olvera, "Los obreros del petróleo y la nacionalización de la industria petrolera: Historia oral, historia oficial y sus límites," *Secuencia, Revista Americana de Ciencias Sociales* 13 (México: Instituto Mora, 1985).

25. Alan Knight, "The Politics of the Expropriation," in J. Brown and A. Knight, eds., *The Mexican Petroleum Industry in the Twentieth Century* (Austin: University of Texas Press, 1992).

26. The workers checked the commissioners' expenses at union assemblies and closely observed their performance of duty. To be an elected union official or to be commissioned to go to Tampico or Mexico City meant extra work and responsibility without implying payment.

27. Alberto Olvera, "The Rise and Fall of Union Democracy at Poza Rica," in Brown and Knight, eds., *The Mexican Petroleum Industry*.

28. See Lorenzo Meyer, *México y los Estados Unidos en el conflicto petrolero, 1917–1942* (México: El Colegio de México, 1977).

29. Lourdes Celís Salgado, *La industria petrolera en México: Una crónica*, vol. 1 (México: Petróleos Mexicanos, 1988).

30. Ibid. The status of "delegation" kept the workers belonging to a work center under the administration of a section that held the collective bargaining contract. This status served small camps or contractors but not the most important oil field in the country.

31. Ibid.

32. They sought acknowledgment by the company that workers performing skilled tasks should be certified and better paid.

33. Celís Salgado, *La industria petrolera*.

34. *El petróleo en México*, 84. The companies protested their exclusion from the Ley del Trabajo provision that granted wage-scale exceptions for small employers who claimed an economic inability to pay more to the workers. The objections of the large oil firms were not successful.

35. *PEMEX* (Poza Rica: PEMEX, 1982).

36. Author's interviews with Eduardo Prez, Ciudad Victoria, March 1985, and with Rafael Suárez, Poza Rica, June 1983.

37. *PEMEX*, 52–53; author's interviews with Martínez and Suárez.

38. *El Universal* (México), September 10, 1937; *El Nacional* (México), September 12, 1937.

39. Author's interviews with Prez and with Martínez, Poza Rica, August 1982; Assembly Proceedings, September to October 1937, Poza Rica, Archive of the 30th Section of the STPRM.

40. Author's interviews with Martínez, Poza Rica, July 1982, and with Gallardo.

41. Assembly Proceedings, September to October 1937.

42. The union members monitored salaries, seeking consistency between wages and job skill levels.

43. Assembly Proceedings, September 30, 1936.

44. Sinesio Capitanachi, *Poza Rica: Apuntes para su historia* (Jalapa: Edition of the Author, 1988).

45. See Alberto Olvera, "The Politics of Expropriation," in Brown and Knight, eds., *The Mexican Petroleum Industry*.

CHAPTER SEVEN

Labor Formation, Community, and Politics
The Mexican Working Class in Texas, 1900–1945

EMILIO ZAMORA

A new chapter in the history of Mexicans in the United States began at the turn of the century as the Southwest quickened its pace of development and Mexican workers assumed a position as the most exploited segment of the working class. After 1848, postwar violence directed against Mexican landowners and merchants had retarded development. The Civil War, however, brought prosperity to Texas and the northern states of Mexico. After the war ended and the shifting of land ownership and businesses away from Mexicans had run its course, a more normal pattern of economic growth ensued. The mining, railroad, and agricultural industries demanded low-wage labor, and they recruited workers on both sides of the border. The increase in immigration and the earlier land and business losses reinforced working-class status on Mexicans. Moreover, anti-Mexican prejudice justified their inferior social standing and a racially defined division of work.[1]

In 1910 the violence of the Mexican Revolution encouraged a sizable migration of workers into Texas as they answered one of the first calls for low-wage labor in the Southwest. Then, after two decades of economic growth, the expansion stopped in the 1930s. As the Great Depression took hold, older immigrants and U.S.-born Mexicans in Texas again lost ground. In the 1940s, however, they benefited from yet another economic swing, the opportunities made possible by the wartime economy, but discrimination and inequality continued despite the occupational gains during the war. Over time, increasing numbers among the occupationally mobile and acculturated segment of the Mexican population in Texas embraced U.S. citizenship despite their minority status and the accompanying discrimination and inequality. The more traditional members of the working class, however, continued to relate to one another through mutualism and a more Mexican sense of identity.[2]

Labor Formation

As a result of the Mexican exodus during the wars with Mexico and Anglo immigration beginning in the late 1800s, the Mexicans lost their majority standing in San Antonio and were engulfed in the smaller settlements in the interior of the state. They maintained their large numbers in deep south Texas, however, and after 1890 they began a demographic comeback across the state. Fueled by births and to a lesser extent by immigration, their numbers by 1920 had increased from 100,000 to 500,000.[3]

Mexicans saw little occupational change between 1900 and 1930. Over 65 percent of the Mexican migrants in Texas worked as general laborers and farm workers. A 5 percent increase in white-collar jobs offset a decline in skilled jobs. Given the growth of the Mexican work force, occupational stagnation underscored the inequality and barriers to mobility. The dramatic unemployment that occurred in the 1930s was followed by a recovery during World War II that continued until 1950. White-collar and skilled workers increased from 34.5 percent to 49 percent of the Mexican work force while the number of unskilled decreased from 65.6 percent to 51 percent. Skilled workers increased in number from 12.5 percent to 27.9 percent, thus outnumbering their white-collar counterparts. Despite these figures, Mexicans continued to be concentrated in the lower-ranked skilled occupations in 1950, while Anglos increased their proportional representation in the higher-skilled ranks.[4]

The agricultural industry employed the largest number of Mexicans. They cleared the land, built irrigation systems, planted, and harvested. Mexican migrant workers crossed the border and traveled through the Robstown-Corpus Christi area toward northeast Texas. The size of the migrant work force varied depending on the phase of the season and the quality of the crop, but during the first two decades it exceeded 20,000 workers. The Mexicans joined U.S.-born and earlier arrivals in their trek that often took them to the beet fields of the Midwest. Many swung back into the Laredo area or the Rio Grande Valley in time to harvest vegetables. Others returned home until the next work cycle. By 1940, 300,000 Mexican workers made "the big swing" across the state.[5]

Mexican railroad workers also constituted a sizable work force. They were first employed to build the lines crisscrossing Texas from inland cities such as San Antonio and Houston to the border. Once the lines were built, the majority of the workers stayed on as maintenance crewmen while a smaller and better-paid group found jobs in urban-based railroad shops. Men recruited along the border or in Mexico, however, often broke their contracts once they reached the interior of the state and realized that they could earn more in the cities or on the farms working as family units. Railroad and agricultural employment thus contributed to the growth and dispersal of the Mexican work force. Moreover, as more migrants decided to remain in the cities and in the towns, patterns of concentration began to emerge.[6]

Urban-based workers were employed primarily as laborers or as semiskilled employees in the service, construction, and manufacturing industries. A significant number periodically traveled to outlying farming areas to supplement their meager family incomes. The continuous arrival of new workers coupled with barriers to mobility bloated the bottom segment of the Mexican working class. Although Mexicans were generally denied access to the higher-skilled occupations during the 1920s, some managed to secure better-paying jobs in expanding industries, some of which catered to a Mexican clientele. Mexican-owned enterprises such as grocery stores, restaurants, tailor shops, newspapers, private schools, and small construction companies also grew and became new sources of employment for the unskilled as well as for the skilled and professional workers. Accompanying this trend, employers in the construction, service, and manufacturing industries began to test local custom by dipping into the enlarged Mexican work force to fill skilled jobs often classified as unskilled.

The 1930s introduced extreme hardship made evident by high unemployment figures and a large-scale return to Mexico. The dramatic fall in the price of cotton and the attendant drop in earnings hit rural economies hard. Mexicans nevertheless joined the 1,800- to 2,000-mile-long migrant route in record numbers. In the urban areas of Texas public campaigns blaming Mexicans for the reduced wages and intense job competition of the Depression underscored their suffering. Local and state officials, producing well-organized and publicized plans for transporting untold numbers to the border, joined in a chorus to deport them. Some U.S.-born Mexican community leaders collaborated by playing on sentimental attachments to the homeland and promises of Mexican government-sponsored colonization projects. According to one estimate, between 500,000 and 600,000 Mexicans were deported or repatriated from the United States, about one-half of them from Texas. The northern Mexican economy, equally hard hit by the Depression, could not accommodate them. The much-touted colonization projects that promised them plots of land, farming implements, and cash subsidies failed due to disinterest. Most of the colonists returned to Texas in the early 1940s as the war boosted the economy to unprecedented levels of production and employment.[7]

The Mexicans in Texas came out of the Depression with an opportunity to improve their occupational standings and alter the effects of discrimination. Significant numbers of them moved out of agriculture and into urban industries, where they obtained better-paying and often skilled jobs. Their decision to move, however, was not always made voluntarily but was forced by the mechanization of agriculture. Moreover, beginning in 1946, when Mexico finally agreed to allow Texas farmers to recruit contract workers, or *braceros*, resident farm workers had to relocate to urban areas or join the migratory work force.[8]

The entry of Mexican workers into wartime industries was one of the most significant developments of the 1940s. They gained employment in the garment, meatpacking, construction, shipping, aircraft repair, and oil industries. Unfortunately, discrimination and inequality persisted in spite of the workers' mobility. They typically took jobs as laborers in the otherwise high-wage firms involved in war production.[9] Several interrelated factors, including labor surpluses, the regulation of the labor supply, and barriers to occupational mobility, contributed to their continued position at the bottom as a racially defined working class. The increase of the Mexican labor supply in Texas during the pre- and post-Depression periods occurred because of industrial growth and expansion. The demand for agricultural labor provided one of the inducements for workers from south Texas and Mexico to travel northward and into urban areas in search of higher wages and more secure jobs. Market demands in the developing northern Mexican region likewise attracted workers from the interior and introduced them to international labor migration as an alternative to poorly paying and unstable jobs. The resulting labor surplus gave Texas employers an advantage in maintaining lower wages and controlling labor organizing.[10]

The active recruitment of workers in Mexico and south Texas joined market forces to regulate the labor supply, thus shaping the size of the work force, the direction of the migrant flow, and the location of unskilled laborers. This deliberate control of Mexican labor partly flooded the market and exceeded the needs of agriculturalists. The workers had little recourse but to take to the road in search of higher wages or new employment after the harvest. The growers continued recruiting with little thought to the surplus that they were creating in the urban areas. Recruiters representing large planters, farmers' associations, and railroad companies brought in Mexican workers.

The mobility of farm workers led to a serious crisis in the towns and cities where Anglo workers accused the growers of disregarding the threat that Mexicans posed as job competitors for their privileged positions in the skilled ranks. As a consequence, agriculturalists entered into a collaborative agreement with Anglo organized labor to regulate the supply of Mexican workers. Repressive measures on the farms, such as vagrancy laws, violence, and labor contracts, had been insufficient to block Mexicans from traveling to the cities. The growers and organized labor successfully lobbied the legislature in Austin to establish the Texas Farm Placement Service and to pass the Emigrant Labor Agency Laws designed to check the movement of workers and the efforts of labor recruiters. The Texas growers went a step further when they joined agriculturalists from other parts of the Southwest and convinced Congress to establish the Bracero Program (1942–1964). Close to 500,000 contract workers entered the United States between 1942 and 1950.

The Depression years witnessed one of the most successful efforts to regulate the labor supply by directing the migrant flow back into Mexico. Recovery came during the war. Again, labor market demands contributed to migration and improved employment opportunities, especially in the skilled ranks. Discrimination, however, continued to deny Mexicans the full advantages of wartime job opportunities. Barriers to occupational mobility during the war were especially disturbing given the prevailing rhetoric of democracy and good neighborliness, but they were by no means new to Mexican workers.

Labor contractors usually recruited in Mexico and south Texas during the early 1900s with the understanding that the Mexicans would take unskilled jobs. An increase in racist thinking that David Montejano associates with the development of commercial agriculture reinforced the Mexicans' position at the bottom in a rural hierarchy of planters, farmers, tenants, sharecroppers, and laborers. The planters and farmers justified discrimination by pointing to the Mexicans' lower standard of living and by alleging negative traits such as laziness, undependability, and a lack of intelligence. Racist thinking associated with a system of labor repression joined with older prejudices that had begun with the Texas Revolution, the War with Mexico, and the continued violence that occurred along the border during the late 1800s.

Cities outside south Texas such as San Antonio and Houston also witnessed racial thinking that justified job discrimination. Former small- and medium-sized growers who had lost their properties when the large planters increased production and lowered the price of cotton adamantly criticized Mexicans. They migrated to the cities thinking that the Mexican work force in agriculture had given planters an unfair competitive advantage. They now concluded that a similar fate awaited them once employers in the urban areas saw the advantages of hiring low-wage Mexican labor. The Anglo labor organizations in the urban areas were the most vocal critics of such immigration. The labor leaders charged that the Mexicans threatened their hard-earned gains by accepting low wages. They called for immigration restrictions and pressured employers against hiring them. They rarely distinguished, however, between Mexico- and U.S.-born Mexicans, thus reinforcing a racial division of labor.

Community Development

The three types of working-class communities that developed in Crystal City, San Antonio, and Houston provide a representative basis for understanding the history of Mexicans in Texas. Other types of communities that are beyond the scope of this study also appeared, including company towns; enclaves in towns outside deep south Texas where few, if any, Mexicans had lived before; and the more established congregations in border cities.[11]

Crystal City

The south Texas rural community of Crystal City with its outskirts dates its beginning to the arrival of migrant workers in search of permanent residence. Although Mexicans inhabited the area during the nineteenth century, the community did not begin to develop until the first decade of the twentieth century, when spinach growers commercialized agriculture and recruited workers and their families. By 1930, Mexicans predominated with a population of 5,166, or 78.2 percent of the total. Their numbers remained relatively stable as the migrant workers returned every winter; indeed, the town became well known as a winter home for Mexican workers. The seasonal nature of spinach production and the short duration of its harvest required periodic travel to the onion fields of south Texas, the cotton farms of central and northeast Texas, and the midwest beet farms of the United States. Crystal City was like other rural communities that supplied a large portion of their Mexicans to the migratory work force. Although the farm worker families earned slightly higher incomes than their counterparts in other rural communities and in San Antonio, their general condition of poverty, discrimination, and segregation was no better.[12]

The Depression brought lower wages and hardship to Crystal City. Farm jobs remained plentiful, however, since the growers maintained a high level of acreage devoted to spinach, but low yields and falling prices cut their earning power. Although the industry did not recover during the late 1930s, the Mexican population remained relatively stable primarily because workers were able to maintain regular employment and supplement their earnings with work in cotton and beets, and the stagnant economy elsewhere offered minimal alternatives.

In 1938 only 20 percent of the families in Crystal City had arrived directly from Mexico; 77 percent had lived elsewhere in the state. A great majority (85 percent) claimed that their families originated in the northeastern Mexican states, especially in Coahuila. Approximately 88 percent of the families included at least one or more U.S. citizens, and most of the children were U.S.-born. The average family had 5.5 persons, of whom 3.1 contributed to the household income.

Almost all of the three hundred families surveyed worked in the spinach fields. More than one-half of them traveled to the North Central and Plains states; a majority of these made the trip directly from Crystal City, while a smaller number first worked in onions for a brief period before moving on to the beet fields. One-third of the families worked in cotton, and a little less than one-half of them also worked in onions before the cotton harvest. Some family members had nonagricultural jobs during the spinach season. They ran stores, fixed cars, did domestic work, or were unskilled laborers. Some benefited from public assistance. Most of the workers performing nonagricultural work and receiving public assistance joined the migratory work force every year. The result was regular employment for eleven months and a low unemployment rate except during April, between the spinach and beet harvests.

The higher earnings and longer work periods in beets and cotton encouraged Crystal City family members to become migratory workers. Spinach work at home provided the lowest income and the shortest period of employment. Beets, especially when seen in combination with cotton and onions, exceeded these conditions substantially. The median annual income of $506 that the three hundred Crystal City migratory families earned represented a significant increase. Fifteen percent of Crystal City's families earned less than $300 per year, while 32 percent earned between $300 and $499.

Low earnings contributed to depressed social conditions in "Mexico Grande" and "Mexico Chico," the Mexican sections of town. The mostly one- or two-room dirt floor shacks were crowded, and the sections lacked paved streets, sewers, and streetlights. The residents often cooked outdoors over open fires during the summer. An impressive number (54 percent) owned their own homes, a fact attributed to a campaign in the 1920s by growers, realtors, and a lumber company that encouraged them to settle and become a permanent labor force. The campaign resulted in a segregated community with homes mortgaged to the local bank.

Low incomes, poor housing, undernourishment, and unsanitary conditions contributed to serious health problems that included a high incidence of diarrhea and tuberculosis. A diarrhea epidemic during the summer of 1939 resulted in two thousand illnesses and fifteen deaths in the county; fourteen of the dead were children below one year of age. Tuberculosis killed twenty-five people. Disease created an unusually high mortality rate of 290 per 100,000.

Mexican children registered low educational levels because of segregation and the joining with their families in the labor migration before the end of the school term. Few of them went beyond the fourth grade. In 1939 only 17 percent of the children between seven and ten years old and 40 percent between eleven and thirteen years old attended the full term. Local school officials segregated the grade school, thus damaging the children while complaining about language difficulties and irregular attendance. Discrimination was also evident in the area of public relief. Between 1932 and 1939, although an overwhelming number of Mexican families met government eligibility requirements, only one out of five families received assistance. Moreover, the U.S. Congress excluded agricultural workers from Social Security Act coverage that included unemployment benefits and old-age insurance.

The migratory workers reconstituted their community on the migrant trail depending on the facilities available and the duration of their jobs. Most beet workers lived in labor camps of temporary dwellings built by companies when they began arriving in large numbers from Texas during the 1930s. Prior to this, families had lived in dilapidated shacks, converted farm buildings, or in the open, either in tents or cars parked alongside the fields. Midwestern beet companies saw the benefit of congregating beet workers in planned communities. The Michigan Sugar Company established a labor camp in the 1930s with nineteen housing units for thirty-five families, or approximately 200 workers. Another camp at Mount Pleasant accommodated 500 residents by 1940. In most cases the growers segregated the Mexicans and African Americans in the camps and placed them in the least desirable houses.[13]

The Mexican agricultural workers in Texas cotton and onion production faced the most difficult conditions during harvests. The poor housing facilities that Texas farmers provided quickly became worse as large numbers of workers arrived for picking. This problem was repeated as they followed the maturation of the crops and congregated in new farming areas. Some families lived in one-room houses or tents provided by farmers, while others slept in their cars or trucks beside the road, or in the open. A smaller number rented in nearby towns. The Texas Farm Placement Service, in cooperation with city and county officials, eventually established campgrounds with running water and toilets at Raymondville, Robstown,

Sinton, El Campo, Levelland, Lubbock, Lamesa, and Plainview. These facilities, however, accommodated only a small minority and led the Farm Security Administration in 1939 to plan the construction of larger camps at Robstown, Weslaco, and Sinton.

Although beet, cotton, and onion growers as well as government officials claimed that they wanted to improve the living conditions of migratory families, they also responded to concerns by local Anglo residents who feared that the migrants would crowd their towns and eventually become permanent residents. The growers wanted to ensure an adequate supply of workers, and Farm Placement Service officials supported this aim in order to ensure high production levels. Making housing available constituted a plan to control the size and flow of migratory labor. It conformed with strategies that included the use of child labor and thousands of labor recruiters delivering the work force.

San Antonio

North of Crystal City, the Mexicans in San Antonio claimed one of the longest urban histories in the state. They had founded the city during the early 1700s, and it became one of the most important colonizing and military ventures on the northern frontier of New Spain. The Mexicans of San Antonio who remained after the Texas Revolution and the War with Mexico faced the sweep of violent domination that included deep south Texas. The economic boom associated with the cotton trade during the Civil War brought a measure of prosperity to Mexican merchants and workers. The Mexican population in Bexar County increased from 1,562 in 1850 to 3,046 in 1900. Their proportional representation relative to Anglos, however, decreased during the same period from 47 percent to 21 percent, reflecting a deterioration in their economic standing.[14]

During the first five decades of the twentieth century the Mexican population of San Antonio grew from 13,722 to 160,410. Their proportional representation also increased, from 26 percent to 39 percent of the city's population. Between 1910 and 1920, during the Mexican Revolution, their numbers grew over 100 percent. The absolute and relative population figures attributed to this group allowed San Antonio to retain its identity as one of the most Mexican cities in the Southwest.[15]

The rural-to-urban and international Mexican migration to San Antonio made it a major labor market by the turn of the century. Newcomers came through El Paso and Laredo, congregated there, and fanned out to places as far away as Chicago. Mexico- and U.S.-born migrants also entered the city on their annual trek through the cotton belt that reached south of Bexar County. The workers and their families hoped to capitalize on improved job opportunities to supplement what they could secure in San Antonio with seasonal cotton-picking jobs in the outlying areas. The San Antonio Mexican community included a small group of skilled workers and an even smaller upper-middle class of merchants and professionals who catered to the working class. Some of the latter descended from older families who maintained their standing through inherited capital, intermarriage, and astute business practices. A greater number arrived as political exiles, especially during the Mexican Revolution. Approximately 25,000 political exiles entered San Antonio during the first major immigration wave into the city between 1900 and 1910. Although most of them returned to Mexico during the 1920s, some remained.[16]

The Mexicans in San Antonio improved their earnings somewhat during the 1920s while remaining impoverished and concentrated in the lesser-skilled occupations. In 1926 close to 50 percent were common laborers or transients who earned less than $14 per week. The laborers with more permanent sources of employment, or regular job holders, included the railroad workers, store clerks, truck drivers, and employees of the city's public works system, the most numerous in the group. Stable jobs meant that they could earn nearly one-half more than the irregularly employed.[17]

The significantly fewer businessmen, small store owners and butchers, slightly exceeded the earnings of the permanent laborers. Skilled workers, including barbers, shoemakers, plumbers, tailors, painters, mechanics, cement workers, and carpenters, represented over 21 percent of the Mexican work force, a figure that was comparable to the one registered by the regularly employed laborers. Businessmen and skilled workers did not earn appreciably higher incomes than the laborers. The businessmen probably registered low earnings because they depended on impoverished clients, while the low earnings of skilled workers suggest a wage ceiling. The professional group, composed of musicians, printers, and journalists, had the highest average earnings yet was the smallest in number.

William J. Knox has argued that the country of birth of Mexican male heads of households explains earning variations. He theorizes that longer residence in the United States and the knowledge of English resulted in continuous and better-paying work. Thus, the recent arrivals, regardless of skills or prior job experience, disadvantaged the entire community. In accordance with his proposition, Knox found that a larger portion, or 65 percent, of Mexico-born male workers whom he surveyed was concentrated in lower-wage occupations. Sixty-three percent of the U.S.-born Mexican workers, however, also were in the laboring occupations. This finding undermines his argument and suggests that Mexicans as a whole were denied upward mobility. Knox's assumptions are more tenable when he points out the greater concentration of Mexico-born workers in the transient occupations; however, the U.S.-born did not record an advantage over the Mexico-born in the business, skilled, and professional ranks.

As San Antonio became one of the major industrial centers in the state with a large number of manufacturing plants and military installations, Mexicans continued to secure better-paying employment. Their condition relative to Anglo workers in the city, however, was relatively worse. Although an increasing number obtained skilled jobs in manufacturing, the great majority of them continued as low-paid laborers during the 1920s and 1930s. The pecan-shelling industry, one of the largest employers of Mexican labor in the city, contributed significantly to the pattern of discrimination and inequality.[18]

By the 1930s pecan-shelling plants in San Antonio produced about one-half of the total national output. This figure was due to the extensive pecan orchards in the area and low-wage Mexican labor. The Southern Pecan Shelling Company discontinued mechanization during the Depression since it was more profitable to employ Mexicans at low wages, as many as 12,000 men, women, and children at about five cents per hour. In October 1938 the already distressed working and living conditions worsened when the industrialists shut down their operations rather than meet the provisions of the Fair Labor Standards Act. That law required industries in interstate commerce to pay a wage equivalent to twenty-five cents per hour. Thousands of unemployed workers sought federal assistance and other jobs while the industry mechanized. It reopened five months later with improved wages and a reduced labor force of 1,800. Before the 1930s a steadily increasing number of U.S.-

born pecan shellers had entered the city from other parts of the state, but most workers came from Mexico between 1901 and 1920. Their numbers dwindled during the 1920s and none arrived after 1931. Some 42.5 percent of the pecan shellers came from other locations in Texas or other states, and 15 percent from San Antonio.

The large companies extended their control through an extensive contracting system. In most cases, they financed pecan contractors who entered into buying and selling agreements. The contractors worked with smaller establishments or groups, including families who shelled at home. If a contractor challenged company prerogatives regarding the supply, price, or quality of pecans, he was taught a lesson. The company withheld nuts, the price was increased, or he was denied a higher grade. The contractor was encouraged to seek higher earnings by subcontracting and increasing production, a strategy that the companies promoted for their own benefit. The development of labor-intensive output had another intent—that is, to maintain a large labor force that could be used to replace workers who either withheld their labor in protests or went to work elsewhere.

Prior to mechanization, pecan shelling began in the fall; peaked in November, and continued until March. Its low point came in midsummer, when cotton was maturing. At this time, one-fourth of the pecan shellers joined the migratory workers to supplement their income. One-quarter of the shellers worked the beet fields of Michigan, Minnesota, and neighboring states. Others found unskilled work in the city or survived on public assistance. Agriculture remained a major source of employment because it provided work for the entire family. Weekly earnings averaged $2.73 in pecans and $3.50 in agriculture.

Life on the West Side of the city attested to the persistence of poverty and inequality. At least 65,000 of San Antonio's estimated 100,000 Mexicans lived in this four-square-mile slum in the late 1930s. They had some of the lowest family incomes in the city and rented dilapidated and overpriced houses without running water, electricity, or indoor toilets. Unsanitary conditions made the West Side a major contributor to the high death and disease rates. Infant deaths and tuberculosis among San Antonio's Mexicans exceeded the national rates. Other problems associated with poverty included illiteracy, low educational attainment levels, prostitution, and poor political participation.[19]

Conditions improved somewhat during the Second World War as the government began to employ Mexicans in record numbers at the four military bases located in the city. Their movement into the skilled ranks was particularly impressive after the military commanders, at the insistence of the Fair Employment Practices Commission (FEPC), implemented a nondiscrimination policy and improved their employment and promotional opportunities. By the 1950s the government had become the largest employer of Mexican workers. The better-paying and more stable jobs at the military camps reflected their growing statewide representation in skilled occupations. Improved job opportunities in other industries also reflected an upwardly mobile trend resulting from wartime economic growth. San Antonio's Mexicans registered occupational gains relative to Anglos primarily because military camp commanders observed the nondiscrimination policy, which contrasted with practices in private industry in Houston.

Houston

The Mexican community of Houston began during the early 1900s as workers settled near the Missouri Pacific railroad yard and the ship channel. As job opportunities improved, additional workers arrived and started to establish distinct neighborhoods, or *barrios*, in the 1920s. The Mexican population grew from 6,000 in 1920 to 40,000 in 1950. By the 1930s, Harris County boasted the third-largest Mexican population outside the border area. In 1950, Houston claimed the fifth-largest Mexican population in the state behind San Antonio, El Paso, Laredo, and Corpus Christi. Their proportional representation of 5.8 percent, however, was substantially less than that of other cities. With time the city grew, public transportation improved, and an elaborated social structure made it less possible to identify the neighborhoods.[20]

Although more than 60 percent of Mexican workers claimed unskilled occupations in 1930, at least 20 percent had skilled jobs while less than 5 percent owned or operated businesses. Unskilled women filled jobs as laundresses, servants, and general laborers; men served as railroad, construction, and general laborers. Fortunate *mexicanas* worked as salespersons in stores, while *mexicanos* operated businesses. In 1944 most families, in substandard housing, earned wages insufficient to support a family. Some of the poorest lived in shacks built along the bayou near downtown; others were in run-down multiple-family units rented from Anglos who migrated to the outskirts of the downtown area. A smaller number of better houses accommodated businessmen, some of whom had migrated to Houston during the Mexican Revolution with sufficient capital to set up small shops. The Mexican business section included drugstores, hotels, cafés, doctors' offices, dry goods stores, jewelry shops, filling stations, grocery stores, and bakeries.

The Depression brought much hardship and discrimination to the Mexican community. As jobs dried up and wages decreased, workers found themselves unable to survive. Moreover, the anti-alien campaigners protested hiring Mexicans for city works projects, and private industry solidified employment barriers. In some cases, relief officials refused to assist them, suggesting that they represented a threat to U.S.-born Anglos. Local officials, however, were more than willing to help them repatriate. Immigration officials contributed to the exodus with mass arrests at work sites. About 2,000, or 15 percent of Mexican Houstonians, left during the early 1930s.

The Mexicans in Houston, however, reflected an urbanization trend in the state. By 1940 the majority of Mexicans in Texas lived in urban areas. Their population in Houston grew from 20,000 in 1940 to 40,000 in 1950 and coincided with the wartime expansion in oil, petrochemicals, and trade. Although the bulk of this population still lived in the original inner-city neighborhoods, new enclaves of the poor appeared during the 1940s. In 1950 the U.S.-born totaled 83.3 percent, or five out of every six Spanish-surnamed persons in Harris County, and suggests that Mexicans entered Houston from other communities in Texas and became permanent residents.[21]

The case of oil illustrates the discrimination practiced in war-related industries. In 1941, Mexicans constituted a small portion, between 6 and 8 percent, of the industry's work force. At that time 5 percent of the 25,000 Mexicans working in industry held jobs in the refineries. During the war many of them found employment in the refineries with their high wages, but this opportunity dried up when the war ended. The employers shifted the Mexicans to unskilled jobs that paid the lowest wages and placed returning Anglo veterans back in the skilled positions.[22] Although more research is needed before we can determine the extent to which Mexicans advanced occupationally during the war, the census data demonstrate

unprecedented, but temporary, gains. These advances resulted from
the opportunities presented by the war effort. They involved a move
from the farms to cities and industry where some workers obtained
better-paying skilled jobs.

In summary, upward social mobility was uneven or even denied. FEPC investigations of Mexican workers' complaints in the
Houston refineries revealed discrimination that denied jobs and
restricted advancement. The Houston case illustrates lopsided development, occupational mobility, and stagnation. Discrimination
in hiring at the refineries reflected a widespread practice that accounts for the low utilization of Mexican workers by industrialists.
Discrimination in promotions created a segregated work force evident throughout the state, although employment in wartime industries represented an important gain, especially for former farm
workers. Furthermore, discrimination created unequal mobility
among Mexicans and between them and Anglo workers.[23]

Political Responses

The history of the Mexican working class in Texas requires a consideration of the varied responses to discrimination and inequality.
The workers challenged this treatment, including segregation in
schools, law enforcement agencies, and governmental assistance
programs. They solicited the intervention of the U.S. and Mexican
governments in labor and civil rights matters, protested low wages
and discriminatory hiring practices, and established alternative institutions such as private schools, newspapers, and community self-
help organizations. These responses were formal and informal,
spontaneous, and sustained.[24]

Seditious groups in the Rio Grande Valley, for instance, staged
running battles with authorities in 1915–16, ostensibly in response
to a formal call to arms by the writer of the Plan de San Diego.
Agricultural workers organized crews who negotiated with farmers and then abandoned fields as an informal bargaining act of
last resort. Groups of workers in rural and urban settings walked
off jobs in protests. Sustained organizing efforts included groups
aligned with the Partido Liberal Mexicano (PLM), Mexican
unions affiliated with the American Federation of Labor (AFL) and
the Congress of Industrial Organizations (CIO), and numerous
mutual aid societies located throughout the state. Reflecting self-

organization, the mutual aid societies achieved prominence at least until the 1930s, and they played an important role in the development of more specialized institutions such as exile groups, unions, and the League of United Latin American Citizens (LULAC).

The most common Mexican working-class groups in Texas were mutual aid societies, or *mutualistas*, which developed during the 1880s and proliferated during the first three decades of the twentieth century. In large part they were a response to the hardships experienced as the economy grew and new waves of immigrants entered a segregated society. In addition to offering social and economic services to their members, mutual aid societies moralistically reflected and reinforced a Mexican sense of nationalist identity.[25] Observers noted the large numbers of mutual aid societies in areas where Mexicans congregated. In 1929, Luis Recinos pointed out that "it is rare to find a city with fifty or more Mexicans that does not have a Mexican society."[26] Some organizations, such as the Sociedad Mutualista Mexicana de Jornaleros of Waco and the Sociedad de Amigos, Beneficiencia Mútua in San Antonio, headed federations that extended throughout the state and beyond. In some cases these federations expanded their scope to include union-like functions as was the case with the Confederación Mexicana de Obreros y Campesinos of Mercedes and the Confederación de Trabajadores Mexicanos en Norte América in Dallas.[27]

In 1911 delegates representing independent and affiliated mutual aid societies and Masonic orders from throughout the state and northern Mexico met in Laredo for the Congreso Mexicanista. They formed a state-wide organization, the Gran Liga Mexicanista de Beneficiencia y Protección. It was short-lived, but the delegates in Laredo demonstrated that mutual aid societies were a prominent force among Mexicans in the state. Their influence continued to be felt into the early 1940s, when they joined with other organizations in the establishment of the Confederación de Organizaciones Mexicanas y Latinoamericanas (COMLA) and the Congreso del Pueblo de Habla Española (CPHE).[28]

Some of the earliest *mutualistas* emerged among immigrants in rural areas. Mexican tenant farmers from Nueces County established three *sociedades* between 1897 and 1905, while Mexican laborers formed seventeen more between 1900 and 1920. Such rural-based mutual aid societies usually had a short life span because of underfunding and migrant instability. They adopted self-help aims, reflecting the almost destitute conditions of agricultural laborers.

The mutual aid societies in urban areas were more stable and had multiple functions, including attempts to build confederations.[29]

The mutual aid societies offered their members services such as death and illness insurance, emergency financial assistance, and help in finding jobs. They also worked with other organizations in sponsoring patriotic holidays and in establishing private schools and newspapers. Mutual aid societies often lent new arrivals from Mexico the cultural and material support that they needed in order to survive the difficult process of adjustment in Texas. The communities, on the other hand, reinforced a Mexican unity and identity on the basis of moralistic values such as mutual responsibility and reciprocity that the societies promoted.

The all-inclusive Mexicanist identity expressed by *mutualista* organizations was particularly evident in their organizing appeals for national unity. Although they were at times led by middle-class Mexicans, they included men and women as well as U.S.- and Mexico-born members. The participants in the Congreso Mexicanista, for example, made no distinction based on country of birth or citizenship. After the conference, one of its organizers, Clemente Idar, added: "We who have been born in this country understand our responsibilities as citizens, but we also feel a profound love for and the most exalted interest in our mother race because we are by destiny her progeny. This nationality and this deep love for the Mexican race runs like blood through our veins."[30]

Mutual aid societies reinforced the organizing impulse with nationalistic language, moralistic statements of purpose, and internal rules of comportment that promoted a national identity and group assistance. The *mutualista* organizations adopted names of historical figures such as Benito Juárez and Ignacio Zaragoza and themes of Mexican unity and well-being such as "La Liga Mexicanista," "La Gran Liga Mexicana," "La Sociedad Benefectora Mexicana," and "La Agrupación Protectora Mexicana." The Sociedad Mutualista Protectora "Benito Juárez," in San Benito, announced that it would "seek that the great Mexican family adopt the principle of mutualism for better understanding." The writers of the constitution of the Sociedad Mutualista Hidalgo y Juárez at Alice added that they would "protect ourselves in a mutual manner against the abuses and violations of our rights and guarantees." Sara Estela Ramírez, a poet, journalist, and teacher in Laredo, summed up *mutualista* tenets during the twenty-fourth-anniversary celebration of the Sociedad de Obreros, Igualdad y Progreso: "Joining souls through the principle of humanity, through the sentiment of innate altruism in the heart, an altruism that permits us to fulfill our obligation to our beloved comrade, to visit him in sickness, to console him in his sorrows and to give him our hand in every bitter hour and in every test, even to bid him farewell when his turn comes to be called to eternity."[31]

Mutual aid societies required their members to adhere to strict rules of comportment that ensured respect and support, sobriety, frugality, and a sense of responsibility toward family and community. Members were expected to refrain from profanity during meetings, to avoid drinking and gambling, and to provide for their families. Failure to meet these expectations led to the loss of membership. These rules were described by members as a necessary means to build righteous and responsible individuals who modeled mutualism as the civic basis for their communities. Mutual aid societies also gave rise to more specialized organizations associated with exile, union, and ethnic politics. Discussions and debates led mutualists to establish separate organizations or to evolve into different ones. Although the new groups pursued more specialized aims, they often remained in the fold by working with mutual aid societies. With the exception of LULAC, they also reflected a Mexicanist identity.

The PLM, a prerevolutionary exile group in Texas, benefited directly from the mutual aid societies. Prior to the PLM's arrival in Texas in 1904, most of the letters of support to Ricardo Flores Magón had come from individual *mutualistas* in the state. Sara Estela Ramírez, an outspoken PLM supporter, voiced a common sentiment when she reminded Flores Magón that the Mexicans in Texas would support his anti-Porfirio Díaz movement. Ramírez had been building such support for the PLM in her writings and speeches. She also participated in the dialogue within the societies on the nature of mutualism and its logical extension into politics.[32]

Ramírez argued that mutualism as practiced by the mutual aid societies corresponded to a law of nature that dictated fraternal behavior. To do otherwise contributed to injustice and exploitation. In calling for the continuous affirmation of the human spirit, she proposed a new society free of class, racial, and gender discrimination. Like Ramírez, José María Mora, a socialist orator and labor leader from Laredo, proposed that fraternity was a natural disposition and that mutualists should always practice it. He called for working-class unity, struggle, and mutualism as essential for Mexican workers in Texas.[33]

The PLM clubs that appeared in the rural area south of San Antonio and Austin during the first and second decades of the century underscore the importance of mutual aid societies. Some of them had prior *mutualista* histories, while others operated as dual organizations active in the Agrupación Protectora Mexicana, a federation of such societies headquartered in San Antonio. PLM clubs and mutual aid societies shared organizers with about twenty sharecropper and labor unions tied to the Renters' and Land League of the Texas Socialist Party between 1911 and 1917. The PLM, Agrupación, and Land League members worked for political unity in Texas while keeping a watchful eye on politics in Mexico.[34] By 1912 the relations between PLM clubs and Agrupación became strained as the exile group openly embraced anarchism and "international class struggle." Political distance, however, did not cause the PLM to renounce national heroes such as Juárez, Melchor Ocampo, and Sebastian Lerdo de Tejada. Even while the PLM grew closer to the socialist unions in the Land League, the latter groups still functioned separately, maintaining relations with other mutual aid societies, expressing Mexican identity, and promoting mutualism and unity.

The political tension caused by the PLM's radical political program did not undermine Mexican identity and mutualism as much as the country-of-birth issue raised by the AFL and its affiliate, the Texas State Federation of Labor (TSFL), when they began recruiting Mexican workers in 1919. The TSFL welcomed Mexicans when the AFL initiated a plan with its counterpart across the border, the Confederación Regional de Obreros Mexicanos (CROM), to discourage immigration. The CROM leaders encouraged their members to remain in Mexico on the condition that the AFL organize the Mexicans already in Texas. The TSFL consented to the AFL's directive, but it only admitted U.S.-born and naturalized citizens.

Samuel Gompers, the head of the AFL, appointed Idar as the organizer for the recruitment of U.S-born and naturalized members. The Mexican workers responded, and by the 1920s at least twenty unions had affiliated with the AFL and the TSFL. Organizing Mexican workers usually involved the recruitment of entire mutual aid societies. The workers would either retain the society as a dual organization or supplant it with the union, which negotiated fringe benefits in lieu of mutualism. Although the leadership, including Idar, questioned the organizing strategy, they understood the value of affiliation and consented. Idar and the unions moved away from the mutual aid societies because of an opportunity shaped by outside forces. This trend achieved greater strength with LULAC's practice of ethnic politics.

LULAC, established in 1929, is usually associated with upwardly mobile, U.S.-born Mexicans who seek change for their communities on the basis of their constitutional rights as citizens. They often spoke in mutualist terms on behalf of the entire Mexican population, but their exaggerated patriotism toward the United States and exclusion of their own nationals dramatized their break with the Mexicanist political tradition.[35] As LULAC's ethnic politics achieved prominence during the Second World War, the mutualist and Mexicanist political traditions continued to hold sway in Mexican communities, as the work of COMLA and CPHE indicates. This division displayed political differences and frayed relations. The COMLA chapter from Houston, the CIO unions of pecan shellers, and unemployed workers from San Antonio often criticized LULAC's exclusionary practices, preferring to include both Mexico- and U.S.-born Mexicans.

Conclusion

The emergence of ethnic politics and the attendant class division that it represented signaled a major development in the history of the Mexican working class in Texas. A small but influential group of predominantly upwardly mobile and U.S.-born Mexicans initiated a dramatic departure from an all-Mexican and binational world of politics. Although they continued to manifest vestiges of the mutualist tradition, they rejected a Mexicanist program of action for an ethnic approach to leverage change. The Mexicanist political tradition persisted, but it was less prominent than its ethnic counterpart by the end of World War II.

The political conservativism of the war and postwar period encouraged the U.S.-born Mexican leadership to embrace ethnic politics. The promise of improvement in social standing for Mexican workers contributed to the popularity of the new political identity, which called for trust in institutions outside the community. LULAC gained prominence after Mexicans had made significant social and economic gains during the war. Working-class mutualism, however, still functions under this veneer, responding to class and racial discrimination and inequality.

Notes

1. See Luis Leobardo Arroyo, Victor Nelson-Cisneros, Juan Gómez-Quiñones, and Antonio Ríos Bustamante, "Preludio al futuro: Pasado y presente de los trabajadores mexicanos al norte del Río Bravo, 1600–1975," in David Maciel, ed., *La otra cara de México: El pueblo chicano* (México: Ediciones "El Caballito," 1977), 243–77; and David Montejano, *Anglos and Mexicans in the Making of Texas, 1836–1986* (Austin: University of Texas press, 1987).

2. Theodore R. Fehrenbach, *Lone Star: A History of Texas and Texans* (New York: Macmillan, 1968), 596–603; William J. Knox, "The Economic Status of the Mexican Immigrant in San Antonio, Texas" (M.A. thesis, University of Texas, 1927), 6–13; Paul S. Taylor, *An American-Mexican Frontier: Nueces County, Texas* (Chapel Hill: University of North Carolina Press, 1934), 71–81.

3. See Manuel Gamio, *Mexican Immigration to the United States: A Study of Human Migration and Adjustment* (New York: Dover Publications, 1971); and Juan Gómez-Quiñones, "Mexican Immigration to the United States and the Internationalization of Labor, 1848–1980: An Overview," in Antonio Ríos Bustamante, ed., *Mexican Immigrant Workers in the United States*, Anthology No. 2 (Los Angeles: UCLA Chicano Studies Research Center Publications, 1981), 13–34.

4. Arnoldo De León and Kenneth L. Stewart, *Tejanos and the Numbers Game: A Socio-Historical Interpretation from the Federal Censuses, 1850–1900* (Albuquerque: University of New Mexico Press, 1989), 39; Montejano, *Anglos and Mexicans*, 298.

5. Carey McWilliams, *North from Mexico; The Spanish-Speaking People of the United States* (New York: J. B. Lippincott, 1949), 172.

6. See Mario Barrera, *Race and Class in the Southwest: A Theory of Racial Inequality* (Notre Dame, IN: University of Notre Dame Press, 1979); and Emilio Zamora, *The World of the Mexican Worker in Texas* (College Station: Texas A&M University Press, 1993).

7. Selden Menefee and C. C. Cassmore, *The Pecan Shellers of San Antonio*, Report of the Works Progress Administration (Washington, DC: U.S. Government Printing Office, 1940), 26–30; Abraham Hoffman, *Unwanted Mexican Americans in the Great Depression: Repatriation Pressures, 1929–1939* (Tucson: University of Arizona Press, 1974), 139–42.

8. Rodolfo Acuña, *Occupied America: A History of Chicanos* (New York: Harper Collins, 1988), 206.

9. See Emilio Zamora, "The Failed Promise of Wartime Opportunity for Mexicans in the Texas Oil Industry," *Southwestern Historical Quarterly* 95 (January 1992): 323–68.

10. The following discussion is based on Montejano, *Anglos and Mexicans*; and Zamora, *The World*.

11. See Andrés A. Tijerina, "History of Mexican Americans in Lubbock County, Texas" (M.A. thesis, Texas Tech University, 1979), 18–19; Montejano, *Anglos and Mexicans*, 103–5; and Zamora, *The World*, 10–13.

12. Selden Menefee, *Mexican Migratory Workers of South Texas*, Report of the Works Progress Administration (Washington, DC: U.S. Government Printing Office, 1941).

13. Dennis Nodin Valdés, *Al Norte: Agricultural Workers in the Great Lakes Region, 1917–1970* (Austin: University of Texas Press, 1991), 64–67.

14. De León and Stewart, *Tejanos*, 10, 12.

15. Richard A. García, "Class, Consciousness, and Ideology—The Mexican Community of San Antonio, Texas: 1930–1940," *Aztlán* 9 (Fall 1978): 30.

16. Idem, *The Rise of the Mexican American Middle Class: San Antonio, 1929–1941* (College Station: Texas A&M University Press, 1991).

17. Knox, "The Economic Status," 15–19.

18. Robert G. Landolt, "The Mexican American Workers of San Antonio, Texas" (Ph.D. diss., University of Texas, 1965); Menefee and Cassmore, *The Pecan Shellers*, 32.

19. The discussion of pecan shellers is based on Menefee and Cassmore, *The Pecan Shellers*, 43–50, 63.

20. Arnoldo De León, *Ethnicity in the Sunbelt: A History of Mexican Americans in Houston* (Houston: University of Houston Mexican American Studies Program, 1989), 8–9, 23–26, 110.

21. See ibid., 11–12, 25–26, 46–53, 98–99.

22. Ibid., 325–26; Pauline R. Kibbe, *Latin Americans in Texas* (Albuquerque: University of New Mexico Press, 1946), 159–61.

23. Zamora, "The Failed Promise of Wartime Opportunity," 340–48.

24. See Guadalupe San Miguel, *"Let All of Them Take Heed": Mexican Americans and the Campaign for Educational Equality in Texas, 1910–1981* (Austin: University of Texas Press, 1987).

25. Roberto Calderón, "Union, Paz y Trabajo: Laredo's Mexican Mutual Aid Societies, 1890's," in Emilio Zamora, Cynthia Orozco, and Rodolfo Rocha, eds., *Recent Scholarship in Mexican History in Texas* (Austin: University of Texas Center for Mexican American Studies, forthcoming).

26. Report by Luis Recinos, Manuel Gamio Papers, Bancroft Collection, University of California, Berkeley. Also "Mexicans Form Honorary Group," *San Antonio Express*, June 16, 1931.

27. Sociedad Mutualista Mexicana de Jornaleros, Waco, 1929, and Confederación Mexicana de Obreros y Campesinos, 1929, Archivo de la Secretaría de Relaciones Exteriores, México, D.F.; Felipe Carvajal, Secretario General de La Confederación de Trabajadores Mexicanos, to Franklin D. Roosevelt, October 21, 1942, War Manpower Commission Records, National Archives, Washington, DC.

28. De León, *Ethnicity in the Sunbelt*, 72–76; Mario García, *Mexican Americans: Leadership, Ideology, and Identity, 1930–1960* (New Haven: Yale University Press, 1989), 146–65.

29. Josef J. Barton, "Land, Labor, and Community in Nueces: Czech Farmers and Mexican Laborers in South Texas, 1880–1930," in Frederick C. Luebke, ed., *Ethnicity on the Great Plains* (Lincoln: University of Nebraska Press, 1980), 190–209.

30. Clemente N. Idar, "El Congreso Mexicanista triunfa: Se discute nuestro proyecto," *La Crónica*, April 13, 1915.

31. Sara Estela Ramírez, "Alocución," *El Demócrata Fronterizo*, April 17, 1909.

32. Emilio Zamora, "Sara Estela Ramírez: Una rosa roja en el movimiento," in Adelaida del Castillo and Magdalena Mora, eds., *Mexican Women in the United States: Struggles Past and Present* (Los Angeles: UCLA Chicano Studies Research Center Publications, 1980); Inez Hernández Tovar, "Sara Estela Ramírez: The Early Twentieth Century Texas Mexican Poet" (Ph.D. diss., University of Houston, 1984).

33. Zamora, *The World*, 104–8.

34. Ibid., 63–65, 142–61, 173–82, 208–9.

35. See Alonso Perales, "El verdadero origen de La Liga de Ciudadanos Unidos Latinoamericanos," in *En Defensa de Mi Raza*, vol. 2 (San Antonio: Artes Gráficas, 1937), 101–3; Benjamín Márquez, *LULAC: The Evolution of a Mexican American Political Organization* (Austin: University of Texas Press, 1993); and Cynthia E. Orozco, "The Origins of the League of United Latin American Citizens (LULAC) and the Mexican American Civil Rights Movement in Texas with an Analysis of Women's Political Participation in a Gendered Context" (Ph.D. diss., University of California, 1992).

CHAPTER EIGHT

As Guilty as Hell
Mexican Copper Miners and Their Communities in Arizona, 1920–1950

ANTONIO RÍOS BUSTAMANTE

Between 1920 and 1950, mining and agriculture dominated the economy of Arizona. Mining employed the largest number of workers, and copper dominated the mining industry. By the 1920s the copper companies had developed hegemonic policies consciously designed to maintain high profitability, prevent effective unionization, and limit the participation of Mexicans and Indians to the role of unskilled laborers. From the 1920s to the 1940s these companies maintained a racial cultural hierarchy with "White Anglo Americans and Europeans at the top and Mexicans and Indians at the bottom."[1]

This study examines the social impact of copper mining on seven important Mexican worker communities through a spatial "snapshot" of them. The geographical area examined includes the seven major copper-mining districts with large concentrations of Mexican Americans: Jerome, Clarksdale, and Cottonwood; Miami, Globe, Claypool, Los Adobes, Inspiration, and Superior; Ray, Sonora, Barcelona, Hayden, San Pedro, and Winkleman; Bisbee, Lowell, Warren, and Tintown; Douglas; Clifton and Morenci; and Ajo-Gibson.[2] One may conclude that the mining companies, through their industrial relations policies, caused the racial-cultural division of the communities. Significant differences developed between the Anglo mining towns and their Mexican counterparts based on differences in company control over the ownership of residential and commercial real estate, the size and composition of the work force, the racially based distribution of the residential population, and the racial hierarchies established for wages and occupations.

Some copper-mining companies had more hegemonic ambitions than others. For example, the Phelps Dodge Corporation emphasized nearly complete control of company-owned towns and aimed at the ownership of all real estate within the community. Other company towns, such as Hayden, controlled by Kennecott, were less complex than those owned by Phelps Dodge. Kennecott adopted a less intrusive policy regarding real estate development and the locations of its employees' residences. Conversely, despite prosperity and extra profits totaling some $2,371,000 annually during World War II, Phelps Dodge fought to maintain segregation in its towns and depressed conditions in its Mexican-American living areas.[3]

Until the successful Congress of Industrial Organizations (CIO) unionization drives of the mid-1950s, the mining companies ran the mines and copper communities as virtual colonial concessions. Only the fierce determination of the miners to organize during the highly profitable years of World War II and the limited degree of government intervention through the National Recovery Act and the Fair Employment Practices Commission (FEPC) created the possibility for unionization. One of the great successes of the workers' unionization effort was their ending of racial segregation.

By 1910 the Arizona copper industry had become the largest in the United States.[4] From 1900 to 1919 escalating labor conflict, culminating in the infamous 1917 Bisbee deportations, characterized the unionizing effort.[5] The mine owners' victory marked the imposition of what has been called the Copper Collar, the companies' version of "industrial progress and labor peace" in the Arizona copper-mining towns.[6] Some historians have called the period from 1920 to 1940 the Quiet Kingdom.[7] During that era Phelps Dodge, the American Smelting and Refining Company, Kennecott, and Anaconda defined wages and labor conditions. They created "Yellow Dog workers associations" (actually company-controlled unions) and dominated the social and economic makeup of Arizona mining communities.[8] For Mexican and Mexican-American workers and their families this Quiet Kingdom included not only open racial discrimination with separate and inferior wages, working, and living conditions but also company actions designed to stimulate anti-Mexican racism among white workers, residents, and officials. However, the Quiet Kingdom was not as silent a realm as it seemed. Labor unrest and resistance characterized the period from the 1920s through the end of the 1930s. Despite violent repression, mine workers of all racial groups sought to organize. And, despite the seeming hopelessness of their position, the miners persisted in organizing from the 1900s, when the Western Federation of Miners initiated their efforts at Bisbee and Jerome.

The organizing efforts of the Great Depression era revolved around the attempts by the American Federation of Labor (AFL) to gain company recognition for skilled Anglo craftsmen such as electricians, machinists, and carpenters. While Mexican workers were almost entirely excluded from these skilled jobs and therefore from participation in the craft unions, the AFL did make a limited effort to organize them in special units called Federal Labor Unions. The AFL, however, kept the Federal Labor Union locals segregated from the other unions to prevent them from becoming more radical. During the 1920s and 1930s the AFL leadership went so far as to warn the Mexicans not to be attracted by the Industrial Workers of the World because as noncitizens they could be deported. The AFL also warned the Mexicans to avoid "Communist organizers" who were "banned from" Miami and Globe.[9]

Meanwhile, the AFL skilled-metal trade craft unions represented only a privileged minority of supposedly more skilled white male workers. They often functioned as pro-company forces during the disputes that management had with the unskilled and semiskilled workers. At other mines such as the Magma, the AFL unions even acted as labor contractors for the companies. They obtained "unskilled Mexican workers." At Magma these "unskilled" Mexican miners bought their jobs from the "skilled" white men and then performed the white men's work as well as their own:

> Here Mexican Workers are hired under ground and at an average rate of pay lower than other underground miners in the state. Anglo miners are given contracts and they in turn employ Spanish-speaking workers to fill the contract. The contractor may take as much as 50% and divide the remainder among several men. The Magma mines are the hottest mines in the U.S.A., which perhaps explains why Anglo workers are given the preference. . . . In Hayden [and] Clarksdale similar conditions exist as those . . . in the Douglas Smelter. . . . In the Feldon properties at Morenci, Arizona, the Mexican workers, who constitute about 50% of the total labor [force of] 2,500, are given jobs in the open

pit mine and then smelter only as common laborers. They are denied promotion and advancement. In Morenci, the company maintains the Longfellow Inn, a recreational center. Mexican workers are denied use of the center. In Ajo, Arizona, at the Phelps Dodge properties similar situations exist as in the other Phelps Dodge properties. In Morenci, Clarksdale, and Ajo, Arizona there are now A.F.L. contracts, but discrimination continues to exist.[10]

The persistent campaign of the companies against unions, higher wages, and improved working conditions continued into the 1970s. In the modern era new open-pit mines have been imposed on the industry with the defeat of the steel workers' union. An examination of the company towns of the "Quiet Era" sheds light on its aftermath, the fate of Mexican-American miners and their families, and the companies' vision of what society should be like.[11]

The Mexicans in Arizona Mining Towns, 1920–1950

Historically, Mexicans and Mexican Americans have supplied the work force needed for copper mining in Arizona. Census data show that Mexicans have long comprised a high percentage of the population in mining towns. In 1910, Arizona's total population was 204,354, of whom 29,454 were counted as being foreign-born Mexicans. U.S. Census Bureau figures from 1910 to 1950 usually identified "Foreign Born Mexicans" only, not Mexican Americans. (In 1930 all Mexicans were counted as a separate race.) In 1920 the Census Bureau counted 334,162 inhabitants of Arizona, of whom foreign-born Mexicans numbered 60,325.[12] Other sources suggest that Mexicans comprised 30 to 40 percent of the statewide population in that year. Between 1900 and 1920 the Mexican population, in search of employment, had concentrated in the mining towns. In most of the copper-mining communities, except for the so-called white man's camps, the Mexicans and Mexican Americans constituted about one-half of the population. In 1919 there were 16,831 persons engaged in mining in Arizona, of whom 105 were owners or managers. Salaried employees, professional or clerical staff, totaled 1,458, while 15,268 were mine workers.[13]

The latter group included so many Mexicans that in 1925 they constituted 43 percent of the copper miners in the state.[14] By the end of the 1920s they had become an even greater majority, especially at Globe-Miami, Douglas, and Clifton-Morenci. For example, at the Miami Copper Company in Globe prior to the shutdown in 1932, Mexican and Mexican Americans made up some 70 percent of the work force. However, when the Miami Copper Company reopened in 1938, the directors adopted a policy of hiring Americans only. By 1942, Mexican workers had been reduced to a mere 5 percent of the laborers.

During the 1920s, Anglo copper miners earned from five to six dollars per day while their Mexican counterparts received under four dollars per day. During the 1930s the racial bias in wages continued, with Mexicans being hired in low-paid unskilled classifications regardless of their abilities, while Anglos were always hired as skilled workers even if they lacked training or experience. The Depression caused a fall in the price of copper and made matters worse. Since many of the mines stayed closed for years, there was a surplus of workers available.

As a result of shutdowns, thousands of miners and their families went without income or sustenance. At that point the government intervened. The politics and administration of federal relief then became highly controversial: it represented an outside threat to the companies' power. While the conservatives attacked welfare programs, the copper companies attempted to hold onto their power by influencing the distribution of benefits. In the copper counties, union organizers and members learned that the companies controlled relief distribution in an anti-union manner. On October 7, 1933, Pierce Williams of the Federal Relief Agency reported that

> we have to operate through volunteers. . . . some weeks ago, there were signs of disturbances in all of the mining camps, due to dissatisfaction with conditions. Of course, as the depression continues, the strain on the unemployed increases, and it becomes likewise easier for agitators to convince them they have a real grievance against the local relief administration. Doubtless, the fact that the local administration is largely managed by copper company men increases the tension. However, in a mining camp, about all the available personnel one can find for relief administration is the staff of executive men employed by the mining companies.[15]

In the late 1930s the growing threat of World War II stimulated the copper industry and large numbers of workers returned to the mines. The employers offered jobs first to the Anglos, but the need for laborers and the growing demand for workers caused them to rehire large numbers of Mexicans. Their number varied from 20 percent of the positions at Bisbee to 80 percent at other sites. However, discriminatory wages continued to prevail, causing complaints and forcing company officials at Miami to explain to FEPC investigators that "another Company, the Miami Copper Company, against which we have complaints, admitted through its superintendent, Mr. Robert Hughes, that there was a double scale of wages for Mexicans and Anglos, admitted it was unjust, said he had written his New York office a time or two to get it abolished, and that he would welcome the abolition of it. The New York office apparently will not support him. The President of the Company is a Mr. Lewisohn. . . . We need pressure from the top."[16]

Phelps Dodge executives offered the following justifications for the lower Mexican wage: "It is not denied by the Phelps Dodge Company that the Mexican workers are kept generally at the lowest wage scale of wages. Tradition and Customary practice is offered as the reason. But the two superintendents with whom I spoke this week argued that (a) They were less capable due to less nourishing food, and (b) they would be demoralized by a higher (or Anglo) wage scale."[17] However, field investigators for the FEPC noted the strong underlying relationship between racially based wage scales and other forms of discrimination: "The whole system of Mexican discrimination as it shows itself by segregation in schools, restaurants, and Anglo clubs will be to a great extent removed when the wage scale for the job is the same for Anglos and Mexicans, and when promotion on the basis of qualification is also equal."[18]

A Spatial Description of the Mining Towns

Arizona's copper industry dominated economically and demographically. During the period from 1920 to 1950 the copper towns constituted one-half of the state's population centers of over ten thousand people. Among the principal factors affecting the spatial characteristics of the copper mining towns were the physical geography and geology of the locations, the changing settlement patterns influenced by the progression of mining and smelting, the development of ore transportation routes, and the hegemonic policies of the copper companies, which included a sharp class and racial hierarchy. The geologic and geographical characteristics of the copper-mining districts gave the mining towns and their Mexican and Anglo communities many similarities.

In general, the miners situated their operations at or near mountain tops in central and southeastern Arizona. After World I, as they exhausted surface deposits, production turned to lower-grade ores and open-pit mining. The mining companies saw to it that they achieved monopolies over property ownership. They cared deeply about the future uses of any terrain being developed. The companies did not want towns located on a barren or mineralized site because it might be subject to mining at a later date. This policy meant the expensive abandonment of the buildings as the open-pit mines grew, the ultimate fate of many Arizona mining communities. Since the mining company usually owned all of the land in the community, the firm's own buildings would have to be torn down.[19]

The center of town usually occupied a level space in the midst of sharp canyons and irregular ground. The company, public, and commercial buildings occupied the small areas of level space at the center. These facilities included company stores for the workers to buy subsistence goods at often elevated retail prices, a hospital, recreation buildings, and schools. The workers built houses on the adjacent hillsides. Independent businesses could exist in the company town only if the dominant firm allowed them to. In some cases they could exist only outside of the property line of the company.

The configuration of the towns and their streets followed the rugged terrain and were highly irregular. The priority given to mining operations often broke up the commercial and residential areas and increased their irregularity. The housing for most of the work force and their families was usually inexpensive but varied according to race: Mexicans could not live with Anglos. Until the 1950s the companies succeeded in maintaining sharp racial divisions in which they classified virtually all Mexican and Native American workers as unskilled laborers and kept them in a distinctly inferior housing subdivision. The nearby White Anglo Americans, duly labeled "skilled," were assigned to superior residences to accommodate their higher status and income. The segregated structure tied housing and jobs together.

The all-white managerial staff resided separated from the workers and occupied quarters ranging from middle-class bungalows with all the amenities to the mansion-like dwellings of the mine managers, top administrators, and engineers. The families of lower-level management and skilled Anglo-American workers lived in bungalows with electricity, running water, and even indoor toilets. The company usually built the residences of the white personnel. Unmarried Anglo-American male employees lived in decent dormitories resembling the railroad hotels of the period. Paved streets and streetlights characterized the neighborhoods of the Anglo employees.

The Mexican and Indian workers, by contrast, occupied sites left over after company and white employees' needs had been met. They usually lived in shacks on irregular and dangerous hillside terrain or at the bottom of canyons and streambeds. Some Mexican and Indian workers were located outside the margins of the company's property on adjacent public or undeveloped land. They rarely enjoyed the benefits of running water or electricity. If the company owned the land, it rented or leased housing sites. Only in a minority of cases did companies in this period erect houses for their Mexican or Indian workers; at best, the companies only supplied building materials. An exception was the mining town of Ajo, in which Phelps Dodge built housing for all the workers, although it coincided with the different needs of the "different races." In some towns the Mexicans occupied older inferior dwellings in which whites had previously lived.

At the beginning of the twentieth century the companies also segregated Italians and Slavs from Anglo Americans. They lived in entirely separate neighborhoods. Sometimes Italians, Spaniards, and Mexicans lived in a mixed area. These earlier ethnic neighborhoods had no more amenities than the entirely Mexican *barrios*. By the 1930s, however, the companies accepted the southern and eastern Europeans to the extent that they were allowed into the Anglo neighborhoods. The Mexicans did not gain that relief.

Racially based wage scales not only affected the types and conditions of housing offered by the companies to the Mexican and Native American workers, but their low wages also ensured cheap and rudimentary dwellings ranging in type from wood frame, stone, tin, or adobe, and in size from one to three rooms. Some had concrete or stone foundations, but others were merely dirt-floored tin shacks or *jacals* built of brush frames plastered with mud. Still others combined these styles to reflect the changing circumstances of their inhabitants and adaptations over time. The houses were frequently packed close together with little yard space. Unpaved paths led to those located far from streets and at the top or bottom of hills.

Mexican and Native American workers shared virtually identical experiences as the victims of company racism. Few of their homes in the 1920s, 1930s, and 1940s offered amenities such as electricity, running water, or indoor toilets. Unmarried Mexican and Native American men lived where they could, sometimes with other families, sometimes camping in crude dwellings. Before 1950 many, if not most, Native American workers lived in so-called Indian camps, where the company provided only the land they lived on: "Mr. Jesse M. Gaylor a Indian employed by Phelps Dodge at Morenci complained that the company withheld from his wages room rent for quarters in the Indian Town maintained by the company, which quarters he did not use because due to his age he could not live in the Indian town . . . and that the withholding of the rent is discrimination in that the company attempted to force him to live in the Indian town against his will."[20] Company officials explained their racist practices in no uncertain terms by stating that "the Indian camp is approved by the Indian Agency, the U.S. Employment Service and the Army; [and] that the rate charged was a flat rate and unless all the Indians paid it the Company would lose money."[21]

Dominant since the establishment of the mines, the companies absolutely controlled property ownership until the 1950s. The federal government exerted little authority in the communities unless the companies requested it. The copper company owners dictated planning in accordance with their view of profitable mining operations. They even influenced private commercial, social, and recreational activities. Pastimes viewed with disfavor could exist only if they escaped notice. In 1917 the companies demonstrated their ability to remove or eliminate anyone whom they considered a threat to their interests by deporting strikers and political undesirables.

Thus, the company owners and management considered the human, social, and cultural needs of Mexican workers subordinate to the profitable operation of the mines. They consulted Anglo employees about issues in a highly limited manner and only to the extent that it benefited the companies. After the destruction of radical unionism by the administration of Woodrow Wilson in 1917, the companies developed a strategy of "dialogue" in the mining towns with the aim of dominating any issue.

Most mining settlements remained unincorporated, while adjacent towns were economically dominated by the huge mining concerns that loudly proclaimed their financial contributions to commerce in the mining counties. Thus, public officials, especially law-enforcement officers, depended upon the copper companies for support. In Miami the sidewalk was for white men only, a policy happily enforced by the chief of police:

> There is a record of indiscriminate beating of Mexican workers by the Chief of Police and his force. There is a record of searches (without search warrant) made of workers who have been told to get out of town. John Welch, the Chief of Police, is the brother of Welch, the employment agent for the Miami Copper Company. There are several cases of union organizers being beaten, and run out of town by the Chief of Police. There have been some searches of some Mexicans to see if they can find C.I.O. buttons.[22]

The companies excluded Mexicans from elected office and municipal and county positions. In Jerome, an incorporated city since 1899, the only Spanish-surnamed person to hold a major public post between 1899 and 1935 was Dr. A. J. Murietta, a company physician who served as the Public Health Officer from 1908 to 1916 and operated a pharmacy.[23] From 1899 to 1935 all Jerome mayors, city councilmen, marshals, magistrates, and postmasters were Anglos,[24] and high-ranking company employees controlled the school board. The ownership of small- and medium-size businesses in mining towns also reflected the racial hierarchy. The company owners largely excluded Mexicans from proprietorship of any but the smallest and least profitable concerns, such as barbershops, grocery stores, and beauty shops. The few Mexican professionals or semi-professionals included pharmacists, teachers, printers, and medical doctors. In Jerome, Mexican-owned businesses included the Paz and Cota groceries, the Marques and Beltran cigar store, pool hall, and barbershop; the Méndez Transfer Company, dealing in firewood; Pena's Place, another pool hall; and the Zaragoza Theater, run by Santiago Tisnado.

Several efforts were made to publish local Spanish newspapers at Jerome, where *El Clarín Dispero* and *Acción Lógica* appeared between 1916 and 1918, *Don Quijote* appeared and disappeared in 1923, and a weekly Spanish insert was added to the *Verde Copper News* between 1927 and 1929. Most of the demand for Spanish-language newspapers was met from the outside by publications such as *El Tucsonese* and *La Opinión*. Anglos owned virtually all of the larger businesses, such as the radio station, insurance agencies, real estate companies, banks, hotels, and jewelry, hardware, clothing, furniture, and appliance stores. They also made up the great majority of professionals and semiprofessionals. The lack of Mexican-owned businesses and the near absence of Mexican professionals was even worse in smaller communities such as Ajo, Ray, and Superior. For example, in 1944 "the Company (Phelps Dodge) owns or controls all businesses in Ajo. These are grouped around a park or square, which forms the center of the mining community. The general merchandise store, the grocery, the café, the soda fountain, and every other business is controlled by the Company."[25]

Jerome is a critically important example of the regime imposed by the companies on the Mexican working class of Arizona. The town is located on the northeastern slope of the Black Hills, on a mountaintop in central Arizona's Yavapai County at an altitude of 5,200 feet.[26] The United Verde Mine was started there in 1876 and established an open-pit operation in 1918. The smelter towns of Clarksdale (founded in 1912) and Clemenceau and the labor town of Cottonwood developed in the valley below.

In 1920 the Clark and Douglas families owned the town of Jerome, and the United Verde Copper Company set up operations there. In 1935 the Phelps Dodge Corporation purchased both the town and the mines. At the time, Jerome had a 50 to 60 percent Mexican majority population. The main street stood on a ridge, but the largest Mexican neighborhood was on the lower part of the hillside. In the *barrio chicano*, dilapidated housing characterized the scene. Chinatown, another segregated neighborhood, was nearby. Further removed were other *barrios* known as El Palomar, El Verde, El Golcho, Gringo Hill, El Tresiento, El Doscientos, and La Daisy on the periphery of the town. The separate and better-quality Anglo housing occupied an area adjacent to the center of town.[27]

On August 10, 1928, a full-page headline in the *Verde Copper News* stated: "Robert E. Tally Separates the Races in New Swimming Pool." After Phelps Dodge took control of United Verde, it used the pretext of a water shortage to assign Mexicans and Americans different periods for swimming for years thereafter. The Americans used the pool exclusively from Sunday through Thursday, then the Mexicans could use it from Thursday evening until Sunday morning when it was being cleaned. Targeting Mexicans, many community social organizations specifically barred from membership anyone who was not a Caucasian American citizen. Until the late 1950s, Mexican children could not join the Boy Scouts.

Out of desperation their parents formed a local branch of the Pioneros Mexicanos, modeled on the principal youth organization in the Soviet Union, which served as a substitute for the Boy Scouts in many Arizona mining towns. While Phelps Dodge ran Jerome, the owners and management refused to consult the Mexican populace, despite its being a majority, regarding important community affairs. In a town characterized by segregated facilities, the Anglos enjoyed tennis courts, shooting ranges, and swimming pools, all of which were off limits to Mexicans.[28]

Around the smelters the company placed the towns of Clarksdale and Clemenceau on flat land reserved for white Anglos only. The Mexican and Apache Indian workers and their families were located in nearby Cottonwood. In 1944, Will Maslow, FEPC Field Operations director, described what he saw:

> The same pattern as that found in other Phelps Dodge plants is followed at Clarksdale. All the Mexicans live in a separate community on company grounds. A Mexican club house is maintained by the company, but the facilities for recreation are inferior to those of the club house for English speaking, or Anglo, employees maintained in the English speaking, or Anglo, section of Clarksdale. In addition to the Mexican community that adjoins Clarksdale proper, there is another small Mexican community, also on company ground, located about a mile above Clarksdale in the direction towards Jerome. This is known as Romita (Little Rome) to the Mexicans and as Centerville to the English speaking workmen.[29]

The Nevada Consolidated Copper Company mine ruled the scene at the Ray mines, located northeast of Tucson. In 1937 the Kennecott Corporation purchased Ray and the nearby site of Hayden. Kennecott's policies differed from those of Phelps Dodge in that it did not seek to own everything, and that attitude probably allowed residents and small merchants greater latitude in shaping the community. Alternatively, it meant a less-developed infrastructure because of company indifference. At Ray the Spanish-speaking communities were known as Sonora and Barcelona.[30] As had occurred so often, the Mexican miners created Sonora through their own labor; miners of Spanish descent built Barcelona in a nearby canyon.[31] In 1943 the Mexican residents in the area complained to FEPC investigators about discrimination. One example was that the company refused to fill the swimming pool for them. When it was filled, the water was allowed to become dirty and rusty unlike the pool for Anglos. The mine superintendent explained to the FEPC that the Mexicans preferred residential segregation and wanted to live together. In order to escape government intervention, the manager lied by claiming that the Mexicans could live in Ray if they wished.

At Hayden, Kennecott adopted a policy of racial segregation. Hayden remained all white while the neighboring Mexican settlements of San Pedro and Winkleman had few conveniences and many hardships. Maslow also described these two communities:

> Just across the canyon from Hayden is located a small community called San Pedro where Latin American workers reside. The company enforces strict segregation within its property. Winkleman which is outside of company property has no segregation, and Anglos and Latin Americans live in perfect harmony. It is the company which enforces segregation in Hayden-San Pedro. This segregation applies to the only moving picture theater in Hayden, is reflected in the school, and in all public establishments in Hayden, all of which is not true of Winkleman. The pattern of segregation just described, which is the result of company policy, is reflected in the wage scheme, the upgrading practices, and the classification of workmen in force.[32]

At Globe and Miami the adobe housing of the Mexican miners stood on hills on either side of Ruiz Canyon. Miami's business section was built on a valley floor called Miami Flats, cut through the middle by Bloody Tanks Wash. The Inspiration and Miami copper mines operated just north of Miami, where the owners established a smelter and concentrator to serve the mines. The *barrios* located on the hills overlooked the town and consisted of wooden shacks, unpaved streets, few or no streetlights, and little or no sanitation facilities.[33] Just over the hill in the next canyon a neat company-built Anglo housing tract enjoyed paved streets, lighting, garbage collection, and sewage lines. The company enforced a policy of segregation even at the Miami Catholic Church, where the Anglos sat on one side of the aisle and the Mexicans on the other. The Mexican children attended segregated *barrio* schools with strikingly inferior facilities. The planned segregation of schools typified Arizona towns until public unrest and political pressure weakened the system during the 1950s.[34]

Following a post-World War I slump, Miami enjoyed an economic boom from 1921 to 1928. During those years the Mexican population increased significantly at Miami Flats, Los Adobes, and the smelter town of Claypool. By 1932 it made up 70 percent of the Miami Copper Company's work force, as noted earlier. Then the Great Depression caused a slump in business and the mine closed. When it reopened in 1938, the directors enforced a policy of hiring only American citizens. They enjoyed some success despite their own inefficiency. In 1942, 75 percent of the 456 employees of Mexican descent were U.S. citizens. In August 1944 the company, by then called Miami Consolidated Mining, employed 1,415 largely Anglo workers. At that point the Pan American League, whose officers included Secretary Jesús Gutierrez, began to actively campaign against discrimination in hiring, housing, and wages.[35]

Across the Pinal Mountains, to the west of Miami, the Magma Copper Company bought the Silver King Mine in 1911. By 1920 the directors of that firm had established a concentrator, smelter, narrow-gauge railroad, and the company town of Superior. Like the mining town of Cananea near the state border in northern Sonora which Arizona capitalist William Greene owned, the company officials divided Superior in half to create an "American Town" and a "Mexican Town." They called the facility-less area of houses built by the company for Mexican workers "Jiggerville," and the well-supplied area for the smelter superintendent, foremen, and Anglo engineers "Smelter Town." Because of their wealth the Magma mines remained open during the Depression while most of the other mines closed, yet even the wealth yielded by the Mexican workers did not overcome the strength of the owners' commitment to segregation and racism.[36]

Farther south, Bisbee, with a population of 9,100 in 1900, became Arizona's largest industrial town. Bisbee exemplified the hegemony of the copper companies. The large smelter loomed over the center of town. The directors of Phelps Dodge had bought the Copper Queen Mine in 1885, and by 1900 it was accelerating its purchases of land near Bisbee. The company brought its policies of racial segregation with it. In 1900, Bisbee was known as a "white man's camp" because Mexicans were not allowed to work at skilled underground mining and because of extreme prejudice toward Chinese. The Anglo working class at the site supported discrimination in housing, jobs, and wages. The Mexican mine workers' housing rose on the steep hillsides north and west of the town. The Mexicans of Chihuahua Hill and Zacatecas, communities that began where the paved streets ended, built their houses on rock platforms because that was all the terrain offered them.

The company, headed by prominent New York bankers Cleveland Dodge and James Douglas, built the housing for its white employees at level sites to the south of Bisbee. Farther south, the workers of the neglected *barrio* of Tintown made their shacks out of tin. Nearby, in 1900, the Mexican workers built the community of Don Luis as a rail junction. They performed an essential task in developing and maintaining communication and supply routes. The settlement patterns in the Bisbee area reflected the hierarchy of the Arizona mining industry as well as the fact that once again segregation prevailed despite highly valuable creativity on the part of the Mexican workers. From 1920 to 1950, Phelps Dodge bought out its competitors and increased its influence over Bisbee. Once again, as in other parts of Arizona, it controlled residential patterns, the ownership of houses, the limits of city boundaries, and the makeup of the population. The company used segregation as part of its strategy in Bisbee through the 1940s.

In 1900, Douglas, located about twenty miles east of Bisbee, became the major smelter town for Phelps Dodge in Arizona. It processed 50 percent of the state's copper. More diversified than other smelter or mining towns because of its location on the border across from Agua Prieta, Douglas also functioned as an agricultural and commercial center. The Mexican work force had formed a majority of the population from the inception of the town. Smelter towns differed from mining towns in that they were located in less mountainous or flat areas, but they shared similar social characteristics. Douglas, named for a high official of Phelps Dodge, occupied a flat site. There, the Mexican *barrio* developed on flatland rather than on hillsides. The housing of poorer Mexicans tended to be near the border, while Anglos and better-off Mexicans lived away from it; indeed, a large part of the Mexican work force lived across the border in Agua Prieta.

In 1931, Phelps Dodge moved to secure its hegemony over the mining industry throughout Arizona. In that year it acquired the smelter of its former rival, the Calumet and Arizona Company. Then, in order to economize because of low copper prices brought on by the Depression, the company laid off most of its new workers. Production did not recover for seven years. In the meantime the directors of Phelps Dodge imposed a new policy of extreme discrimination at the smelter. One hiring strategy called for the recruitment of workers from Arkansas and Texas rather than allowing the promotion of Mexican employees.[37] The episode involving the Detroit Copper Company installations at what are now known as Clifton and Morenci underscores the fact that Phelps Dodge not only acquiesced in segregation but imposed it in areas where it had not prevailed earlier. In the nineteenth century the Detroit Copper Company constructed the first concentrator in the Arizona Territory and attracted a large number of skilled Mexican workers. Unfortunately for the Mexicans, Phelps Dodge bought out Detroit Copper in 1895. By 1922, Phelps Dodge had extended its complete domination of the district to include land ownership, housing, and trade.

The builders of the new town of Clifton placed the Anglo homes on the hills and higher flatland above the town. In contrast, as usual, they relegated the Mexican workers to shacks built in the bed of the San Francisco River, which was prone to sudden flooding, and on the steep hillside across the river from Clifton. The Mexican communities of Morenci and Metcalf grew up on the steep north end of Morenci Canyon. Then, between 1929 and 1939, the Depression paralyzed production and left most of the workers unemployed. For a time the county government offered the use of farmland where the unemployed could grow food. Phelps Dodge, however, refused to pay any taxes to Greenlee County with the claim that its mine and smelter were out of operation. The company's action crippled the finances of the county and its ability to respond in the crisis. Then the federal government began to forcibly repatriate Mexican families. By 1933 the authorities had forced out over four hundred Mexican families, thus significantly reducing the population around Clifton-Morenci. First, the company laid them off at the mine, and then the county government denied them public assistance. The federal government then began its deportation program. And finally, Phelps Dodge supplied the workers with train transportation back to Mexico, presumably to make sure that they all left.

In the absence of mining jobs during the Depression the main source of employment became federal work programs such as the Works Progress Administration and the Civilian Conservation Corps. Most local businesses, both Anglo and Mexican, closed because of a lack of customers. However, the economy decided the outcome. In 1937, when the demand for copper began to increase, the mines reopened and many of the Mexican families returned. The population, which had decreased significantly between 1933 and 1936, immediately recovered.

Since the 1940s the growth of the open pit at Morenci has been the dominant physical characteristic of the area. As a result of the growth of the open pits the old towns of Morenci and Metcalf had to be abandoned. In 1943, Phelps Dodge built a completely company-owned town at Morenci and a smaller residential area called Stargo for foremen. Until the 1960s the company successfully imposed segregated facilities that even reached the Mexicans in death. Their cemetery, built on a steep hillside, still exists. (Ironically, the Anglo cemetery, built on lower-lying ground, has been washed out.) In 1943, Mexicans comprised 60 percent of the Phelps Dodge work force at Morenci. Faced with difficult conditions, the Mexican workers turned to their strong traditions of mutual self-help and community organizations in order to survive. That strategy included burial and disability assistance and orphans' care. It replicated their actions at other Phelps Dodge towns, where such steps were also necessary in order to overcome the dire conditions in which they had been left.[38]

The experience of Mexican miners in Ajo is another important episode in the history of the Arizona mining industry. Located some forty miles south of Gila Bend, the Calumet and Arizona Companies began copper-mining operations there in 1912. Because Ajo was a desert site, water had to be pumped from underground wells and stored in large reservoirs for mining uses and for human consumption. The New Cornelia Copper Company, which took over operations in Ajo, created a town that stood as an exception in Arizona and yet proved that segregated but equal facilities were not possible. Some 7,000 people, including Mexican and Indian workers, lived in Ajo. The firm provided eight hundred houses in the town, and Anglos, Mexicans, and Indians were given segregated yet comparable dwellings.[39] In 1920 the managers of the New Cornelia Company boasted of their achievement: "Around the plaza are the attractive tile or frame dwellings of the American employees, and the new school building. A complete water, lighting, and sewer system was installed before the townsite was occupied. Over the hill toward the mine is the Mexican townsite, with its one, two, and six family hollow tile houses, all harmonizing with the general architectural plan. The Mexicans have taken great pride in their clean and attractive homes."[40]

The New Cornelia Copper Company owned Ajo lock, stock, and barrel until 1931. In that year Phelps Dodge purchased Ajo and everything changed. The new owner expanded the open pit.

Thirteen years later the company's racist policies had once again created an oppressive environment: "The Mexican workers at the mine and mill live in what is known as Mexican town, built on property owned by the company. No direct or open pressure is used in maintaining this arrangement, and to a certain extent, it may be said that it is largely voluntary. Nevertheless, there are numerous ways in which they are made to feel that it is best for them to reside in Mexican town. In the case of the Indians, it is not voluntary. They have to live in the Indian town which is supervised by a special official, and they are treated very much as if they were on a reservation."[41] After nearly forty years of laborious copper mining the population of Ajo in 1956 still held at nearly 7,000, with 4,294 Anglos and 1,452 Mexicans in residence. But by then Ajo was desolate despite the fact that the mine had produced $94,000,000 in copper between 1918 and 1956. Phelps Dodge had taken the profits from those earnings and left the townspeople with neither infrastructure nor assets nor any viable means of support.[42]

In conclusion, the copper companies dominated the economy of the state and the mining communities. In the absence of outside assistance, the Mexican and Mexican-American workers built their own makeshift houses and developed their own health-care services, such as midwifery and nursing care, and mutual aid, such as child care and disability assistance. The companies' ownership of the town sites, near-monopolies of employment, and conscious economic and social policies of discrimination against Mexicans and Mexican Americans maintained an often vicious racial hierarchy. The segregation of Mexicans and Native Americans from Anglos denied the first two groups the opportunities of full citizenship. The far-reaching repression exercised by the companies and local authorities slowed the development of a radical union alternative.

The development of mining and smelting and transportation routes created new communities, and company owners determined which residents would receive services. The owners' segregationist policies of discrimination in occupational assignments and the distribution of benefits, including housing, recreation, education, and health care, provided them with huge profits and left the communities with very little once the copper veins ran out.

Through their monopolistic controls the owners restricted the access of the Mexican workers to nonmining occupations, property ownership, and self-employment. The Arizona copper barons, many of whom sat on boards of directors in New York, exported their racial labor practices and their idea of a desirable social order to Mexico as well. Arizona's copper-mining towns resembled and served as models for the racially segregated copper-mining communities created by the same companies in Mexico, such as the Phelps Dodge facility at Nacozari in Sonora, William Greene's operation at Cananea, and Kennecott and Anaconda in Chile.

Notes

1. This essay owes much to sources identified in Clete Daniel, *Chicano Workers and the Politics of Fairness: The FEPC in the Southwest, 1941–1945* (Austin: University of Texas Press, 1991).

2. Two diametrically opposed perspectives on company towns appear in the literature. One view is exemplified by the company histories of Robert Glass Cleland, *A History of Phelps Dodge* (New York: Alfred A. Knopf, 1952); and James B. Allen, *The Company Town in the American West* (Norman: University of Oklahoma Press, 1966). A labor history perspective is offered by James W. Byrkit, *Forging the Copper Collar: Arizona's Labor Management War of 1901–1921* (Tucson: University of Arizona Press, 1982).

3. Field Investigators Daniel Donovan and Barron B. Beshoar to Dr. Ernest Trimble, August (n.d.) 1942, Reel 28, HQ Files, Fair Employment Practices Commission (FEPC) Records, National Archives and Records Administration (NARA), Washington, DC; Daniel, *Chicano Workers*, 74.

4. Arizona Bureau of Mines, *Mineral and Water Resources of Arizona*, Bulletin 150 (Tucson: University of Arizona Press, 1969), 117–56.

5. See Brykit, *Forging the Copper Collar*, for conflict.

6. Juan Luis Sariego, Luis Reygadas, Miguel Angel Gómez, and Javier Farrera, *El estado y la minería mexicana: Política, trabajo y sociedad durante el siglo XX* (México: Fondo de Cultura Económica, 1988), 101–18.

7. See almost any issue of the *Arizona Labor Journal*.

8. This condition was widespread. See Emilio Zamora, *The World of the Mexican Worker in Texas* (College Station: Texas A&M University Press, 1993).

9. *Arizona Labor Journal*, passim.

10. Statement of Harry Hafner and Leo Ortiz to Dr. Ernest G. Trimble, July 30, 1942, FEPC Records, NARA.

11. Barbara Kinsolver, *Holding the Line* (N.p.: ILR Press, 1989).

12. Fourteenth Census of the United States, vol. 6, *Mines and Quarries, 1919* (Washington, DC: U.S. Government Printing Office, 1922).

13. Charles T. Connell to H. L. Kerwin, April 6, 1925, U.S. Conciliation Service, Untitled file on Mexican Immigration, Box 142, Record Group 280, NARA; Mark Reisler, *By the Sweat of Their Brow* (Westport, CT: Greenwood Press, 1976), 117.

14. Census of General Industries, 1954, vol. 2, *Area Statistics* (Washington, DC: U.S. Government Printing Office, 1952).

15. Pierce Williams to Harry Hopkins, Federal Emergency Relief Administration (FERA), October 7, 1933, FERA Records, NARA.

16. Ibid., August 31, 1933.

17. Ibid.

18. Pierce Williams to Harry Hopkins, FERA, October 7, 1933, FERA Records, NARA.

19. E. G. Trimble to Lawrence W. Cramer, FEPC, August 20, 1942, FEPC Records, NARA.

20. Barron B. Beshoar, Associate Field Representative, War Manpower Commission, to Dr. Ernest Trimble, FERA, September 21, 1942, FERA Records, NARA.

21. Ibid.

22. Statement of Harry Hafner and Leo Ortiz to Dr. Ernest G. Trimble, FERA, July 30, 1942, FERA Records, NARA.

23. Herbert V. Young, *They Came to Jerome: The Billion Dollar Copper Camp* (Jerome, AZ: Jerome Historical Society, 1972), 174.

24. Ibid., 180–84.

25. Report, Will Maslow, Director, Field Investigations, Clifton, to Carlos E. Castaneda, Assistant to the Chairman, Washington, DC, May 4, 1944, FEPC Records, NARA.

26. J. Carl Brogdon, "The History of Jerome, Arizona" (Master's thesis, University of Arizona, 1952).

27. Lily Sahagun Hernandez, "Los Pioneros Mexicanos: The Mexican Pioneers," paper, History Symposium, Jerome Historical Society.

28. Ibid.; H. C. Harding, Jerome, to Grace Sparks, Chamber of Commerce, Prescott, May 31, 1933, FERA Records, Field Reports, Arizona, NARA.

29. Maslow to Castaneda, Washington, DC, June 8, 1944, FEPC Records, NARA.

30. Leonor Lopez, *Forever Ray, Sonora, Barcelona* (N.p.: private printing, 1984).

31. Ibid.

32. Maslow to Castaneda, Washington, DC, May 4, 1944, FEPC Records, NARA.

33. Raymond Johnson Flores, "The Socio-Economic Status Trends of the Mexican American People in Arizona" (Master's thesis, Arizona State College, 1951), 37.

34. Fred G. Holmes, "Close the Breach: A Report on the Study of School Segregation in Arizona," January 12, 1950, Arizona Council for Civic Unity.

35. Flores, "The Socio-Economic Status," 37.

36. Gladys Walker and T. G. Chilton, "The History of Mining at Superior," in J. Michael Canty, ed., *The History of Mining in Arizona*, vol. 2 (Tucson: American Institute of Mining Engineers, 1991).

37. Carlos A. Schwantes, *Bisbee: Urban Outpost on the Frontier* (Tucson: University of Arizona Press, 1992); *The Douglas Report* (Tucson: University of Arizona, Bureau of Applied Research in Anthropology, 1982); Robert S. Jeffrey, "The History of Douglas, Arizona" (Master's thesis, University of Arizona, 1951).

38. Olivia Arrieta, "The Mexicano Community of the Clifton-Morenci Mining District: Organizational Life in the Context of Change," in Mary Romero and Cordelia Candelaria, eds., *Community Empowerment and Chicano Scholarship* (Berkeley: National Association for Chicano Studies, 1992); Mabel Baker Morgan, *Forty Years in Arizona: Miami, Clifton, Morenci* (Phoenix: Butler Printing, 1980); James M. Patton, *History of Clifton* (Clifton, AZ: Greenlee County Chamber of Commerce, 1977); Heather Hatch et al., "Clifton: Photography and Folk History in a Mining Town," *Journal of Arizona History* 23, no. 3 (Autumn 1982); Joseph F. Park, "The 1903 Mexican Affair at Clifton," *Journal of Arizona His-*

tory 18, no. 2 (Summer 1977); and James R. Kluger, *The Clifton-Morenci Strike: Labor Difficulty in Arizona, 1915–1916* (Tucson: University of Arizona Press, 1970).

39. Arthur Train, Jr., *Ajo: Early History of Ajo, Home of New Cornelia Branch, Phelps Dodge Corporation* (N.p., 1941).

40. *Ajo, Arizona: Property, Plant, and Process* (N.p.: New Cornelia Copper Company, 1920).

41. Maslow, Ajo, to Castaneda, Washington, DC, June 13, 1944, FEPC Records, NARA.

42. John Wallace Leonard, "The Economics of a One-Industry Town" (Master's thesis, University of Arizona, 1954).

CHAPTER NINE

Customs and Resistance
Mexican Immigrants in Chicago, 1910–1930

GERARDO NECOECHEA GRACIA

In the early twentieth century, Mexicans emigrated to the United States with the intention of obtaining work, not of changing their way of life. Even though the new jobs they found were distinct from their agricultural and artisanal work, the labor culture learned in Mexico continued to condition their habits and attitudes. This essay explores the new employment and old conduct of Mexican workers and describes and compares how they viewed work in Mexico and Chicago and how they performed it in the latter place. Certain patterns recur that characterize their working experiences at both places, but there are also conflicts that suggest significant changes. In time, many Mexicans acquired new attitudes similar to those of the industrial coworkers who had preceded them.

The changes took place in a context of accommodation and re-sistance. In spite of discrimination, harassment, and prejudice, Mexican workers pursued their own ends, often overcoming the contemptuous attitudes and structural obstacles that hindered the re-creation and modification of their way of life. As both Mexicans and workers, they mixed elements of their culture, nationality, and class experience in resisting subordination.

Early in the twentieth century, few Mexicans lived in Chicago; in 1910, there were no more than 500. Their numbers increased by 1930 to almost 20,000, but they still comprised less than 1 percent of the total population of the city. Nevertheless, the Mexicans' presence was significant for local industry. In 1926 they represented

11 percent of the nearly 66,000 workers employed by fifteen of the largest industrial plants. Mexican immigrants found work in the crews that maintained railroad rights-of-way, a job available to them as soon as they crossed the border and which dispersed them throughout the United States. Those arriving in Chicago found industrial jobs during the 1919 steel strike and the 1922 meatpackers' strike. Later, the Mexican work force entered the large steel mills of South Chicago, East Chicago, and Gary, Indiana, and a smaller number found employment in the packing plants of Swift and Armour, while others worked in the stockyards.

Although the railroads, steel mills, and meatpacking plants provided the main job opportunities for some Mexicans, others looked to different sources of employment, such as in the enormous McCormick machinery-manufacturing plants, or for the many small producers of macaroni, mattresses, candy, garments, and carpets. Perhaps less than 2 percent pursued the far more common practice in Mexico of self-employment as artisans, merchants, or professionals.

While a handful of Mexicans were engaged in skilled work and earned higher wages, the great majority worked at unskilled tasks as assistants and common laborers. The menial jobs they held were usually disagreeable because of exposure to extreme temperatures, filth, danger, and noxious and toxic gases. The workday extended from ten to twelve hours while wages were low. With earnings of less than $100 per month in the 1920s, their income surpassed their potential in Mexico where the average wage was 57 cents per day, but it was not enough to live comfortably in the United States.[1]

Finding Work

The expectations of Mexican workers and the political realities they encountered often clashed. In March 1925, Luis Palacios, desperate after a long period of unemployment, asked the personnel manager at the Inland Steel Corporation for a job. When he was turned down, the supervisor tried to throw him out, but Palacios defended himself. Members of the staff beat him up and left him unconscious in the street. To add insult to injury, the company then filed charges against him. In the meantime some members of the Mexican community formed a defense committee, distributed leaflets describing the incident, and promised to take action.[2] From their perspective the management owed Palacios dignity and the right to work. Palacios and his defense committee disappeared from the historical record, but the episode illustrates the tensions that arose between Mexicans and employers over definitions of fair treatment and managerial hiring practices.

In the 1920s foremen in American industry usually hired and fired plant workers, and their methods of selection varied. Sometimes, after briefly surveying a crowd of would-be employees gathered in front of the factory, they would point out those whom they considered adequate for the vacant posts. When they were feeling magnanimous, they hired those recommended by their employees based on friendship or ethnic and family solidarity. But they also sold job vacancies. The foremen frequently had absolute authority over employment in their departments.

Earlier, during the 1890s, the rise of scientific management methods created experts who suggested that the power to hire and fire should be removed from the hands of mere foremen. The experts concluded that their whimsical criteria brought inefficiency in job performance. But large industries only gradually followed through on this advice by installing personnel departments. Toward the end of the 1920s only one-third of the companies that employed over 250 workers had such departments. In those cases, specialists matched the physical, mental, and moral characteristics of applicants with job requirements. The aim was to eliminate inefficiency.[3]

The personnel managers also sought to destroy solidarity among the workers. When foremen did the hiring, the result was often the predominance of one immigrant group or clique in a department. In this situation, worker dissatisfaction often led to protest demonstrations. The factory managers in Chicago, therefore, began to seek ethnic diversity in the workplace. A steel mill executive explained that job assignments based on country of origin served to "balance" the nationalities and to reduce labor conflicts. Later, a government commission concluded that Chicago-area industrialists deliberately mixed workers of different nationalities with the goal of eliminating protests and limiting the power of unions.

While the owners fostered ethnic divisions among their workers after the 1890s and used personnel experts to do the hiring, they feared reducing the power of the foremen. Many in management believed that without the power of hiring, promoting, and firing, the foremen would lose control of the workplace. This argument was so strong that the process of professionalizing personnel matters took many years.[4] At the same time the employers promoted competition among workers of different nationalities in order to reduce their capacity to act in unison. Sometimes personnel managers placed African Americans and Mexicans together, challenging each group to demonstrate who were the better workers. In one large steel mill, the Mexicans sought to produce more than their Anglo counterparts, commenting among themselves that "we won't let the gringos be better."[5]

Between 1910 and 1930, Chicago became an important destination for Mexican immigrant workers. New arrivals used the contacts of friends and relatives to find employment. The workers had obtained information from friends while still in Mexico about available job opportunities up north. The friends or relatives then recommended the newcomer for a position at the same factory, or even department, where they worked. This practice became commonplace in the small factories of Chicago's Near West End. Mexicans tended to gravitate to the area because it offered jobs and cheap accommodations. For instance, when the overseer at the mattress factory at Marshall Field needed a new worker, he simply told one of his Mexican employees. On the following day a brother, sister, or cousin would apply for the job. In 1925 the factory had 100 workers, and 50 of them were Mexicans; by 1928, 75 of them worked there. Other Mexicans worked at the paper factory in Barret, while the Meinhardt Mop Company employed only Mexicans.[6]

The railroads provided other job opportunities in the Near West End. The railroad companies recruited some of their workers in the Southwest and others through Chicago agencies that depended on word of mouth to circulate job notices. Mexicans commonly exchanged information in front of these agencies or at neighboring eating houses (*fondas*). The information acquired through these informal channels was fundamental for telling workers who could be trusted, which factories offered acceptable meals, and which had the most humane foremen.[7] Work on the railroads and in agriculture also was generally offered through group contracts.

At the larger steel mills and packing plants with their personnel departments, jobs frequently could be obtained through the recommendation of a friend. One Mexican immigrant arrived at Illinois Steel, in Indiana Harbor, looking for work. He found the job, thanks to the mediation of a friend who worked there. Another new immigrant came looking for his brother and ended up working with him at a Swift and Company packing plant. The Mexicans were known to be "magnificent in helping each other to get jobs." Mutual aid, in this context, consisted in offering information and advice, acting as interpreters, or talking to the foreman. According to historian Paul Taylor, everybody acknowledged that Mexicans managed to establish themselves in Chicago through networking.[8]

Those who did not know somebody in the Mexican community resorted to indirect means to find work. In pool halls and *fondas* frequented by Mexicans, owners and patrons offered advice to the new immigrants. Social workers established contact with employers who accepted Mexicans. The workers also received help from Mexican charitable organizations such as Cruz Azul, which gave at least one man a letter of introduction with which he found a job at Illinois Steel. Everybody hoped to obtain this kind of help. Some even complained when they did not receive it.[9]

By networking, the Mexicans struggled to evade the impersonal and unreliable mechanisms of the labor market. Their strategy, however, was not just to avoid the impersonal nature of the job market; they were also following traditional customs of finding work. In Mexico, family connections played a crucial role. Boys in the countryside worked with their parents. They learned to do farm chores prior to inheriting the status of *peón de hacienda* (laborer) or small tenant. Those who lived on ranches worked in family groups, and the sons helped their father, their grandfather, and their uncles. In addition, they worked for the large landholders for a wage. The tenant often asked the hacendado to become the godfather to one or more of his children, and this practice ensured sharecropping contracts. The same bond helped the children of the sharecropper to become *peones de hacienda*. When they sought work, the *peones* went from one hacienda to another, where they had relatives employed.

Small businesses in Mexican towns and cities also depended on the work of family members.[10] In the second half of the nineteenth century, for example, artisans Lidio and Trinidad Santillán wove *rebozos* (traditional shawls) in Jiquilpan, Michoacán. In Chicago their children, grandchildren, nieces, and nephews did the same from 1870 to 1920. Blacksmiths, shoemakers, leather workers, and other rural artisans usually distributed the manufacturing tasks among their wives and children. From time to time, when they needed extra hands, they employed relatives or neighbors.

In urban manufacturing workshops, master craftsmen recruited staff among their relatives or the relatives of their workers. Melitón

Herrera remembered how his father, owner of a cigarette company in Jiquilpan, doled out jobs to relatives. In the same factory, Aureliano Mejía began working with his brother. When faced with high work loads, shoemakers in Guadalajara asked their employees to bring somebody they knew to the shop. In the workshops and factories of Jalisco, workers took on their children as apprentices, usually at the age of ten years.

The Mexican pattern of asking for work or of offering it created bonds of reciprocity that often combined the labor relationship with that of the family. The artisan and the ranchero served as parent and boss; the hacendado and the manufacturing entrepreneur as godfather or distant relative. Bosses and subordinates formed a large, but hierarchical, family. No one involved thought of the relationship as a strictly contractual agreement for the purchase and sale of labor. For that reason, people did not consider labor as a mere commodity.[11]

Mexicans arrived in Chicago with a well-established approach to finding work. Modern industry tried to force them to follow a new pattern of conduct, but they resisted. Even though they were subjected to a labor market ruled by supply and demand, they found ways to personalize their actions. On the one hand, hiring out their services was a commercial transaction, but on the other it was a consequence of social relationships and a way of asserting them. But life in Chicago was not a replica of their previous experience because the American employers did not adhere to the interchange of favors and obligations with which the Mexicans were familiar. Meanwhile, working in the big city and in modern industry helped forge new bonds because individuals were sharing the same experience. A new sense of reciprocity and solidarity was developing among the Mexican workers of Chicago.

This realization allows us to better understand Luis Palacios's conduct with the personnel manager in the light of customs as he knew them. By insisting that he be hired, Palacios appealed for favors and obligations that the manager did not understand. The defense committee thought that Palacios's actions were "natural" and that the manager seemed "not to have a human heart." In their view, Palacios's behavior was normal and the manager was inhumane.

Palacios's experience represented something important to those who wrote and distributed the protest leaflet. To present oneself to a personnel department that bought work without considering the human circumstances of the situation was humiliating. Thus, the defense committee members thought it was important to show the company that Palacios was not alone, that they would organize themselves to defend him. With this aim, they appealed precisely to the expectations of reciprocity: "Let us support him, today for him, tomorrow for ourselves." With this, they demonstrated the solidarity that they owed to each other. They also recognized that the new impersonal, urbanized working environment and language barriers separated them from their employers.

Turnover, Wages, and Job Security

Luis Quintero faced a different situation. Although he had a job in a meatpacking plant with which he supported his family, he was not happy. In Mexico he had worked on a ranch, riding horses in the open air. In Chicago he worked indoors, moving back and forth between the heat of the ovens and the cold of the freezers. The job was unhealthy, and he left it. Unable to find a satisfactory alternative in Chicago he returned to Mexico with his family.[12] At first, Quintero's decision, like Palacios's behavior, seems hard to understand. He devised a plan to live and work abroad in order to improve his material condition, but material advances alone were not enough; Quintero opposed, even rejected, working conditions that were beyond his ability to control. Quintero and Palacios typify the tensions in premodern industrial culture when it comes face to face with the work, uncertainty, alienation, and wages of modern industry in places such as Chicago.

　　Most Mexicans ended up by changing jobs and cities several times in just a few years. They took the first opening available once they crossed the border. The railroads recruited them for temporary jobs across the country. Once their short-term contracts expired, they looked for other positions nearby.[13] Like modern workers, Mexicans always had two questions in mind: where can jobs be found, and which ones pay the best?[14] In search of answers, they wove a complicated pattern of emigration and employment in Chicago and in various places across the United States. High labor mobility was not unique to Mexicans. The problem preoccupied those scholars who analyzed industrial relations during the second decade of the twentieth century. In his book on industrial education, Roy Kelly argued that unskilled workers with less than three months' service were responsible for the high levels of turnover, which in 1918 fluctuated between 100 and 300 percent.[15] Between 1890 and 1920 immigrants experienced this instability.

Most newly arrived Mexicans did not have the skills demanded by the Chicago labor market. They fit the profile of the unstable worker and did not stay long in their jobs. In 1925 a railroad company reported that Mexicans only represented 6 percent of the total work force but were responsible for 22 percent of the job turnover. In 1928 an average overall of 5.25 percent of the workers at one steel mill quit each month, but a higher 7.84 percent of the Mexicans left. In 1925 only a few of the 2,265 Mexicans employed in steel mills and packing plants, smelters, and the railroads had worked at the same job for three years. At the end of the decade, less than one-half of this work force had three years of continuous service in the same industry.[16]

Singling out the instability of Mexicans, even though other workers manifested the same tendencies, many personnel managers chose not to hire them. Some made their preferences clear when they asked for workers at the state employment office. One manager said that he had hired a group of Mexicans, but when the leader decided to leave, the rest followed him. Another asserted that his steel company valued stability: "We give preference to men with home and family, and Mexicans are at the bottom of our list." A worker named Díaz, a young meatpacker, summarized the treatment that many of these immigrants received: "The boss says that he cannot give a good job to a Mexican because he leaves in a short time and then the boss has to train a new worker."[17]

Other employers, however, such as agricultural and railroad companies, preferred Mexicans because of lower wages and the need for large numbers of temporary laborers. The steel industry required the same flexibility because of market fluctuations. Industrialists tried to run their factories at full capacity, but at times they sought to cut back production while waiting for new orders. Temporary unemployment was common, and the alternative was to search for odd jobs in the steel industry.[18]

The Mexicans' attitude toward temporary employment also contributed to the pattern. They were accustomed to periods of intense, hard work alternating with periods of leisure. This pattern had emerged from the practices of agriculturalists, artisans, and factory workers in Mexico. Immigrants from rural areas sought temporary work elsewhere during down times in the crop cycle. Thus, industrial layoffs in Chicago duplicated past labor experiences in Mexico. This situation, combined with the discrimination practiced by many employers, helps explain why Mexicans did not settle in permanent and secure jobs.[19]

Finally, job turnover increased with the politics of the industrial economy and the search for efficiency. After 1870 the steel manufacturers introduced technological innovations and rationalized the working process while reorganizing the management of their mills. They sought to increase productivity while reducing labor costs. In some cases, particularly in the furnaces and conversion departments, they replaced humans with machines. In the rolling and finishing mills, technology increased the speed of work. In both cases, per capita production increased while skilled work lost ground to the semiskilled activity of machine operation.

By 1900 the meatpacking plants had grown enormously. The work done by a single skilled butcher in the small plants of 1880 was carried out twenty years later by rows of machines working in tandem with hundreds of men. Instead of one butcher in 1880 working on one animal, each worker in 1900 performed the same task over and over again on many animals.[20] Three decades later a Mexican journalist visited the slaughterhouse of the Union Stock Yard in Chicago and wrote in amazement:

> I look down. There moves, in the atmosphere charged with vapors and strong emanations, an army of men in shirtsleeves armed with enormous knifes. I vaguely perceive, towards the other end of the room, the way the pigs go in, one by one, squeezed in, and frightened to death in the face of the foreboding danger; how quickly the machine lifts them up by their hind legs and suspends them in the air; and how quickly a hand—or two, or three, or one thousand, I do not know!—stabs them with a knife in the wooly belly. . . . Rivers of blood flow. The dead pigs parade in an endless chain. Their hair is removed. They are put in boiling water. They are flayed. And, I see the uninterrupted row of pink, shiny, fat pig corpses. . . . I think that here, in a blink, the pigs become ham: I see it happening on a massive scale![21]

At the turn of the century the nature of work changed dramatically, thereby requiring a different kind of laborer. The large number of immigrants looking for jobs facilitated the creation of an almost desperate labor force that would accept inhumane conditions. Once machines imposed a rhythm, human limitations on productivity disappeared. The result was a less heavy but more tiring work process because the laborer had to apply energy in an intense and endless way for twelve hours per day, seven days per week. Manual tasks could be done without skill and knowledge; they became simple and repetitive. The distinction between those who had an occupation and common laborers disappeared; so did the expectations of starting a job as an apprentice and moving up. Workers became easily interchangeable from one factory to another, and from one industry to another. By 1910 the industrialists completed the transformation, and, while changes continued, they were not as significant during the next fifty years. Redundant and monotonous factory work generated discontent and encouraged high levels of turnover. In his extensive study on the subject, Sumner Slichter emphasized the underlying contradiction between imposing efficiency and maintaining a stable labor force.[22]

Many Mexicans disliked industrial work because it clashed with their previous experience. In Mexico many had been peasants, artisans, and merchants all at once. Most of them still preferred combining their work in several ways. When artisans and peasants divided their duties, they did so not only to increase productivity but also to integrate the members of the family. When they finished a task, they had time to play, eat, and rest before they started the next one. Although they worked from sunrise to sundown, it was with a slower rhythm than that required by factory labor. Tasks were made more agreeable by conversing together or reading aloud. Their six-day week respected the *san lunes* (Mondays when they did not work) and holy days, which seemed to multiply. Thus, their schedule obeyed the needs of society, or nature and its cycles.[23] These habits caused Chicago industrialists to consider the Mexicans unsatisfactory workers. They criticized their slowness, inconsistency, and lack of specialized skills. The managers reported that Mexicans only reluctantly accepted the logic of industrial employment. This perception reduced job opportunities for Mexicans in heavy industry and left them in the least skilled positions.[24]

As the years went by, however, an increasing number of Mexicans sought regular jobs. Among the alternatives, the meatpacking plants and steel mills offered the best wages and relative stability. Those immigrants seeking work in these industries wanted job stability and higher wages. Their attitude, which became more evident after 1925, coincided with the growing desire among the owners to reduce turnover and the stagnation of wages. By the late 1920s the growing and mutual desire of workers and management for more stable employment secured a growing number of jobs for Mexicans in Chicago's largest industries.

The concern of the capitalists to stabilize the labor force went hand in hand with the transformation of work. In 1913, because of turnover, the Ford Motor Company managers in Highland Park hired four times the number of laborers needed to fill the vacancies. In the following year, Henry Ford announced his decision to pay $5 per day for an eight-hour day. By 1916 the turnover rate had decreased to 16 percent. Meanwhile, the other large companies, including U.S. Steel, introduced reforms that improved working conditions for their skilled workers. An editorialist commented in *Iron Age* that "every entrepreneur knows the problem of keeping a skilled work force." The same writer noted that "nobody pays attention to unskilled workers."[25]

After 1920 the expenses for training new workers and the search for lower labor costs prompted solutions other than higher wages and better working conditions. Planners attempted to coordinate demand and production, and personnel managers tried new criteria of selection and incentives to ensure the retention of workers. Some large companies, including U.S. Steel, even promoted national, racial, and gender segregation in order to play off one group against another, but none of these measures solved the problem.[26]

During the 1920s the increasing flow of workers to Chicago through the movement of Americans from the countryside to the cities and the introduction of a great number of women to the labor market limited job opportunities for Mexicans. Automation also eliminated jobs and reduced the creation of new ones where Mexicans worked. Consequently, after 1925, job demand exceeded supply. Unemployment rose and the turnover rate diminished to one-half of what it had been before World War I.[27]

Wage stagnation during the 1920s also impacted upon job mobility. In the late nineteenth century and first decades of the twentieth the average income for factory workers continued to rise, but between 1919 and 1929 it changed very little. Industrial laborers earned an average of 66.2 cents per hour in 1923 and only 71 cents in 1929. Between 1920 and 1929 the wages of unskilled workers decreased from 51 to 49 cents. The incentive to change jobs in order to receive a better wage lost ground in helping to reshape the lives of Mexican workers.[28] During the 1920s economic circumstances helped to modify the attitude of some Mexicans regarding their willingness to move between jobs. They came to Chicago because of the higher wages there than in Mexico or in the American Southwest. The steel mills and meatpacking plants offered good wages, but those who got jobs had few opportunities to augment their income. They hoped for promotions, but the chances were remote. Moreover, other cities had less opportunity to offer than Chicago. There is no evidence that the Mexican workers of Chicago demanded wage increases in those difficult times.

After all, what they earned in Chicago served to support an entire family back home. That is why they considered their stay in Chicago as transitory. They expected to earn enough to finance a more comfortable life upon their return to Mexico. The immigrant laborers in Chicago may have sent home as much as one-third of their income.[29] To achieve their goal they seized existing opportunities to avoid remaining long without an income. The majority of those who worked in the steel mills stayed for several years but eventually went back to Mexico.

Those who remained usually had left very little behind in Mexico, neither land nor family. Some had planned to stay when they immigrated, but others kept postponing their return until they had developed ties too strong to sever in Chicago. For these men, a living wage meant something different than it did to those who had material obligations and sentimental bonds back home.[30] For example, a Michoacán shoemaker, whose occupation was obsolete in the American economy, had worked in the beet fields, on the railroads, and in a steel mill. In 1928 he explained his needs, stating that "I want to have a job for two or three years in the same place. Then I can buy clothes and food. If I am short of money, I know that I will receive another check. I want a job because I know that I must work in winter. If I do not have money, I can die of cold or hunger in Chicago."[31] For him, returning to Mexico was not an alternative.

Other Mexicans with similar needs remained on the job, especially those who worked in the steel and meatpacking industries. Less fortunate workers worried about not being able to stay in the same job without interruption. This concern may have predisposed them to modify the earlier habits and attitudes that had hindered their success and stability. They contrasted with Quintero, who held onto his customs, kept moving, and then returned to Mexico. The first years of the Great Depression revealed stark differences among the Mexican workers. As a result of the massive unemployment provoked by the financial crash, thousands returned home. Some left voluntarily, while the authorities forced others to leave.[32] Those who remained in Chicago, after one-half century of deportations and unemployment, had learned to value job security and had become distinct from their still unacculturated compatriots.

Paternalism and Despotism

"The boss's girlfriend, Lucille, seemed to always get the easy tasks, but then she found herself in the dirty and slow job of packing couplings for exhaust pipes. The boss reassigned Enriqueta González Flores to the job. At that moment, the Mexican woman threw down the parts and walked toward the door. Someone asked her, 'Hey, Enriqueta, where are you going?' She replied, 'To flirt with the manager so that he assigns my job to Lucille!' The boss soon brought the couplings to Lucille's seat, among widespread laughter." The González Flores incident demonstrates Mexican sensitivities to the power relationships inside the factory. The contrast between working environments in Chicago and Mexico shows how Mexicans had to adapt and cope with unequal working relations.[33]

In the Chicago steel mills, personal contact between workers and bosses was a thing of the past. By 1910 the boss of a family business rarely knew his workers at a personal level. Higher executives delegated everyday plant operations to specialized managers. Planning departments grew. Supervisors specialized in mere phases of the productive process: verifying compliance with instructions, ensuring the supply of materials, effecting quality control, measuring the time and cost of each task, keeping machinery in good working order, and enforcing discipline. Lower-level supervisors kept department heads informed, and the latter did the same for the plant superintendent, who was responsible to top management. This hierarchy in organization reinforced the gap created by the economic, cultural, and educational differences between the Mexican workers and their American bosses.[34]

The relationships among the Mexicans changed with workplace circumstances. No longer aware of the total productive process, they usually had intimate knowledge only of their own group. The workers knew their immediate superiors to some degree but had impersonal relationships with the rest of the managers. The immediate supervisor handled complaints and quarrels. Mexican workers had had limited experience with this managerial hierarchy in their homeland. In Mexico the person who hired them worked with them in direct personal, family, and community ties. And in Mexican factories, which were usually much smaller than those in the United States, most laborers had more contact with the boss.

This personal relationship in the Mexican workplace involved sharing of responsibility for the workers' welfare. The bosses granted loans, supplied food and drink, and founded schools and churches. In return for favors, the workers knew how to reciprocate. They stayed extra hours, secured new employees among their friends and relatives, took work home for their wives and children, and accepted lower wages. Employers and workers frequently spent leisure time and planned important festivities together. These favors and obligations involved ties that surpassed a mere contract.

Paternalistic attitudes characterized the relationship between boss and subordinates. In the workshops and ranchos of Guanajuato, Jalisco, and Michoacán, the father was the boss. His conduct reflected family concerns. A hacendado, as boss, had the obligation to be wise and generous, to behave like a father. The factory owners often behaved in the same way. Personal contact, mutual favors, and obligations relieved the negative effects of an otherwise unequal relationship between employers and employees. The workers within this unique environment solved their disagreements with the boss directly. To behave any other way risked ostracization and criticism from other workers with obligations to the boss. Thus, many of the Mexicans in Chicago knew little of strikes and unions, of organized methods for resolving labor problems. More commonly, laborers and artisans depended on their good relations with the person who employed them. A cigarette maker recalled years later that "everything was solved by means of family contact, there was nothing like a workers' union, the seventh day or anything of the sort."[35] Workers expected their notions of mutual obligation to be respected.

In the emergent modern industry of Chicago such notions of reciprocity did not exist. This situation had three significant implications. First, the Mexicans believed that their bosses acted on their own account, whimsically or with prejudice toward them. A Mexican who worked in a meatpacking plant said that the "bosses know that we do not speak much English, [so] they make us work harder and give us the nasty jobs." To Mexicans, the behavior of their superiors broke with the codes of acceptable conduct. As one put it, "I do not mind working, but I will not have a servile attitude and they want you to be servile. I am not used to that." Some complained about corruption, favoritism, and arbitrary changes in job assignments: "Many of the bosses receive five or ten dollars a day from the other workers so that, in return, they will get better jobs. Us, we are sent to some other task." At a steel mill, several Mexicans protested when a boss made his son a crane operator and transferred the Mexican who had held that job to a common one.[36]

Second, the Mexicans believed that top managers would give them justice if they knew about the arbitrary attitudes of the bosses on the floor. A Mexican steelworker stated that "the company" was good, but "they" did not know about the abuses. Another said that the superintendent ignored, and thus tolerated, the sale of jobs. Indeed, bosses occasionally were dismissed for taking bribes. But it was not easy to skip over immediate authority and complain to the top managers: "When they employ you, the big manager of the office orders you to do one thing, but the security man orders you to do something else and the boss also tells you to do it or else he fires you. If you tell the superintendent that he must sign your card, he reprimands the boss and sends you back to work. But in four or five days the boss can assign you somewhere else and tell you that there is no more work."[37] The "big manager" at the office kept his distance from what was going on while the boss abused his disciplinary power. Perceived mistreatment was the issue that caused the most strain between the American employers and their Mexican employees. For the Mexicans the figure of the despotic boss rather than general industrial discipline was responsible for the conditions that they faced at work.

Third, the unequal relationships between jobs and ethnicity led Mexicans to reassert their horizontal bonds as workers. Because they could not trust the hierarchy, the only protection was whatever they could offer each other. One example of this situation was the committee for the defense of Luis Palacios against Inland Steel. The Mexicans founded several workers' associations such as the mutualist society, Free Mexican Workers of South Chicago. They directed its efforts toward assistance, not the modification of the labor environment. Its members, however, did express their frustration and discontent when they described themselves as "the pariahs of these hells of steel, where we exhaust our existence."[38] The employers reacted negatively whenever the Mexicans acted in concert, even in the founding of mutualist societies.[39]

The despotism in the factories and the breakdown of Mexican paternalism provoked confrontations between American management and the workers, and the latter responded with spontaneous actions. The ephemeral nature of these activities, however, has left little trace. Even so, there was a process of change: the Mexican workers in Chicago faced new labor experiences and problems and created ways of resolving conflicts and supporting each other.

Resistance: Inherited and New Experiences

According to Eric Hobsbawm, labor history in industrial societies went through two significant moments. In the first stage, capital and labor defined the limits, conduct, and legitimacy of their respective positions. In Chicago this phase reached maturity in the early 1920s. In the second stage, the new attitudes and ways of behaving became internationalized. During this second period in Chicago the original disputes seemed to be settled, such as working hours and wages, arbitration procedures, unions, collective bargaining, and strikes. Capital and labor first established the rules of the game, made mutual adjustments, and behaved accordingly. The capitalists of Chicago as well as their Mexican work force epitomize Hobsbawm's argument.[40]

It could be argued that the shaping of industrial relations in Chicago at the beginning of the twentieth century took place during the second moment, but Herbert Gutman has shown that elsewhere, between 1890 and 1920, the two phases lived in a complex and intertwined way. One segment of the working class inherited the process of capitalist transformation developed during the nineteenth century, but, like the Mexicans in Chicago, a growing number of workers were only beginning their confrontation with the industrial regime. Gutman underscores the cultural conflicts and processes of adaptation that defined this transitional period.[41]

Between the Depression of the 1890s and that of the 1930s, three processes shaped American and Chicago society. The first was the transition from the era of dispersed capitalism to a more concentrated system of finance. The second involved the introduction of advanced technology and a transformation of labor characterized by the diminution of skilled work. Finally, the third process was the immigration of millions of young men, whose labor power was indispensable to mass production. The interaction of these phenomena defined the homogenization of labor in the history of industrial capitalism. By 1920 the transforming initiative of capital had established its hegemony in the wake of intense battles fought with labor over the nature of work. The so-called American Plan, promoted by the manufacturing associations, emerged temporarily victorious, banished trade unions from the factories, and endowed factory managers with the authority to hire, fire, and set working hours and wages.

American workers' resistance to the rise of capitalist workplace practices and wages had dramatic moments during this period, including the bloody strike in 1892 at Homestead, Pennsylvania, where union members lost their dispute against the Carnegie Steel Company, to the general strikes of 1919. David Montgomery classified the strikes according to the demands of the workers. Some strikers sought to reduce the working day to eight hours, a demand that had prevailed in Chicago since the second half of the nineteenth century. Other skilled workers walked out in opposition to the mechanization and routinization of their work. Semiskilled workers and common laborers were also involved and fought for wage increases. Between 1916 and 1922 skilled workers staged frequent and important strikes. Montgomery also found that the various complaints and streams of resistance among skilled workers and common laborers fused during the period from 1916 to 1922.[42] Working hours, wages, and control on the shop floor were the key issues, and they caused tremendous strain in the industrial relationships of the time.

Mexicans entered industrial Chicago toward the end of the struggle to set the rules. Second- and third-generation workers had already accepted the attitudes and limits defined as industrial relations. Confrontations between the Mexicans and the bosses in Chicago parallel the broader working-class protests against the new methods of scientific management. In fact, Montgomery includes strikes against unpopular bosses within the category of strikes for control.[43] In addition, the Mexican workers of Chicago repeatedly showed their opposition to the endless rhythm imposed by machines, which contrasted dramatically with their more individualized labor experience back home. Thus, their protests reflected the desire for the control that they had traditionally exerted over their work.

The contrast between the resistance of Mexican workers and their counterparts of other ethnicities in Chicago introduces the cultural dimension of their discontent. Many of them had to learn

to measure their work in clock time and not by tasks, and they had
to overcome the belief that wages merely complemented a family
income intended to sustain and reproduce an artisan or peasant way
of life. Indeed, many of them eventually abandoned industrial life
and returned to Mexico without ever learning the rules. Most Mexican immigrants had had no previous experience with industry. For
this reason, their opposition to management mirrored the different
way that they viewed their working world. They rejected more than
scientific management. Rafael Quijano expressed the sentiments
behind their attitude:

> In Mexico, many of these line workers were shoemakers, car-
> penters, blacksmiths, and so on; they had learned a trade as ap-
> prentices, to later become expert masters. . . .
>   Consider, for instance, the American workers who have their
> tasks distributed according to their abilities: some polish wood,
> others carve it, others shape it in the lathe, others paint it, others
> assemble the furniture, etc. In the meantime, our carpenters sum-
> marize in their work all this experience and each one, by him-
> self, can finish a piece of furniture. . . . If it were possible to
> reunite all our fellow-countrymen who possess a trade working
> by their own account, they would easily achieve economic
> independence.[44]

As Gutman has argued in a wider framework, the attitude of
Mexican workers in Chicago paralleled that of the farmers and artisans who experienced the first stages of industrial capitalism and
the skilled workers who opposed Taylorism at the beginning of the
twentieth century. They perceived mistreatment at work as discrimination because management, without knowing it, attacked the customs that defined them as Mexicans. Thus, they found it unbearable
when bosses singled them out for the dirty and heavy jobs, or refused to call them by their names, or insulted them, or forced them
to work on holy days. The Mexican immigrants also resented being
treated differently because of their physical appearance. José López,
who worked in a meatpacking plant, declared that the Americans
did not want Mexican employees "because our color is different."
Many discovered that being Mexican hindered job searches or promotions. Their complaints indicate that they did not distinguish the
prejudice of the bosses from the features of industrial work.[45] Discriminatory practices led to confrontations.

Their acts of protest were spontaneous both because their motives stood beyond the rules that legitimated industrial relations and because no conciliatory mechanisms existed. The cultural conflict produced several reactions. Quitting a job was the most frequent one. Sometimes a worker, trusting in their goodwill, would present his case to supervisors. A more effective form of protest came when a whole group stopped working. Kinship and friendship created the solidarity necessary for spontaneous work stoppages by Mexican crews in agriculture and on the railroads as well as of groups exclusively formed by Mexicans working in steel mills and meatpacking plants. They resorted to their usual bonds to generate collective protest.

The large steel and packing company executives, however, preferred work crews made up of mixed nationalities. Mexicans worked alongside Poles, Lithuanians, Croatians, Irish, and others, some having been in the industry a long time. This pattern meant that veterans taught new workers the "attitudes towards work and towards the bosses that [the veterans] considered socially acceptable."[46] This learning process took place in the factories of Chicago. Mexicans working in the large steel mills in 1919 joined the industry's general strike. According to one manager, "Mexicans mainly followed the leadership of Spaniards, and there were many radicals among the Spaniards."[47] Many of them attended the homage to socialist leader Eugene Debs upon his death in 1926 and the conference given in the same year by the Communist Albert Weisbord regarding the Passaic strike of 1919, when the Amalgamated Textile Workers closed several mills in New Jersey and demanded higher wages and a wide range of benefits.[48] During the 1930s they took part in the organization of trade unions at steel mills and meatpacking plants.

Daily experiences sustained this participation. Manuel González related how he had ridiculed a factory boss who bothered him. A mixed group of coworkers supported him including, among others, Sam, a huge black man; McBroom, a former rancher from Oklahoma; and Fred, a factory repairman.[49] González emphasized the importance of shrewdness and manhood in building solidarity among heterogeneous workers. When a confrontation involved only Mexicans, their conduct could be even more categorical. A group at the Youngstown Sheet and Tube Company accused the manager of swindling them by not reporting all the hours that they had worked. They decided to protest through a work stoppage rather than by quitting their jobs. The stoppage took place in 1927 and indicates that, by then, Mexicans knew how to play by the rules governing relations between capital and labor.[50]

The work stoppage at Youngstown Sheet and Tube also demonstrated the significance of individual leaders. Basil Pacheco encouraged his workmates to protest. He was fired for his involvement but later reappeared as one of the organizers of the steelworkers' union. As early as 1915, Mexican union workers refused jobs as strikebreakers or scabs at a local foundry.[51] They drew the name of the Society of Free Workers of South Chicago from the Great Circle of Free Workers at Rio Blanco, which had become famous during the textile workers' strikes of 1906–07 for better wages and working conditions. The activists helped bridge the gap between old and new experiences in linking Mexicans to other workers and by politicizing those without previous experience.

The social networks and work attitudes that immigrants brought with them from Mexico challenged the established practices of the Chicago labor market. Relationships within the working groups, where veterans mingled with the Mexican minority, merged the inherited experience with a new one. Mexicans who remained in Chicago joined a situation that in the short term not only strengthened their ties with their countrymen but also broke the more traditional patriarchal bonds that linked them to managers and foremen. Labor conflicts became more significant. Being Mexican defined the terms of the conflict and legitimized the behavior to be followed. Their passage into the American industrial working class was an economic and cultural process that transcended the working environment to embrace everything that clashes when distinct heritages collide.

Notes

1. Ernest W. Burgess and Charles Newcomb, *Census Data of the City of Chicago, 1920* (Chicago: University of Chicago Press, 1931), 21–23; Paul S. Taylor, *Mexican Labor in the United States*, vol. 2 (New York: Arno Press, 1970), 29–31, 36–38, 77–80, 155; Robert Redfield, "The Mexicans in Chicago," Diary (October 5, 1924–April 24, 1925), Redfield Papers, University of Chicago Special Collections Library, Box 59, f. 2, 5–9, 55–57, 67; Elizabeth A. Hughes, *Living Conditions for Small Wage Earners in Chicago* (Chicago: Department of Public Welfare, 1925), 44–47; Irving Bernstein, *The Lean Years* (Boston: Houghton Mifflin, 1960), 63–65.

2. *México* (Chicago), March 21, 1925.

3. David Brody, *Steelworkers in America: The Nonunion Era* (New York: Harper and Row, 1969), 109; Roy W. Kelly, *Training Industrial Workers* (New York: Ronald Press Co., 1920), 119; David M. Gordon, Richard Edwards, and Michael Reich, *Segmented Work, Divided Workers: The Historical Transformation of Labor in the United States* (New York: Cambridge University Press, 1982), 135–38.

4. Gordon et al., *Segmented Work, Divided Workers*, 137; Kelly, *Training Industrial Workers*, 198–215.

5. Taylor, *Mexican Labor*, 78, 94; Gordon et al., *Segmented Work, Divided Workers*, 141–42.

6. Redfield, Diary, 24–26, 51–53, 75–81; Taylor, *Mexican Labor*, 68.

7. Taylor, *Mexican Labor*, 64–66.

8. Ibid., 75, 128; Redfield, Diary, 21; Interview, Jim Martin with Justino and Caroline Cordero, South Chicago, September 11, 1981, Archive of the Southeast Chicago Historical Project, Columbia College, Chicago.

9. Robert C. Jones and Louis R. Wilson, *The Mexican in Chicago* (Chicago: Chicago Congregational Union, 1931), 9; Redfield, Diary, 39–41; *México*, November 6, 1930; Taylor, *Mexican Labor*, 128.

10. Carlos B. Gil, "Life in Provincial Mexico" (Los Angeles: UCLA Latin American Center Publications, 1983), 68–69; Guillermo de la Peña, "Ideology and Practice in Southern Jalisco: Peasants, Rancheros, and Urban Entrepreneurs," in *Kinship, Ideology, and Practice in Latin America*, comp. by Raymond T. Smith (Chapel Hill: University of North Carolina Press, 1984), 204–34; Patricia de Leonardo and Jaime Espín, *Economía y sociedad en los altos de Jalisco* (México: Nueva Imagen, 1978), 66–73, 195–203; Roger Rouse, "Migración al suroeste de Michoacán durante el Porfiriato: El caso de Aguililla," in *Movimientos de Población en el occidente de México*, coord. by Thomas Calvo and Gustavo López (México and Zamora: CEMCA and Colegio de Michoacán, 1988).

11. Patricia Arias, "La industria en perspectiva," in *Guadalajara: La gran ciudad de la pequeña industria*, coord. by Patricia Arias (Zamora: Colegio de Michoacán, 1985), 82–83; idem, "Talleres, comerciantes e industriales: Una trilogía persistente," in ibid., 233–38; Guillermo Ramos Arizpe and Salvador Rueda Smithers, *Jiquilpan, 1895–1920* (Jiquilpan: Cardenas, 1984), 234–44; Jorge Durand, *Los obreros de Río Grande* (Zamora: Colegio de Michoacán, 1986), 61.

12. Redfield, Diary, 39–41.

13. Interview, Gerardo Necoechea with Justino and Caroline Cordero, South Chicago, November 13, 1986, and with Carmen Arias and Natalie Ruiz, South Deering (Chicago), November 24, 1986; Hughes, *Living Conditions*, 10, 22; Anita Edgar Jones, "Conditions Surrounding Mexicans in Chicago" (Master's thesis, University of Chicago, 1928), 22; Taylor, *Mexican Labor*, 75–76; Jones and Wilson, *The Mexican in Chicago*, 17.

14. Taylor, *Mexican Labor*, 95.

15. Kelly, *Training Industrial Workers*, 18–21.

16. Hughes, *Living Conditions*, 49–50; Taylor, *Mexican Labor*, 90–91.

17. Taylor, *Mexican Labor*, 80–81, 94; Redfield, Diary, 21.

18. Brody, *Steelworkers in America*, 38–40.

19. Paul S. Taylor, *A Spanish Community: Arandas in Jalisco, Mexico* (Berkeley: University of California Press, 1933); Hilda Iparraguirre, "Moroleón: Proceso de trabajo y comunidad rebocera, 1840–1920," in *Comunidad, cultura y vida social*, comp. by Seminario de Movimiento Obrero y Revolución Mexicana

(México: INAH, 1991), 55–69; César Moheno, *Las historias y los hombres de San Juan* (Zamora: Colegio de Michoacán, 1985), 76–80.

20. Brody, *Steelworkers in America*, 27–49; James R. Barret, "Unity and Fragmentation: Class, Race, and Ethnicity on Chicago's South Side, 1900–1922," *Journal of Social History* 18 (Autumn 1984): 40.

21. Carlos González Peña, *La vida tumultuosa* (México: Andrés Botas e Hija, n.d.), 219–20.

22. Sumner Slichter in Gordon et al., *Segmented Work, Divided Workers*, 148–49; Brody, *Steelworkers in America*, 80–111; Alfred D. Chandler, *The Visible Hand* (Cambridge, MA: Harvard University Press, 1977), 361–62.

23. José A. Uribe Salas, *La industria textil en Michoacán, 1840–1910* (Morelia: Universidad Michoacana, 1983), 155–63; Mario Camarena and Susana Fernández, "Los obreros artesanos en las fábricas textiles de San Angel, 1920–1930," in *Comunidad, cultura y la vida social*, 178–91; Luis González, *Pueblo en Vilo* (México: Colegio de México, 1979), 98–105.

24. Taylor, *Mexican Labor*, 80–92.

25. Quoted by Brody, *Steelworkers in America*, 109–10.

26. David Montgomery, *The Fall of the House of Labor* (New York: Cambridge University Press, 1987), 234–40; Kelly, *Training Industrial Workers*, 21; and Gordon et al., *Segmented Work, Divided Workers*, 170–76.

27. Bernstein, *The Lean Years*, 55–71.

28. Ibid., 54, 66–67; Gordon et al., *Segmented Work, Divided Workers*, 149–50.

29. Manuel Gamio, *Mexican Immigration to the United States* (New York: Dover, 1971), 30–31.

30. Interview, Necoechea with the Corderos, November 13, 1986; de Leonardo and Espín, *Economía y Sociedad*, 77, 104–5.

31. Taylor, *Mexican Labor*, 98.

32. Neil Betten and Raymond A. Mohl, "From Discrimination to Repatriation: Mexican Life in Gary, Indiana, during the Great Depression," *Pacific Historical Review* 42 (August 1973): 370–88; Louise Año Nuevo Kerr, "The Chicano Experience in Chicago: 1920–1970" (Ph.D. diss., University of Illinois, 1976), 72–76.

33. Manuel González Flores, *Una pareja de tantas* (México: Yolotepec, 1950), 160–61. González Flores published his book in 1950, and it is possible to date the events he narrates during the war years. See Efrain Huerta, "Libros y antilibros," *El Gallo Ilustrado* (México), November 23, 1980.

34. Brody, *Steelworkers in America*, 22–26; Montgomery, *The Fall*, 216–25; Chandler, *The Visible Hand*, 266–67; and Gordon et al., *Segmented Work, Divided Workers*, 132–40.

35. Quoted in Ramos Arizpe and Rueda Smithers, *Jiquilpan*, 244, 148–49, 235; Durand, *Los obreros*, 37–38; Uribe Salas, *La industria textil*, 175; Arias, "Talleres," 237, and "La industria en perspectiva," 99; de Leonardo and Espín, *Economía*, 71–73; Iparraguirre, "Moroleón," 71–73.

36. Taylor, *Mexican Labor*, 101–2.

37. Ibid., 101–4.

38. *México*, November 27, 1926.

39. Taylor, *Mexican Labor*, 94, 118, 122.

40. Eric Hobsbawm, "Costumbre, salarios e intensidad de trabajo en la industria del siglo XIX," in idem, *Trabajadores* (Barcelona: Crítica, 1979), 352–83.

41. Herbert G. Gutman, *Work, Culture, and Society in Industrializing America* (New York: Alfred A. Knopf, 1976), 3–78.

42. David Montgomery, *Workers' Control in America* (New York: Cambridge University Press, 1979), 91–112.

43. Ibid., 98.

44. *México*, November 27, 1926.

45. *México*, May 15, 1926; "Mexican Work," April 30, 1929, and "Report of the Mexican Work at the University of Chicago Settlement of the Year 1930–31," typescript, November 13, 1931, Mary McDowell Papers, Box 21, and "Mexican Work," 1926, April 30, 1929, and 1929–1933, Chicago Historical Society, Manuscripts Collection.

46. Montgomery, *Workers' Control*, 42.

47. Taylor, *Mexican Labor*, 117–18.

48. *México*, October 30, 1926; ibid., December 18, 1926.

49. González Flores, *Una pareja de tantas*, 171–74.

50. Francisco A. Rosales and Daniel T. Simon, "Chicano Steel Workers and Unionism in the Midwest, 1919–1945," *Aztlán* 6, no. 2 (1975): 269.

51. Taylor, *Mexican Labor*, 115–16.

CHAPTER TEN

Historical Perspectives on Transnational Mexican Workers in California

DEVRA WEBER

Superbarrio, Mexico's masked superhero of popular causes, turned up in Los Angeles, California. His appearance before the City Council demonstrated the continuities and changes between Mexican immigrant workers organizing in the 1920s and 1930s and those in the 1980s and 1990s.[1] The *Los Angeles Times* reported the colorful manifestation in February 1989 with an article entitled "Who Was That Masked Man? Ask the INS." Looking out from a photograph was the Mexican wrestler, or *luchador*, wearing red tights, a yellow cape, high laced shoes, a red mask winged in yellow, and the initials "SB" displayed prominently across his chest.

Superbarrrio (literally, super neighborhood) emerged out of the Asamblea de Barrios, a Mexico City-based movement of urban squatters that grew out of working-class areas devastated by the 1985 earthquake. The masked *luchador* appropriated the image of a popular working-class wrestler and framed it within the double cultural context of an anti-Superman fighting for justice. He became a popular political and cultural figure in Mexico, even running as a presidential candidate in the crowded field of opponents to the Partido Revolucionario Institucional (PRI) candidacy of Carlos Salinas de Gortari in 1988. Superbarrio ultimately threw his vote to Cuauhtémoc Cárdenas, the candidate of the major opposition Partido de la Revolución Democrática (PRD), while Cárdenas symbolically voted for Superbarrio.

The impact of Superbarrio's campaign will be analyzed by others. Instead, this essay examines how and why immigrant workers responded to his representation of them. Superbarrio came to Los Angeles to scrutinize the condition of his "brothers on this side of the border." He addressed the City Council on behalf of temporary Mexican workers, met with farm workers and homeless people, and had a heated exchange with the Mexican consul general. The Immigration and Naturalization Service (INS) then abruptly arrested him as an "illegal alien." The INS detention formed another symbolic link between Superbarrio and his compatriots on both sides of the border. Migrants in Los Angeles appropriated the image of Superbarrio in 1992 into a similar figure called Mopman, who stood as a symbol of the Latino-based militant union named Justice for Janitors. Superbarrio had come to represent not only the everyday Mexican of the urban working class but also a transnational working-class hero epitomizing the immigrant concept of terrain *sin fronteras*, or without borders.

Superbarrio personifies the popular culture of contemporary urban unrest. Yet his reception by Latino workers in the United States and their creation of Mopman are symptomatic of deeper and more continuous historical relations between Mexican immigrant workers, social groups, labor organizations, politics, conflict, and culture on both sides of the border. This essay places Mexican migration in historical perspective. Mexican transnationalism is not a new phenomenon, and its character has changed in the late twentieth century, but the concept proves to be a useful tool for understanding the history of Mexican workers both north and south of the border.

Transnationalism and Historical Perspective

Scholars use the term "transnational" to refer to the changes wrought among workers and communities in response to the globalization of the work force by multinational corporations. A forceful interpretation defines it: "Immigrants . . . develop and maintain multiple relations—familial, economic, social, organizational, religious and political—that span borders . . . the multiplicity of migrants' involvements in both the home and host societies is a central element of transnationalism. Transmigrants take actions, make decisions, and feel concerns within a field of social relations that links together their country of origin and their country or countries of settlement."[2]

Migrants develop multiple, overlapping, and changing identities in heterogenous communities in relation to class standing, class shifts, education, gender, and participation in social conflicts. During the 1910s and 1920s local Mexican identities increasingly shared space with a deeper sense of national identity created by, among other things, migration. New experiences formed the basis for new identities, produced either by different workplaces or by exposure to different cultures. The expansion of capitalist development and migration led to the decline of a sense of a "home" through increasing alienation.

A new kind of migrating population emerged, produced by the networks, activities, and patterns of life that encompassed both their host and home societies. This pattern reveals a convergence of two cultures in daily life. The idea of transnationalism focuses on the social connections among immigrants and their relation to the increasing mobility of both labor and capital. The perception challenges the previous historiography of immigration that "evokes images of permanent rupture, of the uprooted, the abandonment of old patterns and the painful learning of a new language and culture."[3]

Transnationalism is not completely new. Barry Goldberg pointed out that, as early as 1916, Randolph Bourne in the *Atlantic Monthly* raised some of the implications presented by immigrants.[4] Nevertheless U.S. immigration mythology precluded much investigation of the concept of transnationalism. Historians for years conceptualized immigration as a process of assimilating primarily white immigrants into a pluralistic society and homogenous culture. Oscar Handlin wrote of the "uprooted" whose break with their past facilitated the effort to become Americans. In the 1960s historians began to back away from this teleological model of pluralism and Americanization and to reconceptualize the immigrant past. Scholars tracked lives in case studies and discovered that the process of immigration was by no means homogenous, complete, or irreversible. While distance and lack of communication cut off some immigrants from their native countries, many others maintained meaningful familial, social, and economic contacts with their hometown. Italian immigrants in Buffalo, New York, in the early nineteenth century, for example, returned home for civil celebrations and family visits. Indeed, the local Italian press advertised $30 tickets for Christmas visits to the homeland.[5]

The new studies of working-class life helped to shift the perception of uprooted immigrants as blank slates toward an understanding of their preservation of cultural, social, and political practices. The discussion of transnationalism in the 1990s came from a broader questioning of the nature of American society and culture.[6] This essay questions more than alleged American plurality by examining society and culture, but it expands on its history. The concept of transnationalism is often presented ahistorically. Some scholars argue that the post-World War II period of late capitalism marks a fundamental break with earlier capitalist development. Further, they argue that "transnationalism" is a new phenomenon. Other historians, however, demonstrate that the postwar period witnessed the intensification, not the creation, of transnationalism.[7] The post-World War II globalization of labor brought increased labor migration and the development of transnational communities. Employing the concept of transnationalism recontextualizes international workers, their communities, politics, and organizations outside the boundaries of the nation-state and helps to capture a fuller picture of earlier immigrants.

Several developments distinguish the 1980s and 1990s. The first is the revolution in technology and communication—advances in airplanes, telephones, televisions, faxes, video recorders, and video tapes facilitate frequent visits home and easier contacts. Another is the great number of transnational immigrants. For individuals, this transnational stage of immigration may be similar to earlier periods in which the first generation maintained contacts with home communities that faded for the second generation. Transnationalism may well remain a phenomenon of only the first generation. Yet, with a continuing influx of migrants, there will be a perpetual first generation bringing their experiences with them. What may distinguish this current period is the ongoing presence of transnational immigrants in societies.

Prior analyses of Mexican immigrants clearly show how historiographical approaches have affected the understanding of this migration. Focusing on workers within boundaries of nation-states minimized the enduring and complex relationship between Mexican migrants, culture, worker organizing, and labor conflicts on both sides of the border. The transnational history of Mexican workers has often been conflated, eluded, or ignored. Eurocentric perspectives on migration, ideology, and labor organization led historians to disregard Mexican workers and the social and labor organizations that they formed.

Diffusionists stress the preeminent importance of the United States on the Mexican immigrant experience and argue that American ideologies and organizations proved pivotal to later social change in Mexico. Yet, as Emilio Zamora points out, the diffusionist perspective has several problems. Among them, first, it assumes that Mexicans who crossed the border were peasants who practiced "traditional" forms of "premodern" or "preindustrial" organization. Second, it ignores the long-term social interactions of generations of migrant workers, the heterogenous situations that they encountered in both the United States and Mexico, and the political and organizational knowledge that workers brought with them. As a result, historians often overlooked Mexican workers as instigators of social change and ignored their continuing interaction with community, political, and social life in Mexico.

Several unique aspects to transnational Mexican migration are rooted in the border shared by Mexico and the United States.[8] The border region is transnational: it possesses economic links, social ties, and political interests that ignore the boundary. In terms of lived experience and identity, people developed a border culture, established towns divided down the middle by the border, and have family members and friends on each side of this imaginary line. The border area is a stepping stone for people from other regions of Mexico who have migrated to find work. In the early twentieth century they toiled on the railroads, in agriculture, and in mines. In the 1990s they work in *maquiladoras*, in agricultural areas, and as day laborers and street vendors in border towns. The border experience is part of the transnationalism of many Mexican migrants.

Because of proximity, these migrants often relate to what social scientists call "daughter communities" in several areas. Cotton workers, for example, from the small town of San Francisco Angumacutiro in Michoacán, migrated to California to Anaheim and the San Fernando Valley, then to Corcoran. Even in the 1920s, as revolutionary fighting still ravaged Mexico and despite slow communication and transportation, strong-enough ties existed so that marriages, deaths, and births of Angumacutiro migrants in San Fernando and Anaheim were recorded in the parish register of their hometown in Mexico.[9]

Political parallels to earlier periods exist as well. Since the 1980s the PRI-dominated government has recognized the political potential of Chicanos and Mexicans in the United States and has increased its involvement with their communities. Mexican opposition parties, such as the PRD and PAN (Partido Nacional Autónoma), raise money and recruit members in California. Likewise, from 1910 to 1930 the United States, and particularly California, was a center of Mexican political activity. The Mexican consuls, linked to the government-backed labor union, the Confederación Regional de Obreros Mexicanos (CROM), organized workers in the United States. Mexican political groups, especially revolutionaries, actively raised money north of the border. The anarcho-syndicalists of the Partido Liberal Mexicano (PLM) moved the party's base to Los Angeles. Supporters of both President Porfirio Díaz and rebel Francisco Madero sought backing north of the border. Later, the protofascist Sinarquistas raised money and stored guns in Los Angeles to be used in impending conflicts in Mexico.

Historically, the transnational experience in work, social organizations, and political movements reflected the migrants' social networks. These interconnections include families, friends, compatriots, and new members acquired in the United States. They provide the social glue of migrant communities and motivate people to move to particular areas. Workers in the California cotton fields of the 1920s and 1930s demonstrated this pattern with family and social networks that helped them respond to challenges in the workplace in both the United States and Mexico.

Migration and Social Networks during the 1920s and 1930s

The bounty of California's agriculture harvested by its workers made the cotton industry the major income producer in the state by 1933. Cotton was the most rapidly expanding sector of California's agricultural economy because of growing demand, technological advances, and capitalization. Cotton production in the state depended upon Mexican workers. Large-scale financial and business operators dominated production, processing, and marketing. They formed associations that worked with agricultural and nonagricultural businesses, banks, and corporations. Although some cotton farmers owned small tracts, the majority in California owned over three thousand acres, and they hired the majority of the farm workers. On these large estates, they lived in private labor camps—rural company towns in which workers lived in company housing, bought from and became indebted to company stores, and sent their children to company schools. A racial hierarchy prevailed in the camps and fields. Anglo owners, managers, and foremen ran the ranches, while Mexican contractors recruited Mexican workers, supervised them in the fields, and acted as intermediaries between workers and employers.

Cotton workers were mostly immigrants. Their experiences emphasized the continuity of Mexican migration. Most workers who picked cotton in the 1920s and 1930s came from Mexico's central plateau made up of Michoacán, Jalisco, Aguascalientes, Zacatecas, and Guanajuato and from the western states of Sinaloa, Sonora, Chihuahua, Coahuila, Durango, Nuevo León, and Baja California. Many came by way of Texas and created new working-class Mexican communities in Southern California, especially around Los Angeles and in the Imperial Valley adjacent to the border.

Mexicans migrated in response to the transformation of their economy that began in the late 1870s. Foreign investment in their country accelerated economic growth and the displacement of workers. Large haciendas producing for the expanding market engulfed small independent villages and decimated the independent peasantry. By 1910, 96 percent of all Mexican families owned no land. Cheap manufactured goods transported by the expanding railroad network displaced thousands of local small producers. Dispossessed peasants found jobs as day laborers, hired hands, and sharecroppers. Displaced workers and artisans found work in the expanding industries. By 1910 almost 700,000 worked in the mines, on the railroads, and in textiles, but others scraped by as beggars, shoeshine boys, or prostitutes in the growing urban centers. Women joined the wage labor force and soon represented one-third of the workers in the burgeoning textile industry.[10]

Displaced from their land, many people migrated in search of work. The expansion of roads and railroads penetrated previously isolated areas and widened the scope of migration. By the early 1900s people left central Mexico for the expanding economic regions in the north of the country and in the southwestern United States. They made their way northward across the border, working on the railroads, in mines, or in agriculture. They helped build the new railroads in the South and Midwest, worked in the mines of

New Mexico, Arizona, Colorado, and even West Virginia, and picked crops across Texas, Colorado, Arizona, and California. They also were hired in the cities as domestics and gardeners.

These experiences in both Mexico and the United States shaped the lives of cotton workers. Due to economic need, most of them held a variety of jobs. Although this variety created instability, their widespread job experiences taught them a wide range of skills despite their designation as "unskilled" labor. The migrant workers learned to endure and adapt to changing working and living conditions. In the rural areas, Mexicans became part of a mobile labor force of sharecroppers and day laborers. The factory, mine, and railroad workers experienced the long hours and dangerous conditions common to the early phases of industrialization. Along the way they accumulated knowledge of different geographic areas, factories, and people. Some cotton workers had previously taken part in spontaneous conflicts with supervisors and employers, walkouts, strikes, labor organizing, and other forms of resistance. Even more had witnessed these clashes. The high turnover in jobs and migration, while disrupting, facilitated the transmission of ideas and organization among Mexican workers in the United States and Mexico.

Examples best demonstrate the experiences of these cotton workers. Braulio López worked on the railroads in both nations, in the mines of Arizona and New Mexico, in a cement plant, on road construction, and picked crops. Elias Garza, a displaced sharecropper from Michoacán, first toiled in a Mexican sugar mill, then worked on Kansas railroads, at a packing plant, a stone quarry, and finally at a railroad station before he began to pick cotton. Gilbert Hernández worked on the Mexican railroads, in the mines of Cananea, and as a day laborer in California. A part Purépecha Indian from San Francisco Angumacutiro, José Bañales, left the Michoacán hacienda where he had labored as a sharecropper and day laborer to work on the railroads in Kansas and to cultivate plants in an Anaheim nursery before he, too, began to pick cotton.[11] Roberto Castro worked on the railroads in Louisiana, Oklahoma, and Texas. Juan Magaña, a laborer from a Guanajuato hacienda, worked on Mexican railroads and the Southern Pacific Railroad. Women also experienced the transition from rural work to a multiplicity of jobs. Juana Padilla, who went to Mexico City when she was fourteen, worked in several factories making shoes, postcards, cigars, bedspreads, and *rebozos*, or shawls.[12]

Mexicans relied on family members and other social ties for stability. In Mexico, families served as the basic social and economic units of society. Not only blood relative ties but also fictive kin through the system of compadrazgo inherited through hundreds of years of mutual assistance formed interlocking networks. These family and social bonds mediated between the individual and society, enabling Mexicans to adapt and respond to the world and the changing demands of wage labor and migration. Rooted in home communities, these networks became the basis for migration and for new settlements in California. Workers migrated to where they had supportive family or friends, creating working-class *barrios* tied together by people from the same home communities in Mexico. They partially re-created their familiar social relations in California. Mexicans augmented these older relationships with new ones that they forged in the north. Work crews migrated from these communities and maintained the social relations of the *barrios* in the cotton camps of the San Joaquin Valley.

The hardships imposed by displacement strained these networks. As a result the migrants adopted mutualism. As Emilio Zamora explains, "Mutualism incorporated . . . fraternalism, reciprocity, and altruism into a moral prescription for human behavior, a cultural basis for moralistic and nationalistic political action that was intended to set things right."[13] A social worker in Los Angeles reported the community spirit among Mexicans living in the Belvedere: "As long as there is a little food in the Mexican district they know that it will be shared by all as far as it will go."[14] They institutionalized this ethos in *mutualista* community groups, or mutual aid societies. Mutualism served as the basis for organized responses by the community and within the work force.

Racism, segregation, working-class status, and the frequent mobility of Mexican men and women narrowed their contacts with Anglo Americans, reaffirming the need to rely on each other. As *barrios* grew, they became less, rather than more, attached to Anglo-American institutions. The growth of the immigrant population, rather than leading toward assimilation, helped to create a stronger identification as working-class Mexicans. In the 1920s and 1930s they identified themselves as *mexicanos*. Eighty-four percent of Mexicans living in Los Angeles had been born in Mexico, and most were antipathetic to becoming U.S. citizens. In 1910, when almost 46 percent of other immigrant groups became naturalized citizens, only 3 percent of Mexican immigrants wanted to be "Americans." By 1920 the number had risen to a still small 5.5 percent.[15]

The transnational aspects of these Mexican workers' proximity to the border, the constant influx of new immigrants, the regular contact with home villages, and the ease of returning home contributed to an enduring sense of Mexicanness even after long periods of residence in the United States. This sense, however, did not preclude deep divisions and bitter conflicts among Mexicans who differentiated among themselves on the basis of ethnicity, region, class, gender, and their length of residence in the United States. For the most part, however, Mexicans operated within a community bound together by common identities and notions of cooperation, sharing, and mutuality. Their attitudes framed the day-to-day lives of the cotton workers.

Growers found Mexican working-class networks essential to recruiting and supervising workers on the camps and ranches. Workers put together labor crews from among family and friends. To obtain crews, contractors and growers relied on these networks, which directly replicated the broader communities from which they came. For example, as noted ealier, Mexicans from around San Francisco Angumacutiro, Michoacán, migrated to Anaheim and San Fernando, California. When they began to work in the cotton fields, their families and friends formed labor crews, signed on with contractors whom they knew from Mexico, and migrated to ranches in an area called Corcoran. As a result, workers migrated in clusters and developed multilayered relationships and obligations stretching back to their home communities in California and Mexico. Those ties helped to define relations among them, and between workers and labor contractors.

The complexity of these relations emerged in the shifting tensions between the two groups. Contractors who had been village leaders or hacienda *mayordomos* in Mexico frequently hired workers who had labored for them back home. This practice, in effect, helped to transfer the hierarchical relationships of haciendas to labor camps in the San Joaquin Valley. One man recalled that contractors would "rule their people just like living on a hacienda."[16] Contractors who had been officers in a revolutionary army supervised their former soldiers and expected military discipline in the fields, even marching workers into the fields in formation. Yet, because a contractor's job depended on obtaining experienced workers and minimizing dissatisfaction with wages and conditions, his relationship with them was mediated by a sense of mutual obligation and expectation that had its genesis in Mexico. Mutuality tended to subordinate individual desires to the needs of the group. Within work crews, the commitments to family, *compadres*, and friends instilled discipline. This sense of mutual reliance also contributed to transforming work crews and labor and social groups into incipient labor organizations and laid the basis for collective action.

Transnational Influences on Labor and Strikes

Mexicans working in the cotton fields responded to the conditions of work based on their past experiences as well as on the immediate situations that they faced. Some cotton workers had been influenced by earlier movements in Mexico. In the areas that had the heaviest out-migration to the United States, Mexicans had engaged in sporadic peasant rebellions against land expropriations by modernizing hacendados. Workers in the industrial sector had begun to form labor organizations in the 1860s, especially in the mining areas and textile mills. By 1906 over 80,000 workers participated in some form of labor organization. Ideologically, these groups were diverse—an amalgam of anarchism, mutualism, and cooperativism. Under increasing repression and economic downturns, Mexican workers organized strikes in the 1890s and 1900s. By the turn of the century, as the work force expanded, inflation deepened and repression increased while the strikes became larger and more militant. One strike in particular came to symbolize worker unrest in the prerevolutionary period. In 1906, Mexican workers struck against the Cananea Consolidated Copper Company, a subsidiary of U.S.-owned Anaconda. Two thousand miners under the leadership of the anarcho-syndicalist PLM walked off their jobs demanding better pay and working conditions and protesting racist practices. This strike and other labor militancy helped lead to the Mexican Revolution.

Durango, Mexico's Laguna cotton-growing district, is an example of an early interrelation between transnational capital and worker and social unrest. The development of the Laguna paralleled that of the San Joaquin Valley in terms of international investment by cotton interests. The American-based Anderson-Clayton Company, the major cotton processor in California, invested heavily in the Laguna's cotton development at the same time that it began to invest in the San Joaquin Valley. Cotton production in both the Laguna and the San Joaquin Valley depended on migrant Mexican labor.

During the late nineteenth century, increased investment transformed the Laguna into a major agricultural and industrial zone. Small landowners and migrant laborers became the backbone for radical peasant challenges to changes that disadvantaged them. The forms of protest ranged from banditry to organized revolt to support for the PLM. Migrants who had been in the United States had a political impact on social movements in the Laguna area. By 1908 officials reported that an armed group called the Mexican Cotton Pickers was planning an attack on Coahuila from its stronghold on the Texas border. By 1918 craftspeople, agricultural laborers, and other workers had organized lodges of the Industrial Workers of the World (IWW), which was an ally of the PLM in the region.

The Laguna district provided a vibrant example of the cross-pollination of social conflicts carried by transnational migrant workers.[17] Mexicans who had been in the United States influenced events in the Laguna. Cotton workers who migrated from the Laguna to the San Joaquin Valley fields carried the knowledge of this experience with them to California. These connections existed in many other areas as well. For example, in 1921 the importation of 2,200 unemployed miners from the Cananea mines to pick cotton in Baja California was significant enough to prompt the American consulate in Mexicali to warn that their arrival would mean trouble: "The laborers of Sonora in general, and the mining element of Cananea in particular, are strictly bolshevistic in their tendencies."[18]

The Mexican Revolution stood as a formative experience for cotton pickers of the 1920s and 1930s. Most had lived through, and some had actively taken part in, the fighting. People remembered the revolution with ambivalence. Their haunting personal memories of death, starvation, and hardship coexisted with a sense of connection to the revolution and the hopes that it held out for social change and increasing freedom from repression and foreign domination. Belen Flores, for example, remembered bodies stacked in heaps along the streets following the bloody battle of Torreón in Coahuila and soldiers who threatened to slice off the soles of the feet of anyone who hid grain from the incoming troops. Other workers, women as well as men, told perhaps apocryphal stories of their relatives' fighting with Francisco "Pancho" Villa, Emiliano Zapata, or Venustiano Carranza. Mexicans who had been in the revolution later applied tactics and strategies that they had learned there as a model of mobilization for the California cotton strike of 1933.

Mexicans gained experience in labor organizing in the mines, agricultural fields, and urban industries in the United States. Ignored by the craft-oriented and nativist American Federation of Labor (AFL), Mexicans had organized ethnic unions or allied with the more inclusive IWW or, later, affiliated themselves with the Communist Party USA (CPUSA). Since the turn of the century, Mexican workers in California agriculture had been organizing ad hoc spontaneous groups that usually disappeared at the end of the season. But, by the mid-1920s, they began to establish more permanent agricultural workers' organizations. In 1927 the Federation of Mexican Societies, composed of mutual aid societies and unions in southern California, formed the Confederación de Uniones Obreros Mexicanos (CUOM). By 1928, the CUOM claimed 3,000 members in twenty-two locals in Southern California and helped spur the formation of the first permanent Mexican agricultural unions. Although it faltered after a few years, the organization was revived in 1933 as the Confederación de Uniones de Campesinos y Obreros Mexicanos (CUCOM) and became one of the major agricultural unions in the state.

The CUCOM union provides one example of binational organizing. The CROM, founded in 1918, had been anarcho-syndicalist but quickly became an organization which, despite lip service to radical ideas, worked closely with the Mexican government. In the 1920s the CROM was making a concerted effort to organize Mexican workers in the United States. It funded the CUCOM, which was allied with the CROM from the beginning. Despite this alliance the CUCOM in the United States did not follow blindly. Political tensions similar to those rending the labor movement within Mexico itself affected organizations in California. In the early 1930s left-wing unionists opposed to consul domination gained increasing control of the union, which led to a split in 1935: the leftist part of the union became a leading political force in agricultural California. The CUCOM was crucial in forming, and then merged with, the United Cannery, Agricultural, Packing, and Allied Workers of America (UCAPAWA), which was affiliated with the Congress of Industrial Organizations (CIO).

Some Mexican workers had been involved in social conflicts which had exposed them to diverse organizations and ideologies that reflected the heterogenous nature of the Mexican working class on both sides of the border. One of the most important influences was the PLM, formed by Ricardo Flores Magón and his advisers. Flores Magón fled to the United States in 1904 and created the organization in Los Angeles. Originally a radical liberal party, the PLM developed into an anarcho-syndicalist organization that advocated worker control over production and the end of U.S. capitalist domination on both sides of the border. Based on common ideology and goals, the PLM formed a close alliance with the IWW. Unlike the CROM or the AFL, the party stressed an international community of workers. Organizers of this impressive alliance worked in both Mexico and the United States. Particularly active in the border areas such as the Sonora mining triangle, Cananea, and the Laguna, they also penetrated industrial zones such as Veracruz and Mexico City. In the United States they organized workers in the mines, agricultural fields, and urban areas of the Southwest. During the Mexican Revolution they joined the revolutionaries' ill-fated attempt to recapture Baja California.[19]

Mexican workers in the southwestern United States were receptive to the PLM. By 1914 it had an estimated 6,000 members, and its newspaper in Los Angeles, *Regeneración*, reportedly was read by over 10,500 people, making it the most widely read Mexican newspaper in the city. Mexicans also joined the IWW, and most of the city's 400 members were Mexicans. Although the PLM declined in size and militancy in the 1920s, it influenced younger Mexican radicals well into the 1930s. Mexican members of the Young Communist League (YCL) received political literature from veterans of the PLM. The left wing of the CUCOM remained anarchist, and its leader, Guillermo Velarde, exemplified the mixture of the various workers' groups. Velarde's father, Fernando, had been a founding member of the IWW and had worked with the Flores Magón brothers, while the younger Velarde remained a member of the IWW.

By the 1920s some Mexicans in the United States turned to the growing Communist party. An interactive relationship arose between Mexican Communists in the United States—many of whom had been born in and remained citizens of Mexico—and the Partido Comunista Mexicano (PCM). Peasants and rural workers in the PCM maintained sporadic and informal contacts with compatriots in the United States, especially along the border. Its newspaper, *El Machete*, circulated widely in the United States, especially in Los Angeles, yet few formal ties existed. The financially strapped PCM, facing increasing repression in Mexico, lacked the resources to maintain broad contacts with Mexicans in the United States and focused more on domestic workers than on migrants who had gone north. Furthermore, by the 1930s, Comintern politics had badly strained relations between the PCM and the CPUSA. The Comintern placed the PCM under the organizations subordinate to the CPUSA in a stunning lack of recognition of the long-standing tensions between Mexico and the United States. PCM leaders rejected taking orders from the CPUSA's general secretary, Earl Browder. This conflict undermined a continuation of the transnational relations that had existed between the IWW and the PLM.

The relative absence of the PCM in the United States forced Mexican Communists in the north to look to the CPUSA for help. Mexicans provided crucial help to the organizing drives by CP-affiliated organizations among their *compadres* in California in the 1930s and later. The CP included Mexican organizations on several levels. Party cells were formed in at least seven towns in Southern California, and younger Mexicans joined the YCL. The numbers were small: for example, by 1933 only two dozen Mexicans belonged to the YCL in Tulare; by 1934 fifteen migrant workers had joined the Mexican CP cell in Brawley. Agricultural workers who followed the harvest helped to organize and lead strikes and served as conduits between Mexican workers and CP organizers. How many Communists worked in the cotton fields is unknown, but despite their small numbers, they, like their Anglo counterparts, played a disproportionate role in labor organizing.[20]

If Mexican leftists provided some leaders, then other leaders and the workers who made up the strike organizers came from the more general force of cotton workers. Many of these individuals had experienced labor conflicts on both sides of the border, and some had fought in the Mexican Revolution. Cotton workers Pedro Subía, Braulio López, Luis Lima, and Narciso Vidaurri, for example, had labored in the triangle towns of Clifton-Morenci, Bisbee, and Cananea where the IWW and PLM had organized miners. Luis Lima had been in agricultural strikes in Mexico, and his uncle was among the Mexicans killed during the 1906 strike in Cananea. Carlos Torres, a cotton worker, took part in the 1919 strike in San Bernardino's orange groves.

Many other Mexicans, of course, had not been involved in labor conflicts and had little or no organizational experience. According to organizer Leroy Parra, "They didn't even know they could organize. It was something new to them and it was something new to a lot of us." Yet, even so, he argued that "the Mexican people are revolutionary. . . . They had (the revolution) behind them that helped them to see the exploitation here in this country."[21] The hard-fought lessons of the Mexican Revolution were applicable in the United States and gave an impetus to labor strikes. As Guillermo Martínez explained, "The experience of pain was carried to various communities over here . . . (and) the know how from organizing came, perhaps, through organizing in the army." Even if only a minority of them actually joined the labor organizations, Mexicans were receptive to organizers who wanted to help the working people.[22]

The cross-pollination of capitalist development, worker migration and organization, Mexican social networks, and workers' mutual aid became apparent in a series of agricultural strikes in the 1930s. When the Great Depression hit in 1929, growers slashed wages. Farm workers responded with a wave of thirty-seven strikes involving 50,000 workers that affected 65 percent of California's crops. The unrest ended in September 1933 when over 18,000 cotton pickers associated with the Cannery and Agricultural Workers Industrial Union (CAWIU) went on strike. They brought work to a stop over a one-hundred-square-mile, four-county area of the San Joaquin Valley. Mexicans comprised 75 to 90 percent of the strikers.

Cotton workers struck to raise picking wages from sixty cents to one dollar for every one hundred pounds of cotton. Such a raise would have increased their average income to two dollars per day. Contractor and strike supporter Roberto Castro explained that "we only wanted them to pay us more. For this the people organized together, without knowing if there was a union or there wasn't. . . . The people got together because they wanted to get more wages, a little more, to be able to give something to eat to their kids . . . if you didn't work you didn't eat."[23]

The strikers walked out of the fields and returned to the labor camps. The growers then began to evict them, and displaced workers established strikers' camps on nearby empty land. Thirty-five hundred strikers formed the largest camp near the town of Corcoran. The camps served as organizational centers and buttressed the sense of community among strikers. Organizers developed mobile mass picketing to cover the vast tracts of cotton fields. Caravans of cars full of men, women, and children went out from the camps to intercept possible strikebreakers on the roads and at ranches where cotton picking was reported.[24] The strike lasted for twenty-seven days. Armed confrontations broke out, and growers ambushed and killed three Mexicans. The violent intensity of the strike ultimately forced the California, Mexican, and U.S. governments to intervene. Mediators settled the strike, and the workers won a raise from sixty to seventy-five cents for every one hundred pounds of cotton picked.

Although historians have focused primarily on the formal labor organizations involved, oral interviews with both leaders and participants reveal the complexity of worker response as well as the importance to this strike of Mexican social networks, past experience, and mutual assistance. Mexican workers used their social networks to precipitate and maintain the strike. Their sense of mutualism undergirded their solidarity, and their past experience in labor and social conflicts supplied tactics and strategies that they then put to use in the cotton fields. Together, these elements from the Mexican experience proved crucial to the spread of the strikes that disrupted California harvests in the 1930s.

Most historical accounts ignore the role played by the workers and have favored the view that the CAWIU was the catalyst for the strike, yet the union did not have the resources to carry out a widespread walkout. It lacked money, had only six organizers to cover the entire valley, and faced a one hundred-mile-long cotton belt. While the San Jose-based union laid out a broad strategy, tactics for the day-to-day organizing took shape in the harsh realities of the San Joaquin Valley. The union played a vital role as an umbrella organization that covered the disparate parts of the strike community. But the major impetus for the strike, its connecting link, was the workers. As CAWIU organizer Pat Chambers remarked, "Although the directives in some superficial way could come from the outside, the actual organization had to come from the workers themselves."[25]

The strike's growth and success depended on the workers' networks as much as on the small but ambitious union. Workers used their personal contacts across the valley to spread and coordinate the strike. Those leaving one strike area brought news with them. The Mexicans transformed bars and pool halls in towns along the migrant route and near the labor camps into meeting halls and information centers. Families, work crews, and friends provided mutual aid: solace, shelter, and food. In the camps, people who were part of the same labor crews settled together into sections based on teams whose members shared a common history. These crew-based camp sections in turn were the basis for an ad hoc governmental structure in which representatives from labor crews spoke for their group within the camp and assigned work to its members. The participation of such crews strengthened local leadership. Such broad-based participation transcended the CAWIU directives to develop rank-and-file leadership and reflected the internal organization of the workers. The leaders and social networks provided an organizational framework that interfaced with the union organizers to facilitate strategy and tactics appropriate to the Mexican work force.

From the perspective of the work force, women emerged as a vibrant and crucial part of the strike, camps, and picket lines. Their participation in the cotton strike had a precedent in the aggressive role that they had played in community concerns in Mexico. There, women had rioted for fair corn prices in the colonial period and had taken part in the anarchist movement of the nineteenth century. Within the life span of most of those in the camps, women had initiated the famous workers' uprising at Rio Blanco, Veracruz, in 1907; carried out strikes in textile mills between the 1870s and 1930s; and had endured or participated in the Mexican Revolution of 1910–1920.

Women went on strike out of concern for their families, the erosion of wages, and declining conditions in the workplaces and labor camps that directly affected their ability to feed and care for their children. Women ran the camp kitchens, distributed food and clothes, and looked after children. In many respects, they continued their usual work of mutual assistance found in nonstrike times. Yet, from the beginning of the strike, older women with long hair and *rebozos*, along with younger women who had adopted the bobbed hair, makeup, and short skirts of flappers, rode with girls barely in their teens to the picket lines.

In Corcoran, women organized and led verbal and physical confrontations with strikebreakers. In at least one instance, exhortations turned to threats and violence. Some women armed with lead pipes and knives, evidently in anticipation of using more persuasive methods than verbal appeals, attacked strikebreakers in a bloody face-off. This pattern recurred in other strikes, demonstrating that the militancy emerged from the women themselves and not from a strike committee's directive.

Strike leaders emerged from the recognized chains of authority within the community of Mexican workers. Literate and experienced in leadership, some were bilingual and some were labor contractors or bosses. Certain leaders had been officers in the Mexican army or in a revolutionary faction. Others were from the small merchant class of barbers, shopkeepers, and cantina owners. Veterans from earlier strikes in Southern California formed the core of this leadership, including Mexican Communists and anarchists who had organized in the earlier strikes of 1928, 1930, and 1933. They acted as conduits between CAWIU organizers and the work force. They did not meet with growers but, rather, organized the camps, planned strategy, directed picketing, and dealt with the day-to-day issues of survival.

Common interests and a sense of mutual aid, reinforced in families and work crews, strengthened the workers' sense of solidarity and resolve during the strike. The strikers utilized their shared experience of the Mexican Revolution as a myth and a model of collective struggle within the context of the strike. Members of the strikers' camps honored the images and stories of the revolution by naming their dusty streets after revolutionary heroes and towns. Men who had been officers organized sentries and patrols composed of veterans. The sentries, armed with crowbars and sometimes guns, protected the camps from armed men hired by the growers to dislodge them.

As the conflict wore on, these interlocking labor crews, families, and social networks stuck together for a prolonged struggle. There were, of course, exceptions—the strikebreakers. But strikers used the strength of these ties and loyalties to appeal to strikebreakers to join the protest. The same social pressure that had once helped enforce discipline in the fields was used to bring together the striking workers and to pressure strikebreakers to leave the fields. Picketing strikers accused strikebreakers as workers, as fellow Mexicans, and as members of the same community of being traitors. Female strikers, for example, at first appealed to strikebreakers as "poor people" and *mexicanos* but then cursed those who remained in the fields and compared them to traitors during the revolution.

The mobility of farm workers facilitated the spread of walkouts to other parts of the state. As the strikes earlier in 1933 had given an impetus to the cotton strike, so did the cotton strikes provide momentum that carried over into the strikes of 1934. As strike organizers in Corcoran promised, the strike moved with the workers back to the Imperial Valley with the January 1934 shutdown by 5,000 workers and then to Arizona and the November 1934 strike by 1,500 cotton pickers. Lacking a strong union base, workers and their networks served as the basis for strike organization.

While their Mexican experience influenced events in the cotton fields, the workers' experiences in the United States also affected political life in Mexico. Migrants returning to Mexico led strikes there. A report in 1918 stated that "most of all the labor trouble in the mining district of Sonora is due . . . to the activities of IWW Mexicans. . . . A number of them are American citizens who have left the United States. . . . They are not as good workmen as the average Mexican and are continually causing trouble. The three murders committed at the different mines during the past six weeks were the work of English-speaking or Americanized Mexicans."[26] In 1919 a consular representative reported to the State Department that "Bolshevism grows all through Mexico. . . . According to Mexican newspapers, *many of the agitators are Americans or Mexicans who have been working in the United States.*"[27]

Primo Tapia, a part Purépecha Indian from Michoacán, represents one of the best examples of transnational influences in labor organizing. He had worked in mines, railroads, construction, and agriculture in the southwestern United States from 1907 to 1919 and joined Ricardo and Enrique Flores Magón in the PLM. He also joined the IWW and by 1916 began organizing Mexican workers. He formed what he called a "revolutionary core" out of family members (all but one Purépecha) from Michoacán. In 1920 he went back to Mexico and organized peasants, again drawing on family and community ties. Tapia established an association of 15,000 peasants by 1925 that became one of the two important rural components of the Communist Party in Mexico.[28]

The most apparent effects of transnational migration on labor organization in the 1920s and 1930s appeared in the economic zones that straddled the U.S.-Mexican border. Examples included the Arizona-Sonora mining triangle, a contiguous area where workers and their organizations moved back and forth across the boundary. For California cotton workers, clear and direct links existed between the Laguna district, the Cananea mining areas, and the California fields. The apparently regional nature of these interrelations expands when we look at the workers who usually came from other parts of Mexico and traveled not as individuals but in groups. They often kept in contact with their hometowns, although the revolution had temporarily disrupted that practice. They worked together in labor crews, lived near each other in camps, and adhered to a sense of mutuality based in older personal and familial relations that stretched back to their practices in Mexico. New relations formed and provided a transnationalism that extended beyond the border region of the time.

Transnational Migration in the 1990s

Mexican migration, settlement, and transnational organization in the 1990s differ from the 1930s. Migration today occurs within the larger economic pattern of globalization, the increased mobility of capital, rising international competition, privatization, deregulation, and the search by businesses for lower costs and higher profits. Since the 1980s, Mexicans have migrated in increasing numbers to the United States. The devaluation of the peso and the economic crisis in the 1980s stimulated this movement. The neoliberal economic policies of the Mexican government under President Salinas de Gortari ended redistribution of land to peasants and encouraged foreign investment and privatization. Moreover, NAFTA officially sanctioned deregulation of international business investment in Mexico.

International competition has contributed to the restructuring of the U.S. economy from one based on heavy industry to one based on technology and services. The demand for cheap labor in these sectors has increased dependence on Mexican immigrant labor, while the economic crisis created by the restructuring has led to a backlash against immigrants. The economic changes, the increasing movement of capital, and the free-trade agreement have also spurred cross-border union organizing. NAFTA provided the rationale, the context, and the basis for international attention for the Chiapas rebellion in January 1994. Technology has altered the face of migration and the nature of community and settlement. The speedier transportation provided by airplanes, trains, and buses facilitates migration between hometowns in Mexico and communities in the United States. Today, migrants frequently return to Mexico to take part in festivals and to visit. Workers phone and sometimes fax their family and friends back home. Many events and celebrations are recorded by video to be savored and sent to the other side for family and friends to share.

Within this changing picture, however, continuities remain. Although economic upheavals of international capital have helped to disrupt family and social networks, they have simultaneously increased individuals' dependency on social groups for support. Mexican migrants still rely heavily on social and family networks that they transplant to the United States. People still tend to migrate with friends and family members, settle in areas where they know someone and have a support system, and find jobs through the same contacts. Their sense of mutualism based on social networks still provides much of the basis for labor organization.

The lives of indigenous workers from the Mexican state of Oaxaca demonstrate these patterns. One Mixtec Indian migrant from Oaxaca asserted, "It is a tradition among us. If a group of *paisanos* arrives to do farm work, they help each other find food and shelter, even if there is little to go around. We are mutualists." Oaxacan migration to the United States began during the 1940s Bracero Program and surged in the 1980s following the economic crisis in Mexico. As of 1994 an estimated 70,000 Oaxacans lived in Los Angeles alone. Familiar with the concept of *el tequio*, or communal work, Oaxacans continue the tradition. On one level, migrants have formed organizations and donate money to improve conditions in their hometowns through potable water, better schools, electricity, and the refurbishing of the local church. Support for the hometown draws on communal labor, which the community expects each member to perform.[29] The size of these groups differs, depending on the size of the population and the degree of attachment to their home community, but these organizations work in both California and Oaxaca.

Migration has also led Oaxacans to redefine and reconstitute their indigenous identities as Mixtecs and Zapotecs in the development of groups such as the Organización Regional de Oaxaca, a federation of Zapotecs in Los Angeles, and the Frente Mixteco-Zapoteco Binacional (renamed the Frente Indigena Oaxaquena Binacional on September 3, 1994, to encompass other indigenous people from Oaxaca). This politically heterogenous coalition has worked in the United States, the San Quintin area of Baja California, and communities in Oaxaca. It has pressured the Mexican government for assistance in building infrastructure in some Oaxacan communities, organized farm workers in San Quintin, and demanded the recognition of human rights for indigenous peoples. This transnational organization, whose basis rests on family and social networks, builds on a complicated web of social relations and social obligations.

Conclusion

The concept of transnationalism is essential both for understanding the historical experiences of migrants and the complexity of immigration and for eliminating the outmoded teleological model of American homogeneity and pluralism. Reconceptualizing the history of immigration and reexamining questions of cultural identity contribute to our understanding of the complex meaning of what it was, and what it is, to be that elusive being called "an American." This approach allows us to comprehend better the heterogeneous society of the United States and to develop a multicultural sense.

Studies on contemporary immigration need to view transnationalism through a historical lens. That perspective enriches our appreciation for the human element in migration and makes clear the importance of the social ties that people crafted in response to the conditions of their daily lives. Those networks formed the basis for labor unions and other formal responses to their experiences. Understanding the continuities of transnationalism refocuses attention on forms of everyday social organization that are obscured by focusing on institutionalized structures of political parties and labor movements. It also includes women, indigenous people, and others often overlooked in traditional accounts. For Mexican workers, thinking of transnationalism makes us take notice of the bonds that have existed between communities in Mexico and the United States over several generations and thus explains the arrival of Superbarrio in Los Angeles.

Notes

1. This essay relies on research found in Devra Weber, *Dark Sweat, White Gold: California Farm Workers, Cotton, and the New Deal* (Berkeley: University of California Press, 1994), and for a forthcoming study on current immigration to California.

2. Nina Glick Schiller, Linda Basch, and Cristina Blanc-Szanton, "Towards a Definition of Transnationalism: Introductory Remarks and Research Questions," in Schiller, Basch, and Blanc-Szanton, eds., *Towards a Transnational Perspective on Migration: Race, Class, Ethnicity, and Nationalism Reconsidered*, Annals of the New York Academy of Sciences 645 (New York: New York Academy of Sciences, 1992), ix.

3. Idem, "Transnationalism: A New Analytic Framework for Understanding Migration," in ibid., 1.

4. Barry Goldberg, "Historical Reflections on Transnationalism," 201–15; Randolph Bourne, "Transnational America," *Atlantic Monthly* 118: 778–86.

5. Virginia Yans-McLaughlin, *Family and Community: Italian Immigrants in Buffalo, 1880–1930* (Urbana: University of Illinois Press, 1982), 76–77. See also Oscar Handlin, *Boston's Immigrants: A Study in Acculturation* (Cambridge, MA: Harvard University Press, 1959).

6. For an introduction to the debate on multiculturalism see George Lipsitz, *Time Passages: Collective Memory and American Popular Culture* (Minneapolis: University of Minnesota Press, 1990).

7. See Ernest Mandel, *Late Capitalism* (London: Verso Press, 1978), 9, on the nature of capitalism after World War II.

8. Aspects of the border are also true for Canada, although there are differences. First, the United States did not conquer part of Canada and has not had the same historical antagonism against that country or against Canadians. Second, the economic relationship is not the same.

9. Douglas Massey, Rafael Alarcón, Jorge Durand, and Humberto Gonzalez, *Return to Aztlan: The Social Process of International Migration from Western Mexico* (Berkeley: University of California Press, 1987), 153–64.

10. Juan Gómez-Quiñones, *Development of the Mexican Working Class North of the Rio Bravo* (Los Angeles: UCLA, Chicano Studies Research Center, Popular Series No. 2, 1982), 18; Rodney Anderson, *Outcasts in Their Own Land: Mexican Industrial Workers, 1906–1911* (DeKalb: Northern Illinois University Press, 1976), 41; *Historia obrera* 5 (Mexico: Centro de Estudios Históricas del Movimiento Obrero, June 1975), 2, 5. Also see the Ramos essay in this volume.

11. Merilee Grindle, *Searching for Rural Development: Labor Migration and Employment in Mexico* (Ithaca: Cornell University Press, 1988): 118–20; Alvaro Ochoa, "Arrieros, braceros y migrantes de Oeste Michoacán, 1849–1911" (Zamora: El Colegio de Michoacán, unpublished, n.d.); Gustavo López Castro, *La casa dividida: Un estudio de caso sobre la migración a estados unidos en un pueblo michoacano* (Zamora: El Colegio de Michoacán, 1986), 16–24.

12. Manuel Gamio, *The Life Story of the Mexican Immigrant* (New York: Dover Press, 1971), 104–9, 149–50. Author's interviews with Roberto Castro and Ray Magaña, Corcoran, California, September 17, 1982; with Juana Padilla, Brawley, California, June 25, 1982; and with Jessie de la Cruz, Fresno, California, June 1, 1981.

13. Emilio Zamora, *The World of the Mexican Worker in Texas* (College Station: Texas A&M University Press, 1993), 86. See also Juan Gómez-Quiñones, "On Culture," *Revista Chicana Riqueña* 5 (Spring 1977): 29–47.

14. Mary Lanigan, "Second Generation Mexicans in Belvedere" (Master's thesis, University of Southern California, 1932), 76–77.

15. Ibid., 72. The rate of naturalizations declined again between 1920 and 1930. See C. C. Young, *Mexicans in California: Report of Governor C. C. Young's Mexican Fact Finding Committee* (San Francisco: R. and E. Research Associates, 1970), 61–74; and Evangeline Hymer, "A Study of the Social Attitudes of Adult Mexican Immigrants in Los Angeles and Vicinity" (Master's thesis, University of Southern California, 1923), 51.

16. Author's interview with Edward Bañales, Corcoran, California, January 1982 and May 1983.

17. William K. Meyers, "La Comarca Lagunera: Work, Protest, and Popular Mobilization in North Central Mexico," in Thomas Benjamin and William McNellie, eds., *Other Mexicos: Essays on Regional Mexican History, 1876–1911* (Albuquerque: University of New Mexico Press, 1984), 243–74.

18. American Consulate, Mexicali, to Secretary of State, September 28, 1921, Microfilm Roll 163, Record Group 59, State Department Records Relating to the Internal Affairs of Mexico, 1910–1929, National Archives and Records Administration (NARA), Washington, DC.

19. Paco Ignacio Taibo, *Los Bolshevikis: Historia narrativa de los origenes del comunismo en México, 1919–1925* (México: Editorial Joaquin Mortiz, 1986); John M. Hart, *Anarchism and the Mexican Working Class, 1860–1931* (Austin: University of Texas Press, 1978); Juan Gómez-Quiñones, *Sembradores: Ricardo Flores Magón y el Partido Liberal Mexicano* (Los Angeles: UCLA Chicano Studies Center, Aztlan Publications, 1973).

20. Author's interviews with Guillermo Martinez, Los Angeles, April 21, 1971; with Leroy Parra, Los Angeles, April 18, 1971; with Miguel Angel Velasco and Arnoldo Martinez Verdugo, CEMOS offices, Mexico City, n.d. Velasco recalled that *El Machete,* the newspaper of the Mexican Communist Party, had a substantial readership in the United States. The records of the newspaper were destroyed in the 1930s.

21. Author's interview with Leroy Parr, Los Angeles, April 18, 1971.

22. Author's interview with Guillermo Martínez.

23. Author's interview with Castro.

24. U.S. Congress, Senate Committee on Education and Labor, Hearings Before a Subcommittee of the Senate Committee on Education and Labor on Violations of Free Speech and Rights of Labor, Part 61, 76th Congress, 3rd Session, 1940, Testimony of Paul S. Taylor.

25. Author's interview with Pat Chambers, Wilmington, California, May 11, 1982.

26. Weekly Report No. 284, Record Group 407, Records of the Adjutant General's Office, NARA.

27. Ibid. Emphasis added.

28. Paul Friedrich, *Agrarian Revolt in a Mexican Village* (Englewood Cliffs, NJ: Prentice-Hall, 1970).

29. Some migrants pay others to perform their *tequio.* They still participate in communal labor even if they have settled permanently elsewhere, because it is required if family members are to be buried in the town.

Index

About the Contributors

Mario Camarena Ocampo is a historical researcher at the Centro de Estudios Históricos del Instituto Nacional de Antropología e Historia, Castillo de Chapultepec, Mexico City, and has written numerous articles on Mexican labor history.

Susana A. Fernández Apango, a historical researcher at the Centro de Estudios Históricos del Instituto Nacional de Antropología e Historia, Castillo de Chapultepec, Mexico City, is the author of an important article on the textile workers of San Angel.

Bernardo García Díaz, a historical researcher at the Instituto de Investigaciones Histórico-Sociales, Universidad Veracruzana, has published *El Estado de Pueblo* and *Un pueblo fabril del porfiriato: Santa Rosa, Veracruz* (1981).

John Mason Hart is a professor of Mexican history at the University of Houston.

Gerardo Necoechea Gracia has written several articles on Mexican labor and the Mexican experience in the United States. He is a historical researcher at the Centro de Estudios Históricos del Instituto Nacional de Antropología e Historia, Castillo de Chapultepec, Mexico City.

Elizabeth Jean Norvell is a Ph.D. candidate in Latin American history at Columbia University, where she is completing work on a history of labor in Veracruz.

Alberto Olvera Rivera, a historical researcher at the Instituto de Investigaciones Histórico-Sociales, Universidad Veracruzana, has published *Historia gráfica de la industria petrolera y sus trabajadores, 1900–1938* (1988).

Carmen Ramos Escandón is the author of *Gender Construction in a Progressive Society: Mexico, 1870–1917* (1990).

ANTONIO RÍOS BUSTAMANTE is a historical researcher at the Center for Mexican-American Studies, University of Arizona, Tucson, and the author of *Los Angeles, pueblo y región, 1781–1850: Continuity and Adaption on the North Mexican Periphery* (1991).

DEVRA WEBER, the author of *Dark Sweat, White Gold: California Farm Workers, Cotton, and the New Deal* (1994), is an associate professor of Mexican-American history at the University of California, Riverside.

EMILIO ZAMORA, an associate professor of Mexican-American history at the University of Houston, has written *The World of the Mexican Worker in Texas* (1993).

Latin American Silhouettes
Studies in History and Culture

William H. Beezley and
Judith Ewell
Editors

Volumes Published

William H. Beezley and Judith Ewell, eds.,
*The Human Tradition in Latin
America: The Twentieth Century*
(1987). Cloth ISBN 0-8420-2283-X
Paper ISBN 0-8420-2284-8

Judith Ewell and William H. Beezley, eds.,
*The Human Tradition in Latin
America: The Nineteenth Century*
(1989). Cloth ISBN 0-8420-2331-3
Paper ISBN 0-8420-2332-1

David G. LaFrance, *The Mexican Revolution
in Puebla, 1908–1913: The Maderista
Movement and the Failure of Liberal
Reform* (1989). ISBN 0-8420-2293-7

Mark A. Burkholder, *Politics of a Colonial
Career: José Baquíjano and the
Audiencia of Lima*, 2d ed. (1990).
Cloth ISBN 0-8420-2353-4
Paper ISBN 0-8420-2352-6

Carlos B. Gil, ed., *Hope and Frustration:
Interviews with Leaders of Mexico's
Political Opposition* (1992).
Cloth ISBN 0-8420-2395-X
Paper ISBN 0-8420-2396-8

Heidi Zogbaum, *B. Traven: A Vision of
Mexico* (1992). ISBN 0-8420-2392-5

Jaime E. Rodríguez O., ed., *Patterns of
Contention in Mexican History* (1992).
ISBN 0-8420-2399-2

Louis A. Pérez, Jr., ed., *Slaves, Sugar, and
Colonial Society: Travel Accounts of
Cuba, 1801–1899* (1992).
Cloth ISBN 0-8420-2354-2
Paper ISBN 0-8420-2415-8

Peter Blanchard, *Slavery and Abolition in
Early Republican Peru* (1992).
Cloth ISBN 0-8420-2400-X
Paper ISBN 0-8420-2429-8

Paul J. Vanderwood, *Disorder and Progress:
Bandits, Police, and Mexican Develop-
ment*, revised and enlarged edition (1992).
Cloth ISBN 0-8420-2438-7
Paper ISBN 0-8420-2439-5

Sandra McGee Deutsch and Ronald H.
Dolkart, eds., *The Argentine Right: Its
History and Intellectual Origins, 1910 to
the Present* (1993). Cloth ISBN 0-8420-
2418-2 Paper ISBN 0-8420-2419-0

Steve Ellner, *Organized Labor in Venezuela,
1958–1991: Behavior and Concerns
in a Democratic Setting* (1993).
ISBN 0-8420-2443-3

Paul J. Dosal, *Doing Business with the
Dictators: A Political History of United
Fruit in Guatemala, 1899–1944* (1993).
Cloth ISBN 0-8420-2475-1
Paper ISBN 0-8420-2590-1

Marquis James, *Merchant Adventurer:
The Story of W. R. Grace* (1993).
ISBN 0-8420-2444-1

John Charles Chasteen and Joseph S. Tulchin,
eds., *Problems in Modern Latin
American History: A Reader* (1994).
Cloth ISBN 0-8420-2327-5
Paper ISBN 0-8420-2328-3

Marguerite Guzmán Bouvard, *Revolutionizing
Motherhood: The Mothers of the Plaza de
Mayo* (1994). Cloth ISBN 0-8420-2486-7
Paper ISBN 0-8420-2487-5

William H. Beezley, Cheryl English Martin,
and William E. French, eds., *Rituals of
Rule, Rituals of Resistance: Public
Celebrations and Popular Culture in
Mexico* (1994). Cloth ISBN 0-8420-
2416-6 Paper ISBN 0-8420-2417-4

Stephen R. Niblo, *War, Diplomacy, and
Development: The United States and
Mexico, 1938–1954* (1995).
ISBN 0-8420-2550-2

G. Harvey Summ, ed., *Brazilian Mosaic:
Portraits of a Diverse People and Culture*
(1995). Cloth ISBN 0-8420-2491-3
Paper ISBN 0-8420-2492-1

N. Patrick Peritore and Ana Karina Galve-
Peritore, eds., *Biotechnology in Latin
America: Politics, Impacts, and Risks*

(1995). Cloth ISBN 0-8420-2556-1 Paper ISBN 0-8420-2557-X

Silvia Marina Arrom and Servando Ortoll, eds., *Riots in the Cities: Popular Politics and the Urban Poor in Latin America, 1765–1910* (1996). Cloth ISBN 0-8420-2580-4   Paper ISBN 0-8420-2581-2

Roderic Ai Camp, ed., *Polling for Democracy: Public Opinion and Political Liberalization in Mexico* (1996). ISBN 0-8420-2583-9

Brian Loveman and Thomas M. Davies, Jr., eds., *The Politics of Antipolitics: The Military in Latin America*, 3d ed., revised and updated (1996). Cloth ISBN 0-8420-2609-6   Paper ISBN 0-8420-2611-8

Joseph S. Tulchin, Andrés Serbín, and Rafael Hernández, eds., *Cuba and the Caribbean: Regional Issues and Trends in the Post-Cold War Era* (1997). ISBN 0-8420-2652-5

Thomas W. Walker, ed., *Nicaragua without Illusions: Regime Transition and Structural Adjustment in the 1990s* (1997). Cloth ISBN 0-8420-2578-2 Paper ISBN 0-8420-2579-0

Dianne Walta Hart, *Undocumented in L.A.: An Immigrant's Story* (1997). Cloth ISBN 0-8420-2648-7 Paper ISBN 0-8420-2649-5

Jaime E. Rodríguez O. and Kathryn Vincent, eds., *Myths, Misdeeds, and Misunderstandings: The Roots of Conflict in U.S.-Mexican Relations* (1997). ISBN 0-8420-2662-2

Jaime E. Rodríguez O. and Kathryn Vincent, eds., *Common Border, Uncommon Paths: Race, Culture, and National Identity in U.S.-Mexican Relations* (1997). ISBN 0-8420-2673-8

William H. Beezley and Judith Ewell, eds., *The Human Tradition in Modern Latin America* (1997). Cloth ISBN 0-8420-2612-6   Paper ISBN 0-8420-2613-4

Donald F. Stevens, ed., *Based on a True Story: Latin American History at the Movies* (1997). ISBN 0-8420-2582-0

Jaime E. Rodríguez O., ed., *The Origins of Mexican National Politics, 1808–1847* (1997). Paper ISBN 0-8420-2723-8

Che Guevara, *Guerrilla Warfare*, with revised and updated introduction and case studies by Brian Loveman and Thomas M. Davies, Jr., 3d ed. (1997). Cloth ISBN 0-8420-2677-0   Paper ISBN 0-8420-2678-9

Adrian A. Bantjes, *As If Jesus Walked on Earth: Cardenismo, Sonora, and the Mexican Revolution* (1998). ISBN 0-8420-2653-3

Henry A. Dietz and Gil Shidlo, eds., *Urban Elections in Democratic Latin America* (1998). Cloth ISBN 0-8420-2627-4 Paper ISBN 0-8420-2628-2

A. Kim Clark, *The Redemptive Work: Railway and Nation in Ecuador, 1895–1930* (1998). ISBN 0-8420-2674-6

Joseph S. Tulchin, ed., with Allison M. Garland, *Argentina: The Challenges of Modernization* (1998). ISBN 0-8420-2721-1

Louis A. Pérez, Jr., ed., *Impressions of Cuba in the Nineteenth Century: The Travel Diary of Joseph J. Dimock* (1998). Cloth ISBN 0-8420-2657-6 Paper ISBN 0-8420-2658-4

June E. Hahner, ed., *Women through Women's Eyes: Latin American Women in Nineteenth-Century Travel Accounts* (1998). Cloth ISBN 0-8420-2633-9 Paper ISBN 0-8420-2634-7

James P. Brennan, ed., *Peronism and Argentina* (1998). ISBN 0-8420-2706-8

John Mason Hart, ed., *Border Crossings: Mexican and Mexican-American Workers* (1998). Cloth ISBN 0-8420-2716-5 Paper ISBN 0-8420-2717-3

Brian Loveman, *For la Patria: Politics and the Armed Forces in Latin America* (1999). Cloth ISBN 0-8420-2772-6 Paper ISBN 0-8420-2773-4

Guy P. C. Thomson, with David G. LaFrance, *Patriotism, Politics, and Popular Liberalism in Nineteenth-Century Mexico: Juan Francisco Lucas and the Puebla Sierra* (1999). ISBN 0-8420-2683-5

K. Lynn Stoner, ed./comp., with Luís Hipólito Serrano Pérez, *Cuban and Cuban-American Women: An Annotated Bibliography* (1999). ISBN 0-8420-2643-6

ISBN 0-8420-2716-5

90000>